D1706553

TEACHING THE BILINGUAL SPECIAL EDUCATION STUDENT

Edited by

Angela L. Carrasquillo
Richard E. Baecher

ABLEX PUBLISHING CORPORATION
NORWOOD, NEW JERSEY

Library of Congress Cataloging-in-Publication Data

Teaching the bilingual special education student / edited by Angela L. Carrasquillo, Richard E. Baecher.
    p. cm.
  Includes bibliographical references and index.
  ISBN 0-89391-623-4
  1. Special education—United States. 2. Education, Bilingual—United States. 3. Handicapped children—Education—United States. I. Carrasquillo, Anjela. II. Baecher, Richard Emeran, 1941-
LC3981.T43 1990
371.97'00973—dc20   90-37630
                                                                CIP

Ablex Publishing Corporation
355 Chestnut Street
Norwood, New Jersey 07648

CONTENTS

The Authors   *v*

Preface   *ix*

Overview   *1*
  Richard E. Baecher

1   Bilingual Special Education: The Important Connection   *4*
  Angela L. Carrasquillo

2   Using Language Assessment Data for Language and   *25*
  Instructional Planning for Exceptional Bilingual Students
  Alba A. Ortiz and Shernaz B. Garcia

3   An Overview of Issues on the Implementation of   *48*
  Bilingual Special Education Programs
  Nivia Zavala

4   Teaching a Second Language to Limited-English-   *67*
  Proficient Learning-Disabled Students
  Angela L. Carrasquillo and Maria A. Reyes Bonilla

5   Instructional Language Preferences of Bilingual   *90*
  Elementary Learning-Disabled Students
  Angela L. Carrasquillo

6   Planning and Implementing English as a Second   *106*
  Language Program
  Nancy Cloud

7   Developing Literacy Skills in Two Languages   *132*
  Frances Segan

8   Written Communication For Exceptional Students from   *148*
     Culturally and Linguistically Diverse Backgrounds
          Debra A. Colley

9   Content Area Instruction in Bilingual Special Education   *169*
     Classes
          Ana Rossell

10   The Cognitive Academic Language Learning Approach: *196*
     A Bridge to the Mainstream
          Anna Uhl Chamot and J. Michael O'Malley

11   Adaptations of the Cognitive Academic Language   *218*
     Learning Approach (CALLA) to Special Education
          Anna Uhl Chamot and J. Michael O'Malley

     Author Index   *225*

     Subject Index   *230*

THE AUTHORS

Richard E. Baecher. Richard E. Baecher is a professor in the Graduate School of Education, Fordham University, where he directs the Bilingual Teacher Education Program. Dr. Baecher has written widely on issues related to the assessment and instruction of LEP students (e.g., Two-Way Bilingual programs, second language learning, educational cognitive styles, teacher training). A firm believer in the benefits of knowing more than one language (which he discovered as a Peace Corps volunteer in Venezuela), Dr. Baecher received his Ph.D. degree from the University of Michigan.

Angela L. Carrasquillo. Angela Carrasquillo is a professor at Fordham University, where she is coordinator of the Teaching English to Speakers of Other Languages Program. She has written two books in the area of teaching reading to the bilingual student and several articles dealing with issues on bilingual and second language learning.

Anna Uhl Chamot. Anna Uhl Chamot is an adjunct professor at Georgetown University, where she teaches bilingualism. Formerly she was an assistant professor at the University of Texas at Austin and research manager for the National Clearinghouse for Bilingual Education. Her publications include numerous professional articles and chapters on second language research, curriculum, and classroom applications. She is co-author, with J. Michael O'Malley, of a new book on learning strategies in second language acquisition and is co-developer, with Dr. O'Malley, of the Cognitive Academic Language Learning Approach (CALLA) for limited English-proficient students. Dr. Chamot received her Ph.D. from the University of Texas at Austin and also holds degrees from Teachers College, Columbia University, and from George Washington University.

Nancy Cloud. Nancy Cloud is Special Assistant Professor, Department of Curriculum and Teaching, Hofstra University, and formerly served as Assistant Director, Division of Training, Evaluation and School Services of the Institute for Urban and Minority Education, Teachers College, Columbia University. Having worked as a bilingual/ ESL classroom teacher and program coordinator for seven years on the west coast, and as a teacher trainer in the midwest and northeast for the past ten years, she possesses considerable knowledge and broad-based experience in non-biased assessment, bilingual education and second language education. She specializes in the area of bilingual special education and has contributed monographs as well as articles in journals and edited books concerning program planning, educational assessment and instruction of exceptional bilingual youngsters. Recently she co-developed a media-based training curriculum to be used by training centers and colleges charged with improving teachers' capability to deliver appropriate instructional programs to culturally and linguistically diverse exceptional children. Ms. Cloud, A.B.D., received her degrees from Syracuse University, the University of San Francisco, and is currently completing her doctoral work at Teachers College, Columbia University in the area of mental retardation and bilingualism.

Debra A. Colley. Debra A. Colley is an associate in teacher education in the New York State Education Department, Division of Academic Program Review. In this position, she is primarily responsible for the focus on special education teacher preparation in a statewide review of baccalaureate programs in teacher preparation. Prior to this position, Dr. Colley taught in the Bilingual Special Education Master's Degree program at the State University College at Buffalo. She has been involved in the development of bilingual special education teacher training programs and has worked as a bilingual special education teacher in the public schools. Her major area of research and writing is information processing and metacognition among bilingual students who exhibit handicapping conditions.

Shernaz B. Garcia. Shernaz Garcia is a Lecturer in Special Education at the University of Texas at Austin and Coordinator of the training programs in bilingual special education. Over the past four years, she has been actively involved in the research conducted through the Handicapped Minority Research Institute on Language Proficiency, on issues related to the identification and placement of limited English proficient Hispanic students in special education, as well as effective instructional practices in the education of LEP exceptional students. Dr. Garcia holds degrees from Poona University, India, and George Peabody College for Teachers, Nashville, TN. Her doctoral degree in special education administration is from The University of Texas at Austin. She has collaborated extensively with Alba Ortiz on research and training in prereferral intervention, effective instructional practices for exceptional language minority students, and policy analysis and development to improve services provided to these students. Dr. Garcia has presented frequently at local, state, and national levels on these and other issues in bilingual special education.

J. Michael O'Malley. J. Michael O'Malley is director of the Evaluation Assistance Center-East at Georgetown University. Dr. O'Malley has directed a number of studies concerning minority language students and most recently completed a series of projects investigating strategies for second language learning and ESL students. Dr. O'Malley received his doctorate in psychology from George Peabody College with a specialization in cognitive development in special education.

Alba A. Ortiz. Alba Ortiz is a Full Professor in the Department of Special Education at The University of Texas at Austin where she directs Bilingual Special Education Programs and the Innovative Approaches Research Project on Exceptional Children. She is also the director of the College of Education's Office of Bilingual Education. Dr. Ortiz was trained as a speech and language pathologist at Southwest Texas State University in San Marcos, Texas and received her doctorate in Special Education Administration from UT Austin. She has focused her career on improving educational services provided to language minority students in regular education and has written extensively with Dr. Shernaz Garcia on prereferral intervention as a mechanism for decreasing inappropriate referrals of language minority students to special education. She is also interested in the assessment of language skills to distinguish second language differences from handicapping conditions and in the teaching of oral language and literacy skills to handicapped bilingual students using whole language approaches. In 1988, Dr. Ortiz and Dr. Bruce Ramirez edited the text, *Schools and the Culturally Diverse Exceptional Student: Promising Practices and Future Directions,* for the Council for Exceptional Children.

Maria A. Reyes Bonilla. Maria A. Reyes Bonilla is an assistant professor of education at Universidad Central in Puerto Rico. For 10 years she was general supervisor of the Learning Disabilities Program at the Puerto Rico Department of Education. Currently she is a doctoral candidate at the Graduate School of Education at Fordham University working on her doctoral dissertation on second language and learning disabled students. In 1983 she wrote a teacher's manual for the learning disabilities specialist. In 1988 her proposal "Images" won a contest held by the Council of Learning Disabilities.

Ana Rossell. Ana Rossell is an adjunct professor at Fordham University and Adelphi University, where she teaches in the special education and bilingual education graduate programs. Dr. Rosell is also a bilingual special education administrator with the New York City Board of Education. For most of her professional life she has worked with handicapped students and has been involved in the development of policy, programs, and curriculum guides for teaching the bilingual special education student. She has conducted research on acculturation. She received a doctorate in educational research from Hofstra University.

Frances Segan. Frances Segan is a staff member of the New York City Board of Education's Division of Multilingual and Multicultural Education. Dr. Segan is a practitioner who has created curricula and professional development activities to help teachers make learning exciting for students in bilingual general and bilingual special education programs. Her university experiences include serving as a bilingual program developer and an adjunct assistant professor for CUNY and Fordham University and as a former project associate for the National Origin Desegregation Assistance Center at Teachers College, Columbia University. In addition to having served as a Title VII project director for special education and bilingual career education projects, she has written articles on bilingual/multicultural curriculum development and chapters on reading and the bilingual child. Dr. Segan holds degrees from Hunter College (CUNY) and a Ph.D. from Fordham University.

Nivia Zavala. Nivia Zavala is an administrator at the Division of Special Education at the New York City Board of Education. She is the director of the Office of Bilingual Services which has been instrumental in the implementation of bilingual special education policy. Ms. Zavala is presently working on her doctorate at Fordham University.

PREFACE

Given some recent and startling estimates that 12 percent of language minority students of limited-English-proficiency (LEP) are handicapped, this book focuses on teaching those students who are bilingual, handicapped, and in need of special instruction. We believe that these students are capable of learning—provided the instruction fits their ways of knowing. This book responds to the complex and practical issues in reaching the goal of teaching these students in an effective way. The common underlying belief of the book is that such ways can be found and implemented in creating diversity of opportunity for teaching bilingual exceptional children.

The book has three central themes. One is to present an overview of the emerging and interdisciplinary "field" of bilingual special education. We contend that the connections between bilingual and special education, respectively, need greater exploration. Neither one should exclude the other; nor are they alternatives to one another. Discovering their interconnections can be a fertile and challenging area for teachers. A second theme is to highlight the function of language in the classroom—the student's as well as the teacher's. The different uses that language can take on is particularly important within bilingual settings. For instance, selecting the appropriate language for teaching is a sine qua non in planning and carrying out effective instruction for bilingual exceptional students. In the last part of the book, we present comprehensive coverage of the instructional features of a bilingual special education classroom in such wide-ranging curricular areas as: English as a second language, reading, writing, mathematics, science, and social studies.

The overriding concern of the book is the subject of teaching the bilingual exceptional student. We allowed all contributing authors as much flexibility as possible in making the connections they valued. Once LEP students are placed in an appropriate classroom setting, effective instruction becomes vital to their educational lives. Instruction within multiple perspectives was the outcome: instructional models, individualized instruction, the role of language in teaching, literacy development in both languages, content area teaching.

The book is divided into 11 chapters. Both theoretical and practical issues related to teaching bilingual exceptional students are addressed. The emphasis throughout the book is on the relationship between appropriate assessment, sound planning, and effective instruction. Language and culture are integral components of this process within bilingual special education classrooms.

The content of the book should be of interest to a wide range of educators and practitioners who are involved in teaching language minority students in bilingual special education. The book can be used as a primary or secondary resource in courses on assessment, instruction, and curriculum development in bilingual special education. Inservice specialists will find relevant materials in the book in planning and implementing instructional programs for bilingual exceptional children. In addition, educators who may not be familiar with the area of bilingual and special education will find useful ideas and practices in this book. Each chapter includes an up-to-date reference list for those who want to pursue a selected topic in greater depth.

We wish to thank those individuals who helped us in preparing this book. Above all, to those language minority students who inspired us to write about their instructional needs and rights. We want to acknowledge the contributing authors for their insightful articles on bilingual special education. Anne Goldstein diligently typed the manuscript. The support and encouragement of our spouses—Ceferino Carrasquillo and Marie Baecher—as well as our children was invaluable in making this book become a reality.

Angela Carrasquillo

Richard E. Baecher

OVERVIEW

Richard E. Baecher

The chapters you are about to read allow you to think differently about teaching the bilingual special education child. What does this phrase mean? How can its purpose be accomplished? Are the authors simply asking us to think by joining two semantic phrases—"special education" and "bilingual"—and then magically, a facile response will pop up? I don't think so. Much more meaning is conveyed than simply linking two separate categories. I invite you to think seriously about the structure of this book and its connections, to think critically about how the authors relate their topic of special interest to the overall structure of teaching the exceptional bilingual child.

An important distinction (Gould, Johnson, & Chapman, 1984) may help the reader in appreciating and relating the numerous ideas and practices contained in each article. Think about teaching the exceptional bilingual child as the "backcloth" or common structure against which or on which things exist and happen. And the things that happen in this book—the "traffic," so to speak—are all the ideas (practical and theoretical), suggestions, and issues that can be found in every article. However, whereas on the stage of a theater, backcloth simply sets the scene, the backcloth of this book is richer since it may have the capacity to shape the things that can exist and move on it. And we encourage the reader to apply these ideas—to "make your own traffic" as it were—on this structure so that positive change does occur. In other words, the structure of teaching the bilingual special education student supports and allows for the ideas of each article. Let's look closer at some of the traffic of ideas that occur in each chapter on teaching the exceptional bilingual student.

In Chapter 1, Angela Carrasquillo views the emerging field of "bilingual special education" as a real possibility, whereby each body of information (Special Education and Bilingual Education) can complement the other. Given her emphasis on the benefits of bilingual education—its focus on the knowledge and experiences of bilingual learners—she firmly believes an important connection can be made between them. One wonders if any other path can be taken on the backcloth of teaching the bilingual special education student? Alba Ortiz and Shernaz Garcia in Chapter 2 continue to weave this connection by concentrating on the all-pervasive role of language in assessing and planning for the instruction of exceptional bilingual students. Their framework for decision making, what they refer to as a "profile of language dominance and proficiency," goes a long way to helping practitioners and support personnel understand the subtle interactions between an individual's severity of handicap and language ability. They strongly remind us that behind the label of "exceptional bilingual student" is a human being with thoughts, experiences, and knowledge who makes up the backcloth of whatever we do in bilingual special education. The issues behind language assessment, the formulation of IEPs, and effective programming for the bilingual special education child within a local setting (New York City) are taken up by Nivia Zavala in Chapter 3. Tracing the origin of these issues to the way we think about and do educational assessment leads her to recommend strongly that the *current* structure of special education needs to be changed in the case of bilingual handicapped learners.

Can learning disabled (LD) children learn a second language as they develop their first language? Angela Carrasquillo and Maria Reyes (Chapter 4), from their review of the literature on second language acquisition, give a positive response to this paradoxical question. The clue lies somewhere between the nature of the meaningful activities in which this child gets involved (under a professional's guidance) and level of motivation of the LD child. In Chapter 5, the reader can take a closer look at this question by reviewing some empirical data on the language preferences and uses of L1 and L2 (Spanish and English, respectively) in a bilingual special education class. Angela Carrasquillo's conclusions, although necessarily tentative, point in the direction of more research in this area, both of a qualitative and quantitative nature. Her message is obvious: The structure of teaching children, who are handicapped and bilingual, calls for it and allows for it.

Nancy Cloud (Chapter 6) begins to define a set of relations between exceptional limited-English-proficient (LEP) students and specialized English as a Second Language (ESL) services. She "traffics" these relational ideas on the structure of teaching bilingual special education students: Special Education-ESL curriculum models (e.g., developmental ESL, content-based ESL, functional/life-skills ESL, career-based and vocational ESL) and instructional strategies (including computers, peer tutoring, learning styles, whole language approaches) are her main foci. Frances Segan in Chapter 7 relates L1 and L2 (first and second language) research to biliteracy, or learning to become literate in two languages. While some readers may be skeptical about how realistic it is to think about this connection, the backcloth allows for this to come forth. Just imagine if a multidisciplinary team of special educators, bilingual and ESL personnel, general education teachers, and other support staff began to collaborate in such an endeavor: The traffic of ideas and activities could be enormous! One definite outcome of such traffic is a holistic, pragmatic approach to teaching which is how Debra Colley describes written communication for exceptional students from culturally and linguistically diverse backgrounds (Chapter 8). Basing the act of writing within a cognitive perspective, three elements stand out in her article: (a) language abilities, (b) cultural/learning experiences, and (c) cognitive processing. To this author, written communication can provide exceptional students an opportunity to become actively involved in the communicative process. Ana Rossell in Chapter 9 extends this traffic on curriculum to grapple with the dual responsibility of teaching language skills and content area concepts and skills to bilingual handicapped learners. Integrating the different content areas of language arts, math, social studies, and science, for example, with the media of language and culture, she provides the reader with exemplary lesson plans on how this can be accomplished. Ana Chamot and Michael O'Malley (Chapters 10 and 11) describe their ground-breaking CALLA, or Cognitive Academic Language Learning Approach, and its potential for teaching the bilingual special education student. CALLA has some unique features which can further define the backcloth of teaching bilingual handicapped learners, such as its grounding in cognitive theory, academic language use, integration of language and content area, and the use of learning strategies to support the acquisition of language and content area knowledge. Teachers and support personnel are encouraged to apply this approach to LEP students with learning disabilities.

There you have the overview of this text. The reader is invited to examine, explore, relate, and think about the backcloth of this text—teaching the bilingual special education student—and the traffic of ideas and suggestions that each author makes on this structure, and to alter it.

REFERENCES

Gould, P., Johnson, J., & Chapman, G. (1984). *The structure of television. Television: The world of structure.* London: Plon Limited.

chapter **1**

Bilingual Special Education: The Important Connection

Angela L. Carrasquillo

In the last decade, the field of special education has received a great deal of attention. This educational field reached its peak in 1975 with the passage of PL 94–142 as part of the Education of All Handicapped Children Act requiring that all handicapped children be provided a free and and appropriate public education. Seven years before, the Bilingual Education Act was enacted providing bilingual schooling for students with limited English proficiency (LEP). Bilingual education came at a time when the United States Civil Rights Commission challenged school authorities to devise ways of providing equal educational opportunities for children from various ethnic minority groups who did not speak English. Thus, the Bilingual Education Act provided a legal recourse to address the cognitive and linguistic needs of language minority students through bilingual instruction. In spite of having bilingual instruction since 1968 and mandatory special education since 1975, it was not until recently that the special needs of language minority handicapped students have been addressed in what is called bilingual special education.

Bilingual education and special education are not mutually exclusive and they are not alternatives to each other. They can complement each other when there is a recognition that language minority handicapped students can benefit from special assistance if they are to have an opportunity to succeed in school. This chapter presents an overview on what has been called the field of bilingual special education. It intends to describe a rationale for providing bilingual instruction and services to language minority handicapped students.

BILINGUAL EDUCATION: GOALS AND IMPACT

Bilingual education is the provision of instruction through the medium of two languages. In the United States, bilingual education means

4

teaching content through English and another language, as well as teaching skills in English. Instruction in the primary language of language minority students allows them to participate in the school's activities and to acquire the skills and knowledge covered in the curriculum while they are learning English. It allows them to make use of skills, knowledge, and experiences they already have, and to build on these prior assets and resources in school.

The principal goal of bilingual education is to improve the educational achievement and subsequent social adjustment of the large numbers of children among minority groups in the United States today who have a less than adequate command of English when they arrive at school because they speak some other language as their mother tongue. A secondary goal of bilingual education is to provide students with a functional language competence as well as with an in-depth understanding of the history and culture influencing the values, beliefs, and attitudes of a different cultural group.

Bilingual education is based on the assumption that alternating between the home language and the school language results in academic retardation and eventual failure among language minority students (Ramirez, 1985). For language minority students, attending school is a very difficult experience because home and school are two different institutions and cultures. Through bilingual education children can make the transition from home to school much easier by reducing the differences between the language and culture of the home and that of the school.

Bilingual instruction has been federally funded since 1968 when Congress established the Bilingual Education Act, Title VII of the Elementary and Secondary Education Act. The United States government funded bilingual education programs as a means of assisting minority language students to attain equality of educational opportunities. This reform movement promotes the concept of the right of every student to an equal educational opportunity. Since the goal of public education is to provide the basic skills and knowledge needed for participation in American society, equal opportunity means that all students should have the same chance to acquire those skills and knowledges. Since federally funded bilingual education programs are transitional in nature, students are given instruction partially through their primary language until they attain enough proficiency in English to benefit from instruction in English. It also promotes primary language improvement, the study of the culture and history associated with the students' mother tongue, and the enhancement of the students' self-esteem.

The Bilingual Education Act was followed by a series of court cases which demanded bilingual instruction for students for whom English was not the primary language. The Supreme Court decision reached in *Lau v. Nichols* (1974) had the most extensive impact on the education of language minority students in the United States. A class action suit was filed on behalf of 1800 Chinese-speaking students in San Francisco. The case argued that students were denied meaningful instruction because they could not participate meaningfully in English-speaking classrooms and thus the lack of equal access to education violated the 1964 Civil Rights Act. The court decision indicated that some type of special language program be provided for students of limited English proficiency. Although the *Lau* decision did not specifically mandate bilingual instruction, it suggested bilingual instruction as one of the alternatives and indicated that action was needed to serve the needs of non-English speakers. Other legal actions (*Aspira v. New York Board of Education,* 1974; *Rios v. Read,* 1977; *Serna v. Portales,* 1974) contributed to the implementation of appropriate language instructional programs.

The Bilingual Education Act has been amended several times since 1968. The use of the native language has been maintained, but there is a greater emphasis on the development of English language skills. At the present time, the definition of bilingual education has been expanded to include special alternative programs, such as English as a second language (ESL). ESL, being an integral part of American bilingual education programs, is designed to meet the immediate communication and academic needs of the students, teaching them the language skills they need to communicate with teachers and peers, and academic content matter in English. Formal instruction in English as a second language enables students to get started in learning the language.

Bilingual education, then, has a positive impact on limited English proficient students. Bilingual education has cognitive, linguistic, sociocultural, and affective benefits for language minority students. Each of these benefits is briefly discussed in the following section.

Cognitive Benefits of Bilingual Education

The development of language is crucial to the cognitive and affective growth of students. There is considerable evidence that bilingual instruction for nonhandicapped students improves academic achievement in English, as well as in academic subjects taught in the native language. Some researchers (Ben Zeev, 1977; Grosjean, 1982; Peal & Lambert,

1962) have found that bilingualism is a great asset to students. Peal and Lambert's pioneering study showed that bilingual students demonstrated better awareness of language differences and were better at learning new languages than monolingual students. Their study indicated that bilingual students scored higher on both verbal and nonverbal IQ tests. Subtests revealed that bilingual students had a more diversified structure of intelligence, more flexibility in thought, greater cognitive flexibility and creativity, and greater divergent thought.

Bilingual proficiency is a worthwhile goal of an educational program. Other studies, likewise, have shown positive effects of bilingualism in several intellectual areas such as: (a) general cognitive development, (b) divergent thinking, (c) orientation to language, and (d) sensitivity to linguistic cues. Swain and Cummins (1979) reviewed most of these studies identifying the positive effects of bilingualism. For example, they concluded that bilinguals are more sensitive to semantic relations between words than monolinguals, are more advanced in understanding arbitrary assignments of names to referents, are better able to treat sentence structure analytically, are better at restructuring a perceptual situation, have greater social sensitivity and greater ability to react more flexibly to cognitive feedback, are better at rule discovery tasks, and have more divergent thinking (cited in Grosjean, 1982, p. 223). Years later, Willig (1985), reviewing studies and evaluations of bilingual programs, revealed positive effects of bilingual programs in all major academic subjects.

DeAvila and Duncan (1979) suggest that the control of more than one language helps the child to develop a metalinguistic awareness and a cognitive metaset which gives the bilingual child an advantage in learning over monolingual peers. However, there is a widespread belief that for limited English-proficient students who are experiencing developmental disability, it is an additional burden of having two languages used in the instructional program and that a monolingual instructional program may be encouraged, even at the expense of the students' home language. In the United States, many minority students with severe academic difficulties are educated in monolingual English programs because it was felt that the learning problems of these students would be further complicated if they are required to cope with two languages of instruction. However, there is no empirical evidence that minority students who are academically at risk experience difficulty coping with two languages of instruction. Instead, there is some evidence related to the success of dual and native language instruction for students with learning handicaps (Baca & Bransford, 1982; Cummins, 1984; Ortiz, 1984b). For these students, bilingual education is the best instructional approach since it teaches students subject matter concepts, knowledge, and skills through the language they know best and reinforces this information through the second language. The underlying assumption is that students are able to learn more effectively in a language they understand more completely. Students are able to learn new concepts and skills in the language they are familiar with while at the same time learning English.

Linguistic Benefits of Bilingual Education

Academic growth, career expectations, and achievements are all influenced by the students' linguistic ability or lack of ability. Language does not operate without meaning or function; it is intimately related to cognitive and affective development. An important benefit of bilingual education is the acquisition of proficiency in English: the student learns through his or her primary language, and becomes proficient in two languages. The assumption is that in bilingual programs, students are allowed to use and develop the language they know best. They use the language they can understand best to explore, interpret, and construct meaning. Students need to develop the ability to use oral and written language effectively. Language skills are needed for learning and students need to learn in the language they manipulate best. It is more efficient and psychologically healthier to fully develop the child's primary language in building verbal ability.

By the age of five or six, bilingual students have acquired, to some degree, basic interpersonal communicative skills in a variety of ways in their primary/home language. The quality and quantity of that home language has an effect on how ready and able students are for the academic demands of the school. For many of these students, these communicative skills may not be able to be used in school.

Learning experiences in the primary language do not harm the acquisition of English academic skills. On the contrary, student interactions through the primary language with parents, relatives, peers, and teachers contribute to their academic progress in English. Ortiz (1984b) found that children who show language problems in both languages appear to benefit from instruction in the primary/predominant language. Langdon (1983) also found that instruction in the primary language is useful for bilingual handicapped students.

Acquisition of English listening skills and fluent speaking does not necessarily imply commensurate development of English conceptual or academic proficiency (Cummins, 1984). Cummins indicated that comments made by teachers on English characteristics suggest that among most immigrant students who arrive after first grade, English communicative skills appear to be relatively well developed within one to two years of arrival. On the other hand, difficulties in English academic skills appear to persist for a longer period of time. Cummins (1984) has posed the following question: "What is the relationship between the acquisition of face-to-face conversational skills in a language and the development of academic and conceptual skills in that language (e.g., reading proficiency, range of vocabulary)?" (p. 63). He answers this question by referring to the nature of language proficiency and its relationship to academic progress. According to Cummins, there exists a common underlying language proficiency, and the rapid transfer of cognitive academic skills from one language to another is possible, given adequate exposure to literacy skills in the other language. Rather than being a waste of time, the development of first language literacy skills among minority students constitutes a basis for the acquisition of English language literacy. The primary language is the means through which communicative proficiency underlying both the first and second language is developed.

Bilingual special education programs need to monitor the language development process for language minority handicapped students. This monitoring will include comparison of the data received at the time of placement decision and the information used in the preparation of the Individual Educational Program (IEP) with recent information relative to the language development progress of the students (Garcia & Yates, 1986). Programs need to establish a clear policy that, for handicapped students from linguistic minorities, the initial and continuing major instructional task is the development of language proficiency. The literature indicates that language proficiency is strongly related to academic achievement regardless of the particular language. Thus, there is a need to provide for the development of language proficiency primarily in the students' primary language. This primary language proficiency will be demonstrated at a level appropriate for movement into academic learning in the second language.

Sociocultural Benefits of Bilingual Education

Culture is the way of life of people or society, including its rules of behavior, its economic, social, and political systems, language, religious beliefs, and laws. Culture is acquired, transmitted, and communicated in large part by language. Many people in contact with two cultures may at first seek to belong solely to one or the other, but with time they realize that they are most at ease with people who share their cultural experience. Adjustment to two cultures can be especially difficult for students. The need to identify themselves with peers in domains such as values, attitudes, clothing, and the fear of being ridiculed, may lead to a state of conflict between the home and the society. Going to school is considered a socialization process requiring students to build a new repertoire of behavior that is very different from what was learned at home. In a sense, what is learned at school should link what one learned at home with what one will need to know to be competent as an adult. Potential conflict between the norms operating at home and those at school may arise if the rules of discourse in each area are very different.

Bilingual education programs develop and maintain the minority students' cultural heritage as they are introduced to the majority culture while helping students in the process of learning. These programs provide a linguistic and cultural continuity between the minority and the dominant group and prepare students to live in a multilingual-multicultural society. An important objective in public schools is the aspect of the language and cultural traditions of the various ethnic and linguistic groups that have contributed to and have been an integral part of the rich diversity of the American nation. The culture of the students is used in the content of the instructional program. The curriculum presents the history and the contributions the particular culture has made in the development of America as a nation. Encouragement of the use of the mother tongue and a demonstration of respect for a student's cultural and family roots effect how children think and feel the school contributes in preparing them to respect and appreciate their own culture and the new culture. Such encouragement also affects how they feel bilingual education holds the promise of helping to harmonize various ethnic elements in a community into a mutually respectful and pluralistic society. Maltitz (1975) indicated that the purpose of bilingual education is twofold: "to instill in children from those minority groups, who have often been subject to prejudice, a pride in their own language and culture, and to promote among persons from other segments of the population an understanding and respect for Americans who may be different from themselves" (p. 1). It provides members of the school community with the chance to become better acquainted with other cultures, incorporating into the curriculum units on the history and cultural characteristics of language minority students. It also includes the study of American history. An emphasis is placed on the concept of preserving and valuing the cultures that make up the United States and the students' culture. The students' mother tongue is part of their sense of identity and an instrument for learning.

Affective Benefits of Bilingual Education

Positive self-esteem is regarded as essential to the learning process. There is evidence establishing a positive relationship between self-concept and academic achievement (Gardner, 1985; Gardner & Lambert, 1972). This relationship is to be expected because students with positive attitudes toward school and toward learning a second language probably are more attentive and concerned about assessment and achievement in the language. Attitudes toward language are significantly related to academic achievement. Among various attitudes that seem to underlie motivation for second language learning and which have been related to achievement are positive attitudes toward the target language group and favorable attitudes toward their own culture group.

Self-concept also plays an important role in a student's academic and cognitive development. After the family, school represents the most decisive role in the development of self-concept because students spend a great deal of time in school. Students' self-images are affected by the success they experience in various subject areas, the manner in which teachers relate to them, their experiences with school peers, and the manner in which textbooks portray students' cultural group. Students who view themselves as being loved, accepted, and respected develop a positive self-concept; they are motivated to learn because they approach learning with optimism and confidence in their abilities. It is suggested that a program that accepts and shows respect for the language and culture of students will do more to enhance the self-concept of its students than a program that does not accept and respect the language and culture of its students.

LANGUAGE MINORITY HANDICAPPED STUDENTS: WHO ARE THEY?

Bilingual handicapped students are defined as those language minority students who exhibit discrepancies in growth and development due to health-related impairments, hearing impairments, mental retardation, orthopedic-related handicaps, serious emotional disturbances, learning disabilities, speech impairment, or visual impairments. Figure 1.1 summarizes the federal definition of handicapped students, applied here to bilingual handicapped students.

Bilingual handicapped students are found in all the categories shown in Figure 1.1, but especially with those labels of "mentally retarded" and "learning disabled."

Language minority students whose impairment adversely affects the student's ability to benefit from a regular educational program and who require special education and related services.

---

1. A severe hearing impairment affecting the processing of information through hearing (Deaf).
2. A communication disorder such as stuttering, impaired articulation, a language impairment, or a voice impairment (Speech Impaired).
3. Imperfect ability to learn, think, speak, read, write, spell, and perform mathematical calculations due to a disorder in the basic psychological process (Learning Disabled).
4. Significant subaverage general intellectual functioning (Mentally Retarded).
5. A hearing imapirment (Hard of Hearing).
6. Physically handicapped-limited strength, vitality, or alertness due to chronic or acute health problems (Other Health Impaired).
7. Severe physical/orthopedic impairment (Orthopedically Impaired).
8. Severe disturbances of developmental rates and/or sequences of responses to sensory stimuli of speech or language, and cognitive capacities (Autistic).
9. Inability to learn that cannot be explained by intellectual, sensory, or health factors (Emotionally Disturbed).
10. A visual handicap which even with correction affects a child's educational performance (Visually Impaired).
11. Two or more handicapping conditions resulting in multisensory or motor deficiencies and developmental lags in the cognitive, affective, or psychomotor areas (Multiply Handicapped).

(Adapted from *Federal Register,*
1982, 33845)

Figure 1.1 Handicapped Bilingual Students.

It is important to note that labels such as the above and especially those of "language impaired" or "learning disabled" do not clearly explain the behaviors involved and often serve only to gloss over the ignorance that presently exists (Cummins, 1984). According to Cummins, current theory is not sufficiently advanced to enable educators to specify the interactions that take place among the causal factors involved in each of the label's disabilities. In other words, it is a complex task made more difficult when language minority students are labeled "handicapped" and "limited English proficient." In many instances, students from language minority backgrounds have been placed in special education programs because these students have not been able to meet the school's expectations for functioning in English. On the other hand, there is a significant group of language minority students who clearly manifest learning impairments.

Bilingual handicapped students are those who, ideally, have been screened and evaluated using nondiscriminatory procedures, including assessment instruments in both languages and requiring the development of an educational program for each student designed to meet the student's specific needs. Bilingual handicapped students may be defined as individuals who are exposed to two languages and cultures and through bilingual instruction are engaged in communication in more than one language. These students are not expected to have equal mastery of both languages, but it is assumed that they can understand the communication of others, and can communicate and achieve goals in both languages (Ortiz, 1984a).

There is a significant percentage of bilingual students who are "English limited," referring to students who come from homes in which a language other than English is most relied on for communication and who have sufficient difficulty in understanding, speaking, reading, or writing the English language, denying them the opportunity to learn successfully in classrooms in which the language of instruction is English. The linguistic level of language proficiency of these students falls at varying points on a continuum (Ortiz, 1984a). At one end of the continuum are monolingual speakers of the first language. These are students who are monolingual in another language, such as Spanish or Chinese, and who do not understand or speak English. A significant number of these students are presently attending schools in the United States. There is another group of students who are dominant in a language other than English but who have some English ability, especially in the communicative speaking phase. In the middle of this continuum, there are those students who are bilingual with some degree of proficiency in both languages. There is a small percentage of these students in bilingual special education programs. For the majority of bilingual handicapped students, the use of their native language seems necessary for a longer period of time since their handicap precludes rapid progress in second language acquisition. Also, for other students, the first language would not be intact to a sufficient degree needed to serve all of their learning and communication needs. De Blassie (1983) has described the environment of these limited English proficient students as mostly sharing the following characteristics: an experiential background that does not fit the school environment, economic impoverishment (self-perpetuating, moral, aspirational, and economic poverty), a feeling of rejection by the dominant society, a poor self-concept, aggressiveness, and frequently linguistically handicapped. Often they live in a negative environment that could be described as disorderly. Poverty influences most of these characteristics since many of the characteristics attributed to culturally different students also characterize low socio-economic class students, regardless of race and ethnicity. But these students can learn if the school provides them with an appropriate learning environment.

TOWARD A DEFINITION OF BILINGUAL SPECIAL EDUCATION

Bilingual special education is the use of the home language and culture, along with English, in an individually designed program of special instruction for students. Bilingual special education considers the students' language and culture as foundations upon which an appropriate education can be built.

Bilingual special education is encouraged by federal legislation law as a means of providing educational opportunities for language minority handicapped students. During the past decade, two federal directions, one related to educational funding and the other to the civil rights of individuals who are handicapped, have had an impact on special education services in the United States. The passage of Public Law 94–142, a revision of Part B of the Education of the Handicapped Act of 1975, focuses on the manner in which appropriate education for handicapped students should be implemented. PL 93–112 is a civil rights law that states that no handicapped individual in the United States, solely by reason of this handicap, be excluded from participating in, be denied the benefits of, or be subjected to discrimination under programs or activities receiving federal financial assistance.

The requirement of PL 94–142, that the unique educational needs of each child be met, provides the groundwork for bilingual special education. Walker (1987) points out that the law provides an opportunity to handicapped children in these ways: (a) the right of access to public education programs, (b) the provision of individualized services, (c) the principle of a least restrictive environment, (d) broadened services provided by the schools and a set of procedures for determining them, (e) guidelines for identification of disability, and (f) the emphasis on state and local responsibilities. Thus, the unique educational needs through the learning of basic skills may be facilitated considerably if a student's culture and language become the foundations upon which an appropriate education is built. Bilingual special education programs are sensitive to the diverse cultural backgrounds of bilingual handicapped students. Sensitivity is shown when the students' cultural experiences are considered and instruction is provided within the students' cultural framework, thus enhancing students' self-concepts, valuing, and cultural backgrounds.

Court mandates have contributed to the field of bilingual special education by requesting appropriate educational assessment and instruction for students for whom English was not the primary language. Among these cases were *Diana v. California State Board of Education* (1970), *Rios v. Reed* (1977), and *Jose P. v. New York Board of Education* (1979). The "Jose P.," one of the most recent cases, was named for a deaf boy who sued the New York City Board of Education on behalf of handicapped Hispanic students. As a result of the case, a federal judge ordered the New York City Board of Education to evaluate and provide educational services to all handicapped students. All these court cases have contributed to identifying and educating language minority students. Furthermore, the Educational Amendments of 1978 (PL 95–561) mandated free and appropriate education for all handicapped children, whereby testing must be done in a nondiscriminatory manner and an individualized educational program must be established, implying that the instruction be carried out in a bilingual manner.

Presently, in accordance with legislative and court mandates, special education services are provided to meet the needs of students with handicapping conditions whose primary language is other than English. These services are part of the educational program to provide both the basic instructional modifications and adaptations prescribed which will enable students to maintain appropriate levels of academic achievement while developing English language skills. In keeping with the regulations of PL 94–142, it is the local school's responsibility to provide students with an instructional program that includes all the components indicated in Figure 1.2.

Bilingual handicapped students, due to their different linguistic and cultural background, need to be served by a program that includes these three elements.

1. *A least restrictive environment.* PL 94–142 requires that, at a moment of students' placement, a factor to consider is the least restrictive educational alternative. This legal provision requires that handicapped students be educated to the maximum extent appropriate and that special classes be substituted for the regular classroom only when the severity of the handicap is such that education in regular classes cannot be achieved satisfactorily. However, subsequent sections of these regulations note that a full continuum of alternative placements must be available. In other words, an attempt should be made to keep handicapped students in the classroom (provided they receive the nec-

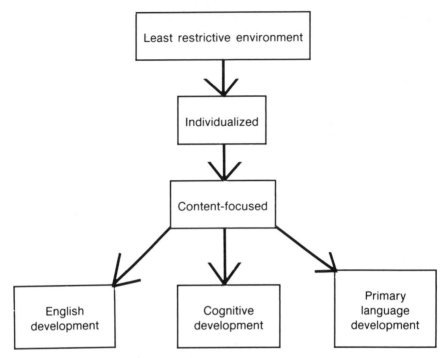

Figure 1.2. Instructional Program for Language Minority Handicapped Students.

essary services), but if specialized services are needed, they must be provided.

The law requires that a continuum of placement possibilities be provided and the one that is the least restrictive be utilized to serve students' special educational needs. It is questionable, then, if the significant number of language minority students enrolled in special education classes (especially in classes for the learning disabled) are placed in the least restrictive environment when it is known that many of these students reflect language differences and not necessarily learning disorders.

Bilingual students, due to their limited English skills, tend to be isolated from the rest of the school. They need an environment that provides for the delivery of bilingual special education services, while at the same time allowing students the opportunity to relate to the surrounding world.

2. *An individualized program that provides the acquisition of academic concepts and learning skills designed to meet the unique needs of each student.* PL 94–142 defines an individualized education program (IEP)

as one that includes the level of educational performance of the student, indication of the annual goal including short-term instructional objectives, the educational services provided, and evaluation procedures. The primary purpose of a bilingual special education program is to help each student achieve a maximum potential for learning. The current national emphasis on instructional planning requires that an individualized education program (IEP) be written for all handicapped students. There is a need for a clearer understanding of the educational needs of the students so that adequate information can be included in the IEP. Developing an IEP for handicapped bilingual students requires an understanding of the students' cognitive, cultural, and linguistic background. Every school district should assure that all handicapped bilingual students and their parents or guardians be provided with an IEP in both English and the parents' primary language.

Bilingual special education is operationalized at each local level with each individual student in mind. All instruction is prescribed in a manner that accommodates and remediates the students' exceptionality. For language minority students, programs must be appropriate not only in terms of special education needs, but also in terms of linguistic and cultural needs.

3. *Content-focused.* Bilingual special education instruction is focused on basic academic skills, including the acquisition of the concepts and skills specified in different subject areas, such as mathematics, reading, writing, social studies, and science. Language development and literacy skills must be emphasized in all subject areas involving decoding, interpreting, and articulating messages within appropriate sociocultural contexts. Concept acquisition includes learning concrete referents and abstract ideas found in the curriculum of the different subject areas of the curriculum.

The major thrust of bilingual education is the promotion of learning and the fullest development of students' potential by creating an atmosphere in which students feel confident in themselves. Cognitive demands increase as students are moved from lower cognitive levels to higher cognitive levels (Tikunoff, 1984). Which subject areas are taught in the primary language and which ones in the second language will depend on students' level of relative proficiency in both languages. The less proficient students skew in the second language, the more instruction in the primary language is given. A content-focused curriculum includes the development of the primary language and English as described below.

Emphasis on the development of primary language skills. The primary or dominant language is the language through which students acquire more of their conceptual and academic development. It is necessary to determine students' strongest language and build on that language development. For most handicapped bilingual students, this primary language is a language other than English which is determined in the evaluation and assessment of the students' linguistic strengths and weaknesses. Primary/native language instruction needs to emphasize development of a high level of proficiency to include literacy. Student-centered literacy activities in the native language can exercise a positive effect on literacy achievement in the primary and second language.

The student's stronger language must be employed in instruction to insure an understanding of the intent of instructional tasks. The primary goal is development of cognitive skills which is best achieved when the student's primary language is the medium of instruction. Growth in linguistic ability is interrelated with intellectual growth since language is a means to represent thought and a vehicle for thinking.

Emphasis on English development. A very important element is the second language component. For most bilingual students, the acquisition of English is an activity undertaken when students have acquired the basic structures and vocabulary in their first language. Many first encounter English when they go to school and find that the language of the school and home are not the same. Thus, English language learning needs to be provided in the best possible environment for students to learn it well and in the least time possible.

Students learn English by imitating the speakers of the language, by using the language creatively, and by using the language to learn. Language acquisition is not only based on grammatical structures, but also (and more importantly) on meaning. When students acquire a second language in meaningful situations, speech emerges in natural stages. Second language instruction should be provided in a meaningful context wherein communicative competence is primary. Through an English as a second language (ESL) program, students can familiarize themselves with meanings, concepts, sounds, basic grammatical structures, and the vocabulary of the second language. Acquiring an adequate vocabulary is an important step in learning the second language. Vocabulary is not learned in grammatical isolation; it is learned to understand cultural referents that words represent in English, its meaning, and its components.

ISSUES IN THE FIELD OF BILINGUAL SPECIAL EDUCATION

The following issues need to be mentioned when presenting an overview of bilingual special education: (a) the role of language in the classroom,

(b) the need for continual evaluation of student progress, (c) components of a successful instructional environment, and (d) the role of parents in the educational planning and instruction of their children's education. Although these issues are briefly identified in this chapter, they are discussed throughout this book, establishing the important connection between the fields of special and bilingual education.

The Role of Language in the Classroom

The language of classroom instruction is a special language. For students, it requires not only understanding of new concepts and new information, but also knowing the rituals of classroom life and how to participate competently in instructional activity. Students learn the language of instruction when engaged in classroom instructional tasks using that language. Language and literacy are best learned when presented in authentic situations reflecting real needs, purposes, and functions. If LEP students are to develop proficiency in English, that proficiency is best developed in relation to learning the language of instruction while learning to participate in instructional activities.

Language needs to be used to be learned. It can be facilitated both as a process and as a product of learning. It is a form of communication providing students the opportunity to participate in learning in different ways. A successful classroom is one in which language is used to communicate and clarify instruction in both languages, in which there is understanding and awareness of cultural differences at the students' expressive and nonverbal communication, and in which both languages are used to develop language skills during the whole day and not just during language instruction.

Cummins (1981a, 1984) addresses the type of communication which should be emphasized in the schools. Acquisition of fluent English-speaking and listening skills does not necessarily imply commensurate development of English conceptual or academic proficiency. It has been suggested that the levels of proficiency bilingual students attain in their two languages may be an important intervening variable mediating the effects of bilingualism on students' cognitive and academic development. It has been hypothesized that there may be threshold levels of linguistic proficiency that bilingual students must attain in order to avoid cognitive deficits and to allow the potentially beneficial aspects of becoming bilingual to influence cognitive growth. This theory assumes that those aspects of bilingualism that might positively influence cognitive growth are unlikely to come into effect until students have attained a certain minimum threshold level of proficiency in the second language. Given this conceptual distinction between basic interpersonal communication skills (BICS) and cognitive academic language proficiency (CALP), Cummins (1981b) has emphasized the importance of the latter in learning a second language. He has established that there is a reliable dimension of language proficiency which is strongly related to literacy and other decontextualized, verbal academic tasks on which policy decisions about language proficiency must be based. For Cummins, the importance of teaching bilingual students is in promoting those academic tasks or literacy skills in two languages.

Effective teachers actively work at engaging students in tasks and communicate their expectations so that students can complete them successfully during instruction. Teachers monitor students' work and provide immediate feedback with relation to task completion. Teachers must be trained in informal assessment so that they can determine when activities and assignments are at the appropriate difficulty level and whether students are comprehending instruction.

Need for Ongoing Evaluation of Student Progress

Students identified as in need of special services must receive services based upon individual need, and not on specific categories of handicap or preexisting service offerings. PL 94-142 explicitly requires a multi-disciplinary individual evaluation that is nondiscriminatory and useful in the development of an individualized education program aimed at improving students' academic, social, and affective skills. One objective of this assessment is the identification of the students' cognitive, linguistic, physical, and social abilities to insure a meaningful and appropriate educational plan. Ideally, for bilingual handicapped students, an individualized education program identifies the mechanism for the establishment of (a) an accurate diagnostic base for the identification of particular handicaps, (b) an appropriate instructional program, and (c) an effective delivery of services.

Students need to be assessed in both languages, the primary language and English. For bilingual special education students, assessment includes an initial screening of the students' language abilities in English and in the primary language, respectively, to determine which language should be used mostly in assessment and instruction. Bilingual students who score at a low proficiency level in both languages need further assessment to probe speech, hearing, language disorders, mental retardation, or emotional disturbances requiring special education services. Assessment personnel should collect information to rule out, to the extent possible, linguistic, cultural, or ethnic differences as the primary explanation of the stated referral problem. They should document that the educational need is not due primarily to unfamiliarity and difficulty with the English language.

Once the initial screening has been completed, the next step is an in-depth evaluation of the students' entire range of communicative abilities, including speech, language-receptive, and expressive elements of discourse. It is important that the speech and language evaluation be performed in the language the students are most exposed to and understand best.

Another component of the assessment process is the evaluation of the students' linguistic abilities in English to provide important information in determining the type and nature of English instruction. Choosing the language of instruction is a crucial component of a bilingual special education program. Once the assessment results indicate which is the students' stronger language, this language should be the language of instruction. In some cases when no clear dominance is established, other factors, such as students' language preferences, motivation, previous language experiences, and attitudes or wishes of the parents should be included in the evaluation.

A Successful Instructional Environment

Bilingual education and special education programs have looked at the work done in regular education in the areas of school effectiveness and successful learning/classroom environments, especially from the perspective that school improvement must involve both quality and equity. The research available on effective schools identifies factors that characterize schools that achieve quality and equity. The following factors have been repeatedly mentioned in the literature: (a) high expectations for all students, (b) a safe and orderly environment conducive to learning, and (c) a clear and focused mission concerning instructional goals. These are the same factors that make a bilingual special education classroom successful.

There is a wide variation in the organization of bilingual programs from school to school due to different community and school district educational goals and parental educational priorities. It is up to local school boards, administrators, parents, and teachers to work out the patterns that best suit their specific needs and objectives. Different objectives require a wide variety of methodologies to put bilingual education into practice. Districts need to have policies to provide special education instructional methodologies to limited English proficient bilingual students who are handicapped.

A bilingual special education program needs to use reciprocal interaction modes which are based on the concept of learning as a process
of constructing a student's own language and the use of a holistic
perspective, that is, the salient environmental features that facilitate
the acquisition of a new language and culture and provide for the
academic development of students. Cummins (1984) and Ortiz (1984a)
suggest a holistic classroom instructional approach. Swedo (1987) defines
the holistic approach as providing students opportunities to be active
constructors of meaning in both languages and literacy, with the construction built on cues from the context of the activity. The interaction
of students with adults in meaningful and relevant ways is very important in this process.

The Role of Parents in Educational Planning

Parents are often mentioned in the literature as an essential element
of effective instructional programs. Responsibility for the child's education is a responsibility of the parents. Parents are the primary helper,
observer, and decision maker for students. PL 94-142 requires parental
participation. Under this law, parents must be provided information,
assessment, and advisement to ensure that they understand the various
proceedings, deliberations, and decisions that may result in relation to
their children's education. Matters related to identification, evaluation,
and placement need to be presented to parents in their primary language.
     Many parents are unaware of the rights and services available to
them as parents of language minority handicapped students. One is the
need for information. That is why parents need to be involved with
their children's school so that PL 94-142 can be explained to them,
in order for them to know their rights and responsibilities under the
law. For example, the right to due process is very seldom understood
by parents. They need to know they have the right to talk to school
personnel about their child's schooling, to see all decisions in writing,
and to appeal any decision made with respect to their children.
     One of the responsibilities of parents is to understand the child's
diagnosis and educational recommendations in terms of placement and
instructional services. Every school district will assure that parents or
guardians of bilingual students are notified in their native language
regarding permission to test, IEP participation, and due process.

SUMMARY

Bilingual special education is the use of the home language and culture
and English in an individually designed program of special instruction

for students. Bilingual instruction provides bilingual handicapped students with the necessary cognitive and linguistic skills to learn in two languages. This appropriate instruction includes a least restrictive environment, a content-focused curriculum, and the development of literacy skills in students' primary and English languages. If these aspects of bilingual special education are followed, an important connection will be made.

REFERENCES

Baca, L., & Bransford, J. (1982). *An appropriate education for handicapped children of limited English proficiency.* Reston, VA: ERIC Clearinghouse on Handicapped and Gifted Children.

Ben-Zeev, S. (1977). The influence of bilingualism on cognitive strategy and cognitive development. *Child Development, 48,* 1009-1018.

Bilingual Education Act, 20, U.S.C. 880(b) (1968) Washington, DC (1968).

Bilingual Education Act Educational Amendments of 1984 (PL 98-511). Washington, DC: Education Department.

Cummins, J. (1981a). Four misconceptions about language proficiency in bilingual education. *NABE Journal, 5*(3), 31-41.

Cummins, J. (1981b). The role of primary language development in promoting educational success for language minority students. In California State Department of Education (Ed.), *Schooling and language minority students: A theoretical framework* (pp. 3-49). Los Angeles, CA: National Dissemination and Assessment Center for Bilingual Education.

Cummins, J. (1984). *Bilingualism and special education.* Clevedon, England: Multilingual Matters.

DeAvila, E.A., & Duncan, S.E. (1979). Bilingualism and the metaset. *NABE Journal, 3*(2), 1-20.

DeBlassie, R. (1983). Emotional and behavioral disorders in bilingual children. In D.R. Omark & J.G. Erickson (Eds.), *The bilingual exceptional child* (pp. 55-68). San Diego, CA: College-Hill Press.

Diana v. California State Board of Education, No. C 7037 RFT, Dis. Ct. No. Cal. (1970).

Garcia, S.B., & Yates, J.R. (1986). Policy issues associated with serving bilingual exceptional children. *Journal of Reading, Writing and Learning Disabilities, 2,* 123-137.

Gardner, R.C. (1985). *Social psychology and second language learning: The role of attitudes and motivation.* Baltimore: Edward Arnold.

Gardner, R.C., & Lambert, W.E. (1972). *The role of attitudes and motivation in second language learning.* Rowley, MA: Newbury House.

Grosjean, F. (1982). *Life with two languages.* Cambridge, MA: Harvard University Press.

Jose P. v. Ambach, 557 F. Supp. 11230 (E. D. N. Y.) (1983).

Langdon, H.W. (1983). Assessment and intervention strategies for the bilingual language-disordered student. *Exceptional Children, 50,* 37-46.

Lau v. Nichols, 414 U.S. 563, 39L. Ed 2 1, 94 S. Ct. 786 (1974).

Maltitz, F.W. (1975). *Living and learning in two languages: Bilingual bicultural education in United States.* New York: McGraw-Hill.

Ortiz, A. (1984a). Choosing the language of instruction for exceptional bilingual children. *Teaching Exceptional Children, 16,* 208-212.

Ortiz, A. (1984b). Language and curriculum development for exceptional bilingual children. In P.C. Chin (Ed.), *Education of culturally and linguistically different exceptional children* (pp. 77-100). Reston, VA: Council for Exceptional Children.

Peal, E., & Lambert, W.E. (1962). The relation of bilingualism to intelligence. *Psychological Monographs, 76,* 1-231.

Ramirez, A. (1985). *Bilingualism through schooling: Cross cultural education of minority and majority students.* Albany, NY: SUNY Press.

Rios v. Reed, 75 C 296(E. D. N. Y.) (1977).

Serna v. Portales Municipal Schools, 351F Supp. 1279 (D. N. M.) (1974).

Swain, M., & Cummins, J. (1979). Bilingualism, cognitive functioning, and education. *Language Teaching and Linguistics: Abstracts, 12,* 4-18.

Swedo, J. (1987). Effective teaching strategies for handicapped limited English proficient students. *Bilingual Special Education Newsletter, 6*(1), 3-5.

Tikunoff, W.J. (1984, September). *Student functional proficiency: Towards specifying a practitioners' operational model.* Paper presented at the New York Bilingual Education Multifunctional Support Center.

United States Department of Education. (1975). *Education of the Handicapped Act.* Washington, DC: U.S. Government Printing Office.

Walker, L. (1987). Procedural rights in the wrong system: Special education is not enough. In A. Garner & T. Joe (Eds.), *Images of the disabled/disabling images.* New York: Praeger.

Willig, A.C. (1986). Special education and the culturally and linguistically different child: An overview of issues and challenges. *Journal of Reading, Writing and Learning Disabilities, 2,* 161-173.

chapter 2

Using Language Assessment Data for Language and Instructional Planning for Exceptional Bilingual Students

Alba A. Ortiz
Shernaz B. Garcia

Selecting the language of instruction is a prerequisite to planning effective instructional programs for limited-English-proficient (LEP) students. For LEP students who are also handicapped, language choice is influenced not only by their levels of native language and English skills, but also by the nature and severity of the handicapping condition. Individuals who are involved in assessment, instructional planning, and in choosing the language of instruction for these students must understand the interaction of language skills with handicapping conditions. Otherwise, students are at risk of being placed in instructional settings in which they are expected to acquire English proficiency *and* profit from English instruction simultaneously. Effective planning for language minority students would incorporate the following principles related to bilingualism and second language acquisition:

1. Threshold levels of proficiency in both languages may be a prerequisite to academic and cognitive success for bilingual students (Cummins, 1984). If bilingual children attain only a low level of proficiency in one or both languages, their long-term interaction with academic environments using these languages will be impoverished.
2. Bilingualism can be a positive influence on students' cognitive and personal development and can enhance their knowledge of, and control over, language (Bialystok, 1984; Cummins, 1984). In order for such benefits to accrue, however, bilingualism must involve nativelike proficiency in both languages.
3. Because there is a common underlying proficiency, bilingual individuals can transfer literacy-related and academic skills across lan-

guages (California State Department of Education, 1985; Cummins, 1981b, 1984). Instruction in the native language thus allows students to master content and stay on grade level as they acquire English proficiency.

4. Students acquiring English as a second language must become proficient in the conversational *and* the academic dimensions of language. It takes approximately one to two years for LEP students to master the conversational aspects of English (basic interpersonal communication skills, or BICS) to the extent that they have nativelike control of the surface structures of the language. However, the development of literacy-related skills in the second language (cognitive/academic language proficiency, or CALP) requires approximately five to seven years before students can perform comparably to their native English-speaking peers (Cummins, 1981a, 1984). Given this, students should not be prematurely exited from special language programs.

5. Handicapped students can benefit from bilingualism in the same way as nonhandicapped students (Greenlee, 1981; McConnell, 1981; Weiss, 1980). For these students, just as for the nonhandicapped, instruction in the native language provides the foundation upon which to build English proficiency. When instruction in only *one* language is appropriate (e.g., to avoid confusing the student), English would not necessarily be the language of choice; consideration must be given to the student's family and language community, age, preference, and career or vocational opportunities (Ortiz, 1984).

6. Acquisition of English is facilitated when communication and input are modified to make messages comprehensible to LEP students (Krashen, 1981, 1982). Comprehensible input is contextualized, that is, it relates to students' backgrounds and experiences, and provides linguistic and paralinguistic cues to aid understanding. Teachers' verbal interactions are geared to students' linguistic proficiency and are characterized by clear articulation, repetition, slower rate of delivery, paraphrasing, and summarizing. New content draws upon students' prior knowledge of the topic.

In this chapter, the above principles will be considered in relation to selecting the language of instruction and planning instructional programs for handicapped LEP students. A framework for decision making will be presented which considers language assessment, a language use plan, and examples of language interventions which can be incorporated into individualized educational programs (IEPs). Recommendations for making instruction culturally and linguistically relevant for LEP exceptional students will be offered and, finally, examples of approaches or strategies which are particularly successful with language minority populations will be discussed.

ASSESSING AND PROFILING LANGUAGE SKILLS

A major outcome of the special education comprehensive assessment should be adequate information to establish the student's language dominance, patterns of language use, and relative language proficiency. Language *proficiency* refers to the level of skill or the degree to which a student exhibits control over the use of language (Payan, 1984). According to Mattes and Omark (1984), the *dominant* language is generally the one which (a) is more developed; (b) is preferred, when, from the point of view of both the speaker and the listener, the two languages are equally appropriate; or (c) the one which intrudes on the phonological, syntactic, lexical, or semantic system of the other (e.g., when Spanish syntax is used in English utterances, as in the case of the *car blue* for the *blue car*). Using equivalent tests or evaluation procedures in two languages allows a comparison of the child's proficiency in each language; the relative difference between assessment results in the two languages provides the basis for determining dominance (Oller, 1979). While dominance data suggest the language of instruction, proficiency data indicate the type of intervention program most likely to meet students' needs.

Traditionally used norm-referenced language assessment instruments often provide an incomplete profile of students' language skills because they do not usually assess language in natural communication situations and tend to focus on mastery over the structural aspects of language (e.g., syntax, phonology, vocabulary, grammar). It is important, then, that these instruments be supplemented by other procedures which describe both spontaneous conversation and cognitive/academic language skills (Cummins, 1984). These language assessments should be current, that is, should not be more than six months old (Ortiz et al., 1985), and should describe receptive as well as expressive skills for both the first and the second language.

Figure 2.1 provides a format for aggregating language assessment data to establish language dominance and relative language proficiency and to select the language(s) of instruction. As is evident in the language profile, these judgments are made on the basis of comparative data in both languages. The next few sections delineate some of the categories included in Figure 2.1.

Name:_____ Grade: _____ Age: _____

School:_____ Teacher:_____ Room: _____

Length of Residency in the U.S.: _____ Country of Origin:_____

Program Placement: Reg. Ed. _____ Bil Ed. _____ ESL _____ Migrant Ed. _____ Other _____

If appropriate, percent of English instruction _____ Native language instruction _____ ESL_____

Grades in bil. ed. program (circle those which apply): preschool K 1 2 3 4 5 6 7 8 9 10 11 12

Grades in ESL program (circle those which apply): preschool K 1 2 3 4 5 6 7 8 9 10 11 12

A. Language Use

1. Home Language Survey Date _____

  1. _____First language learned by student

  2. _____Language most frequently used by student at home

  3. _____Language most frequently used by parents with student

  4. _____Language most frequently used by adults with each other at home

  5. _____Language most frequently used by student with siblings

Based on the above, indicate primary home language: English ____ Other language ____ Both____

2. Observation of Relative Language Usage (to be completed by a bilingual observer):

  Observer(s)_____ Date(s) of Observation _____

  Check (✔) the language(s) the student uses with monolingual and bilingual individuals in each of the following contexts. If the student's language is characterized by code-switching, place a "C" beside the check (✔C).

Contexts	Only English		Mostly English		Equal Use		Mostly Other		Only Other	
	*M	B	M	B	M	B	M	B	M	B
1. Informal with peers (playground, cafeteria, bus, etc.)										
2. Informal with adults (hallways, play areas, cafeteria, off-campus)										
3. Formal with peers (classroom, lab, library, etc.)										
4. Formal with adults (classroom, lab, library, etc.)										
Number of checks in each column (✔)										
Number of checks involving code-switching (✔C)										

*M= With monolingual speakers   B = With bilingual individuals

Based on the above, the most frequently used language is: English_____ Other language ___ Both ___

Comments:

Figure 2.1. Profile of language dominance and proficiency.

B. Tests of Language Skills

1. Norm-Referenced Oral Language Proficiency Test Results

DATE	LANGUAGE	INSTRUMENT/PROCEDURE	AREAS ASSESSED	RESULTS

2. Criterion-Referenced Oral Language Proficiency Test Results

DATE	LANGUAGE	INSTRUMENT/PROCEDURE	AREAS ASSESSED	RESULTS

C. Achievement Test Results

1. Norm-Referenced Achievement Test Results

English:

Subject	Instrument	Norms Appropriate for Student?	R.S.	S.S.	%ile	G.E.	A.E.	Date
Language								
Reading								
Math								
Other								

Other Language:

Subject	Instrument	Norms Appropriate for Student?	R.S.	S.S.	%ile	G.E.	A.E.	Date
Language								
Reading								
Math								
Other								

Figure 2.1 (cont.)

2. Criterion-Referenced Achievement Test Results

English:

Subject	Instrument/ Procedure	Score	% Correct	G.E.	A.E.	Other	Date
Language							
Reading							
Math							
Other							

Other Language:

Subject	Instrument/ Procedure	Score	% Correct	G.E.	A.E.	Other	Date
Language							
Reading							
Math							
Other							

D. Please record any available information about the nature of prior instruction and adaptations attempted to improve performance.

Modifications or Interventions	Date Begun	Date Ended	Amount of Time	Results

E. Language Dominance (Check one):

English _____   Other Language _____   No clear dominance established _____

Other Comments:

Form Completed By: _____   Date: _____

Source: Based on a form presented in: California State Department of Education (1981). *Individual Learning Programs for LEP Students.* Sacramento, CA: Author, which was revised by Nancy Cloud, December, 1986.

Language Use Patterns

A comprehensive language assessment should establish patterns of language use; without this information, there is a risk that the wrong language will be selected for assessment and instruction. For example, in a study of LEP Hispanic students placed in programs for the learning disabled, Ortiz et al. (1985) found that 49 percent of 108 students who were described by teachers as being English-dominant at school used Spanish as the primary language at home. This finding is consistent with literature which suggests that language dominance can vary for the same students across a variety of settings, speakers, topics, or even specific aspects of the languages being assessed (Burt & Dulay, 1978).

Home Language Survey. Every district is required to conduct a Home Language Survey (HLS) to determine whether a language other than English is spoken in the home. Students who have been exposed to other languages are tested, using a standardized language assessment instrument, to establish their language dominance and proficiency and to determine whether they are eligible for special language programs such as bilingual education or English as a second language (ESL) instruction. The HLS questions (Figure 2.1, Section A.1) can reveal language use patterns in the home; interviews with parents and others can also provide valuable information about language use in the home and community, language preference, and children's level of proficiency in each language.

Observation data. Assessing students' ability to engage in spontaneous, natural conversation yields information about their knowledge of the rules of conversation and about functional language use (i.e., pragmatic language skills). Observations should focus not only on interactions with peers and adults in informal settings to describe interpersonal communication skills but should also focus on language use in more formal, academic contexts to determine whether the student has adequate proficiency to master literacy skills (Cummins, 1984). Further, observation of the student's language use with monolingual as well as bilingual individuals will provide further insights related to language dominance and proficiency (Figure 2.1, Section A.2).

A pragmatic approach to language assessment focuses on the child's ability to function in daily life and to communicate meaning while taking into account the likelihood that LEP students will make errors in grammar, pronunciation, or syntax since they are in the process of learning English. If second language learners make errors in their use of English syntax and grammar, but are able to engage in and maintain a conversation in English (i.e., have good pragmatic skills), the structural errors are probably normal developmental errors. On the other hand, if they make structural errors and also have difficulty with language use (e.g., poor topic maintenance, long delays before responding, frequent revisions which interfere with meaning making, etc.), it is more likely that a language disorder is present. Thus, using pragmatic criteria to screen for language disorders results in more accurate identification of children with true disorders (Damico, Oller, & Storey, 1983; Oller, 1983).

Tests of Language Skills

Section B of the Language Profile underscores the need to establish *relative* language proficiency, that is, students' abilities in English as compared to those in their native language.

Norm-referenced language tests. Districts use a variety of norm-referenced language proficiency instruments, for example, Language Assessment Scales (De Avila & Duncan, 1977), Bilingual Syntax Measure (Burt, Dulay, & Hernandez-Chavez, 1976), IDEA Oral Language Proficiency Test (Dalton, 1979), and Basic Inventory of Natural Language (Herbert, 1979). These instruments usually report scores on a five-point scale, with 1 indicating little or no knowledge of a language and 5 indicating native or nativelike proficiency. It is important to establish a clear dominance whenever possible because the results of language dominance and proficiency tests are used not only to determine the primary language of instruction, but in the case of students referred to special education, to determine the language of assessment. Inaccurate decisions about the dominant language can lead to inappropriate placement of LEP students into special education. A guiding principle in assessment of limited-English-proficient students is that the child is not handicapped unless the handicapping condition can be documented in the child's dominant language.

Students referred to special education are usually tested employing other norm-referenced language assessment instruments, for example, the Peabody Picture Vocabulary Test (Dunn, 1965), or the Test of Oral Language Development (Newcomer & Hammill, 1977). Most of these instruments are not normed on LEP students and thus cannot be used to make special education eligibility decisions. Moreover, few standardized English-language instruments have equivalent forms in the native language, making it difficult to compare abilities using similar data across the two languages, a requirement for distinguishing language differences from handicapping conditions. The results of norm-referenced language testing should be compared against results of criterion-referenced assessments.

Criterion-referenced language assessment. Literacy-related activities, which involve problem solving, synthesis, and/or analysis of information (e.g., test taking), demand high levels of cognitive language proficiency to be successfully completed. As the level of language becomes more complex, LEP students who do not possess comparable levels of CALP would be expected to have increasing difficulty in completing such assignments. Consequently, assessment of CALP skills is important to understanding academic performance and insuring that language limitations are not inaccurately interpreted as deficits in intellectual or cognitive development.

As indicated previously, comprehensive language assessments involve evaluation of both receptive and expressive language skills. Dictation and story-retelling activities assess students' receptive language skills, that is, how well they understand messages. Receptive skills are important given that so much school time is spent receiving messages from teachers and others, as, for example, in class lectures, reviews, or when directions for completing assignments are given. Storytelling activities, when used to assess expressive language skills, can reveal information about a child's ability to organize information, sequence events, draw conclusions, and evaluate actions. Assessment of narrative competence also reveals information about cognitive development when the *content* of the story is the focus of analysis, rather than the linguistic accuracy of structures. Cloze procedures, which require students to fill in missing words in a passage, measure expectancy grammar, or the ability to predict the missing word on the basis of knowledge of the context and understanding of the structures which surround the missing word. Cloze procedures also tap into a student's experiential background, familiarity with the topic, vocabulary associated with the subject, and his or her knowledge of the rules of syntax and grammar.

Assessment of Achievement

Since poor academic achievement is a primary reason for referral of LEP students to special education (Ortiz et al., 1985), and determination of a specific handicap is based on the relationship of academic achievement to intellectual potential (e.g., learning disabilities versus mental retardation), assessment of achievement is another critical aspect of the comprehensive assessment for special education. As with language assessments, eligibility decisions which are based, in part, on academic achievement require that equivalent measures of achievement in both the native language and in English be available. However, it is important to understand that assessment of achievement in the native language presupposes instruction in that language.

The limitations of language assessment instruments, discussed previously, are also limitations of traditionally used achievement tests. It is necessary, then, to supplement outcomes of norm-referenced instruments with criterion-referenced measures (Sections C.1 and 2 of Figure 2.1). Curriculum-based assessment (Tucker, 1985) and other informal procedures for assessing academic progress can be extremely valuable in overcoming problems associated with the lack of appropriate, standardized achievement tests for LEP students, and can provide data that are more relevant and sensitive to prior, as well as future, instruction. For example, if it is determined, using curriculum-based assessment, that the instructional materials being used are too difficult for the student, these materials can be changed or modified and progress monitored to determine whether the adaptations resolve learning difficulties. A judgment about the presence of a possible handicap cannot be made without evaluations of prior instruction provided the student, as well as the level of skill attained in the problem area(s).

Exposure to the curriculum. In evaluating prior instruction, a primary goal is to determine whether the student received adequate exposure to the curriculum, that is, whether there were sufficient opportunities to acquire desired skills. Some students fail to master academic content because their education is interrupted for a variety of reasons (e.g., absenteeism, frequent moves, etc.). These interruptions can have cumulative negative effects on future success. Prereferral intervention (Section D of Figure 2.1) is necessary in order to rule out the possibility that learning problems are associated with a lack of opportunity to learn rather than with a learning disability (Ortiz & Garcia, 1988).

Instruction must also be evaluated to determine whether there were sufficient opportunities for students to practice skills or content to reach desired levels of independent performance. Students are sometimes allowed to engage in independent practice before they have demonstrated adequate understanding of the task and thus may actually be learning incorrect responses as they work on their own. It is important to remember that independent functioning requires mastery of material at the level of 95–100 percent (Rosenshine, 1983). This raises concern about goals and objectives that are written with evaluation criteria established at the 70–80 percent level.

If LEP students are to experience academic success, instruction must be provided in their dominant language. When students who are dominant in their native language are placed in submersion programs, where English is the only language of instruction, failure is most likely a function of their inability to understand the language in which the content was presented. In evaluating prior instruction and the adequacy of exposure to the curriculum, questions such as the following should be asked (Garcia & Ortiz, 1988):

1. Was the child given ample opportunity to master native language skills and academic content before being transitioned to English instruction?
2. What resources were used to provide native language support for students who were not in bilingual education programs?
3. Was the teacher adequately trained to provide dual language instruction? English as a second instruction?

These questions can focus the types of instructional activities and curriculum to be planned for LEP pupils.

LANGUAGE PLANNING

The dominant language should be the language of instruction. In only a few instances will it be impossible to determine language dominance. The notion of a "balanced" bilingual, that is, a person who has equal skills (or lack of skills) in all aspects of listening, speaking, reading, and writing has been refuted in the second language acquisition literature (McCollum, 1981). Determining dominance, then, requires *multiple* data sets which allow examination of pragmatic skills as well as phonological, lexical, semantic, and synactic characteristics, in both the receptive and expressive domains. The need to investigate both receptive and expressive language competence cannot be overstressed. For example, some children *speak* English exclusively, but have greater *receptive* skills in the other language. This might be the case if parents understand, but do not speak English. In such instances, parents use their native language in interactions with their children who, in turn, respond in English. It would be inaccurate to simply describe these students as being English-dominant.

The data in each of the categories of the language profile should be carefully examined to establish patterns of use and strength (Section E of Figure 2.1). As indicated previously, the dominant language will be (a) the one the student uses in the greatest number of contexts; (b) one in which the child most frequently receives the highest scores or ratings; (c) the one the child consistently prefers to use, when either language would be appropriate; and/or (d) the one whose rules and structures seem to influence production in the other language most frequently. In examining performance, it may be necessary to disaggregate data to establish patterns of performance. For example, if a child scores a 2 in English and a 2 in Spanish on the Language Assessment Scales, it is helpful to look at the individual subtests to determine whether he or she received higher scores in more of the subtests in one of the languages, a pattern that is not evident when simply looking at global ratings.

Students dominant in a language other than English should receive instruction in that language; children dominant in English should be instructed in English. If no clear dominance can be established, other variables may be taken into consideration, including (a) the child's age, (b) the child's language preference, (c) motivation, (d) previous language experiences, and (e) attitudes or wishes of the parent. As a rule of thumb, if dominance cannot be established, the dominant language of the parents is most likely to be the child's dominant language.

Type of Language Intervention Required

Beyond choosing the language of intervention, educational plans should also specify the type of language intervention that the child needs (Ortiz & Yates, 1989; Willig & Ortiz, in press). Some students will have intact language skills and will simply require that teachers help them refine and expand their linguistic abilities. Instruction for this purpose can be characterized as *language enrichment.* Other students need *language development* programs because, while their language skills are adequate for communicating in their home and community, these skills do not match the language demands of the classroom. For example, children who are classified as "English-proficient" (i.e., not eligible for bilingual education or English as a second language programs) are usually placed in regular classroom programs where only English is used in instruction. While they demonstrate good interpersonal communication skills, these children may need more time to attain cognitive/academic language proficiency required for mastery of literacy skills (Cummins, 1984). A language development program would help assure that English skills of these students are commensurate with those of Anglo peers. Students with language disorders will need *remediation* programs. It is critical that these student receive special education services in their dominant language since it is competence in this language that facilitates the acquisition of high levels of proficiency in the other language (Cummins, 1984).

Another critical decision in choosing the type of intervention is whether, or which, students will receive English as a second language instruction. There will be some circumstances, usually because of lack of bilingual special educators, under which the only option available will be to teach LEP handicapped students in English. In such cases, special education instruction must be modified using English as a second language strategies.

Language Use Plan

Because handicapped students are likely to receive services from several instructional or related services personnel, it will be important to develop a language use plan to coordinate instruction. The language use plan essentially describes *who* will be using *which* language, for *what* purpose (why), and in which skill or subject. For each objective specified in the IEP, a person is designated as responsible for instruction leading to attainment of that objective. For bilingual students, the IEP should specify the language in which instruction or other services will be provided, not only by special education and regular classroom teachers, but also by speech pathologists, counselors, occupational and physical therapists, and so forth. Specifying the language of instruction will assure that instruction is consistent with the student's language status.

PLANNING THE INSTRUCTIONAL PROGRAM

Considerations related to the language of instruction comprise but the first step in determining an appropriate instructional program for handicapped LEP students. The selection of instructional materials, approaches, and strategies should also be made on the basis of what is known to be effective for the student's handicap as well as linguistic and cultural background. Since language minority students also represent culturally and/or ethnically diverse environments, it is important that curricular as well as instructional planning be guided by a philosophy that will maximize the success of these students in school.

Cultural Relevance

Understanding cultural characteristics is an important aspect of providing appropriate instruction and selecting relevant curricula for language minority students. While some student behaviors do not conform to the desired or expected behaviors of the dominant society, they may, nonetheless, be appropriate, given the student's ethnic or cultural group (Ortiz & Yates, 1989). Special educators must learn as much as possible about the cultures represented in their classrooms, including the effects of socioeconomic status, religion, or gender differences. For example, since some minority groups tend to be overrepresented at the lower socioeconomic levels (U.S. Bureau of the Census, 1983), behaviors which may be a consequence of social class differences are sometimes mistakenly attributed to ethnic differences.

To ensure that curriculum and instruction are appropriate for culturally and linguistically diverse students, special educators must be familiar with principles of multicultural and pluralistic education. The following are offered as a general framework to guide instructional planning (Gollnick & Chinn, 1986):

1. Curricular materials and instructional approaches must be sensitive and relevant to sociocultural backgrounds and experiences.
2. Teachers must understand and identify their own teaching and learning styles, as well as the learning styles of their students, so that instructional strategies are responsive to any differences in cognitive style and they maximize opportunities for success. Cultures may vary in their approach to learning, problem solving, and so on, with the result that these cognitive style patterns are acquired as part of the children's enculturation within their own group. Awareness of such differences will assist teachers in being more responsive to learning difficulties that may, in fact, result from an incompatibility of the teaching approach with the student's preferred learning modality.
3. Oral and nonverbal communication patterns between students and teachers should be analyzed and modified, if necessary, to increase the involvement of students in the learning process. Communication conflicts between students, and between teachers and students, can sometimes be the result of different sets of expectations and interpretations ascribed to the same behavior. For example, some behaviors that are frequently reported as problematic (e.g., lack of eye contact) and possibly considered to be evidence of a learning or behavioral disorder could, in fact, be appropriate in a culturally different context (Ortiz & Maldonado-Colon, 1986).
4. Multicultural education must be integrated throughout the curriculum, rather than taught in isolated, fragmented units. Often, attention to cultural diversity in the curriculum tends to be restricted to celebrations of festivals, religious holidays, food, music or dance, with little or no attention to the social, cultural, and historical contributions of minorities to the United States. Further, limiting attention to traditional aspects of the culture also creates the risk that contemporary characteristics of the group will be ignored, thereby perpetuating the very stereotypes that multicultural edu-

cation seeks to avoid (Oritz & Yates, 1989). In fact, it is extremely important to realize that individuals' cultural identity and characteristics cannot be defined without consideration of cultural differences within the group. It is preferable to think of culture as a continuum, with individuals demonstrating characteristics ranging from traditional to atraditional (Ramirez & Castaneda, 1974). While members at one end of the continuum will display characteristics traditionally associated with the culture, atraditional members may possess few or none of these behaviors and values, but may be totally assimilated into the dominant, mainstream culture.

5. Multicultural education can be enhanced by utilizing community resources. Given that there is a shortage of teacher preparation programs and inservice training to adequately prepare educators to work with language minority students, members of the students' community, including parents, professionals, volunteers and others, become an invaluable resource for the school system. Particularly in the case of newly arrived immigrant groups, community participation in the activities of the school, in developing materials, and in assisting with linguistic issues can increase the school's sensitivity to the students' needs as well as increase the community's participation in their children's education.

Specifically, the following questions should be addressed in planning and implementing instructional programs for LEP handicapped students (Garcia & Ortiz, 1988):

1. How is the student's cultural background different from the culture of the school and larger society?
2. To what extent are the individual student's characteristics representative of his or her community?
3. Is the student able to function successfully in more than one cultural setting? If not, how can opportunities to acquire bicultural competence be incorporated into the curriculum?
4. Is the teacher familiar with cultural information specific to students and their communities?
5. How will these aspects of the student's culture be incorporated into the curriculum?

Linguistic Relevance

The results of the language assessment provide the basis for selection of the language of instruction and the type of language program the student will receive (i.e., enrichment, development, remediation, or ESL). While the assessment process considers and evaluates aspects of language such as proficiency, dominance, interpersonal versus academic skills, it does not necessarily provide information on how the student uses language to accomplish social and cognitive goals. From a sociolinguistic perspective, students' "academic success depends less on the specific language they know than on the ways of using language they know" (Heath, 1986, p. 144). Differences in styles and uses of language, and patterns of verbal interaction can be a function of culture as well as social class (Heath, 1986; Westby, in press). Since the culture of the public schools reflects the values and expectations of the middle-class dominant culture, students from varying backgrounds may find that their linguistic styles and interactions are at odds with expectations at school.

It is often assumed that children enter school already equipped with specific linguistic skills, not only in terms of grammatical structure and form, but also in their ability to use language to accomplish specific goals (e.g., to label objects, recount or recast past events or information, follow directions, sustain and maintain appropriate social interactions, and obtain information from individuals with whom they may not be familiar) (Heath, 1986). The range and function of language use in school has also been described in the literature as restricted or narrow (Applebee, 1981; Langer, 1986). Students who come from different language communities (e.g., working-class English-speaking groups and language minorities) may not share the school's expectations about when, where, and how children learn language (Heath, 1986). For these students, it is important that special educators understand the nature of their language learning, and identify those linguistic functions and skills the student may need to be taught so that these may be incorporated into the individualized educational plan.

Teacher Variables

Much of the discussion in this chapter related to linguistic and cultural issues in instructional planning presupposes that individuals involved in the decision-making process are knowledgeable about second language acquisition, cultural and linguistic diversity, and the effects of these on student achievement. However, since few institutions of higher education offer specialized training in serving exceptional language minority students, training special educators to serve this population relies heavily on effective staff development programs and continuing professional growth, often initiated by teachers themselves. It is critical that preservice programs incorporate bilingual special education and special education/ESL competencies into the curriculum, given the increasing numbers of language minority students in the schools. Specific competencies—particularly those related to language and linguistic considerations—which should be included in inservice and preservice training are discussed below.

Teacher knowledge and training. When handicapped students are also limited-English-proficient, instructional programs must be planned to facilitate acquisition of English as a second language as well as academic achievement. Unless teachers are knowledgeable about current theories of second language acquisition, the relationship between the first and second language, the role of the first language in second language acquisition, bilingual education and second language instruction, and characteristics of instruction which promote language learning for LEP students, they will be unable to provide appropriate instruction to these students.

LEP handicapped students preferably should be served in bilingual special education programs where instruction in the academic areas can be provided in the native language, accompanied by ESL instruction as appropriate. However, one of the dilemmas of recommending native language instruction is that there is a lack of bilingual special educators to provide such teaching. It is therefore critical that monolingual special educators recognize that LEP students will not profit from specially designed instruction until they develop adequate English language proficiency. It is, therefore, important that English as a second language instruction be part of students' IEPs and that special educators become familiar with the most current practices and research on second language teaching.

Teaching style. Teachers must be aware of their own teaching style and their students' learning styles. Unless an effort is made to the contrary, teachers are likely to use a teaching style that best reflects their own learning style (Ramirez & Castaneda, 1974), and which, consequently, maximizes opportunities for those students who share a similar style. While it may not be realistic or desirable to consistently expose students to all material in ways that utilize their preferred cognitive style, teachers should be able to provide instruction using a variety of approaches to be responsive to various styles. This can be achieved by using multisensory teaching aids, diversified grouping patterns, learning centers, variations in reinforcement systems, as well as allowing students to participate in selecting a process that best accomplishes their learning goals and objectives. Exposure to other styles can be a valuable learning tool for students and will increase the likelihood of success under a variety of task conditions.

Teacher Expectations. Teacher judgments and predictions about student performance have been known to significantly affect student outcomes. Research on teacher expectations (Good & Brophy, 1973) suggests that teachers who hold low expectations for certain students tend to interact differently with this group as compared to others for whom they have high expectations. Teacher behaviors that reflect low expectations might include: waiting less time for a response, accepting incorrect or partially correct responses, providing fewer opportunities to learn, focusing on behavior rather than academic performance, seating low expectation students further away, and calling on these students less often. Groups which have traditionally been victims of low expectations include the handicapped, females, the economically disadvantaged, and those who are culturally and linguistically different. It is important to note that, for exceptional LEP students, expectations for academic performance are likely to be mitigated by their handicap as well as the teacher's perception of their linguistic ability. If linguistic differences are interpreted as deficiencies to be remediated, students are liable to be perceived as "disadvantaged" and programs will reflect similar philosophies of instruction. On the other hand, if limited English proficiency is treated as a language "difference," instruction will be aimed at enriching student experiences and adding school language competence by presenting academic content in the native language, while simultaneously providing opportunities for acquiring English proficiency.

PROMISING INSTRUCTIONAL STRATEGIES

The preceding discussion alerts teachers to student variables which will influence the teaching-learning process. The first step in educational planning is to personalize the instructional environment so that compatibility between student characteristics and teacher/teaching characteristics is accomplished. The second step is to select instructional strategies which complement student characteristics and increase the likelihood that learning will occur. Ortiz and Yates (1989) and Willig and Ortiz (in press) summarize the characteristics of effective instructional practices for exceptional LEP students as follows.

Transmission Model

Cummins (1984) suggests that the nature of instruction provided in special education classrooms serves to maintain students' low functioning. According to Cummins, instruction is characterized by an emphasis on transmission models of teaching which emphasize task analysis and sequence instruction from simple to more complex activities, with content transmitted by means of direct instruction, highly structured drills, and independent seatwork. Transmission-oriented teaching presents difficulty for limited-English-proficient students because activities are frequently stripped of context and therefore lose meaning and purpose. Of particular concern is that language lessons, which emphasize sentence patterns or drills and which focus on linguistic structures, may actually interfere with the second language acquisition process.

Reciprocal Interaction Model

Reciprocal interaction teaching models are more effective than transmission models for exceptional minority language students. Reciprocal interaction teaching is characterized by genuine dialogue between student and teacher, in both oral and written communication, and focuses on development of higher levels of cognitive skills, rather than on basic skills (Cummins, 1984). For example, reading is taught using approaches that emphasize comprehension rather than those that emphasize word recognition. Literacy skills are fostered using approaches such as language experience stories, dialogue journals, shared book experiences, and creative writing tasks, with an emphasis on developing high levels of competence in the native language. Moreover, teachers do not teach language as a *subject,* but, instead, consciously integrate language use and development into all curricular content.

Language instruction. According to Krashen (1982), language acquisition takes place best when input is provided that is comprehensible, interesting, relevant, not grammatically sequenced, and when it is provided in sufficient quantity. Methods such as the Total Physical Response Approach (Asher, 1979) or the Natural Approach (Krashen & Terrell, 1983) seem to be more effective because they allow students to develop comprehension skills, attempt to reduce student anxiety, and provide comprehensible input. An advantage for many handicapped students is that these approaches offer simplified language codes and active involvement in the learning process.

Learning to learn. Motivation problems in academic learning situations are usually linked to poor learning histories, cognitive deficits, and negative attributional states (Borkowski, Weyhing, & Turner, 1986). Underachieving students fail to see that their own intellectual efforts may contribute to the solution of the problem and, instead, see themselves as passive recipients of information. Henderson (1980) suggests that teachers provide opportunities for students to set goals and to help determine their own activities. Students can be taught to evaluate tasks, plan various options, select appropriate strategies to achieve goals, and to modify their own behaviors as they encounter problems (Paris & Oka, 1986). Teaching problem-solving strategies increases the likelihood of academic success. In turn, success enhances the student's own perception of competence and helps maintain on-task behaviors. Moreover, success helps foster intrinsic motivation and appreciation of learning for learning's sake. IEPs should recommend reinforcement systems which emphasize task engagement and performance in relation to a standard, rather than systems which focus on tangible rewards and maintain external motivation.

Collaborative learning. Collaborative learning provides excellent opportunities for students to develop leadership, to learn how to make decisions, to resolve conflicts, and to enhance communication skills— all critical to independent functioning. Teachers can foster positive interdependence by establishing that the goal of the group is to ensure the learning of all group members, giving rewards based on the overall achievement of the group, structuring tasks so they require cooperation and coordination among group members in order for the goal to be achieved, and giving complementary roles, sequenced for successful completion, for all members of the groups. Cooperative learning strategies are particularly effective for learners who have difficulty operating from a framework of independence and intrinsic motivation. An additional benefit for limited-English-proficient students is that collaborative learning groups offer natural contexts for development of both conversational and academic learning proficiency.

SUMMARY

The suggestions provided in this chapter are obviously not exhaustive. They do, however, suggest some promising practices in language assessment, educational planning, and instructional strategies which can improve the performance of language minority students in special education. It is important that educators, and particularly special educators, explore these areas more fully and evaluate the efficacy of these recommendations so that the growing number of language minority students who are being placed in special education programs have the best possible opportunity to achieve their social and academic potential.

REFERENCES

Applebee, A.N. (1981). *Writing in the secondary school: English and the content areas.* Urbana, IL: National Council of Teachers of English.

Asher, J. (1979). *Learning another language through actions: The complete teacher's guidebook.* Los Gatos, CA: Skyoak Productions.

Bialystok, E. (1984). *Influence of bilingualism on metalinguistic development.* Paper presented at the Symposium on Language Awareness/Reading Development: Cause? Effect? Concomitance? Held at the National Reading Conference, St. Petersburg, FL.

Borkowski, J.G., Weyhing, R.S., & Turner, L.A. (1986). Attributional retraining and the teaching of strategies. *Exceptional Children, 53*(2), 130-137.

Burt, M., & Dulay, H. (1978). Some guidelines for the assessment of oral language proficiency and dominance. *TESOL Quarterly, 12*(2), 177-192.

Burt, M., Dulay, H., & Hernandez-Chavez, E. (1976). *Bilingual Syntax Measure.* Oakland, CA: Harcourt, Brace, Jovanovich, Inc.

California State Department of Education. (1985). *Beyond language: Social and cultural factors in schooling language minority students.* Los Angeles, CA: California State University, Evaluation, Dissemination, and Assessment Center.

Cummins, J. (1981a). Age on arrival and immigrant second language learning in Canada: A reassessment. *Applied Linguistics, 2,* 132-149.

Cummins, J. (1981b). Empirical and theoretical underpinning of bilingual education. *Journal of Education, 163*(1), 16-29.

Cummins, J. (1984). *Bilingualism and special education: Issues in assessment and pedagogy.* Clevedon, England: Multilingual Matters Ltd.

Dalton, E. (1979). *IDEA Oral Language Proficiency Test.* Whittier, CA: Ballard & Tighe, Inc.

Damico, J.S., Oller, J.W. Jr., & Storey, M.E. (1983). The diagnosis of language disorders in bilingual children. *Journal of Speech and Hearing Disorders, 48,* 285-294.

De Avila, E.A., & Duncan, S.E. (1977). *Language Assessment Scales.* Corte Madera, CA: Linguametrics Group.

Dunn, L.M. (1965). *Peabody Picture Vocabulary Test.* Circle Pines, MN: American Guidance Service.

Garcia, S.B., & Ortiz, A.A. (1988, June). *Preventing inappropriate referrals of language minority students to special education.* (New Focus monograph No. 5). Wheaton, MD: National Clearinghouse for Bilingual Education.

Gollnick, D.M., & Chinn, P.C. (1986). *Multicultural education in a pluralistic society* (2nd ed.). Columbus, OH: Merrill Publishing Company.

Good, T.L., & Brophy, J.E. (1973). *Looking in classrooms.* New York: Harper & Row.

Greenlee, M. (1981). Specifying the needs of a "bilingual" developmentally disabled population: Issues and case studies. *The Journal of the National Association for Bilingual Education, 6*(1), 55-76.

Heath, S.B. (1986). Sociocultural contexts of language development. In California State Department of Education, *Beyond language: Social and cultural factors in schooling language minority students* (pp. 143-186). Los Angeles, CA: Evaluation, Dissemination and Assessment Center, California State University.

Henderson, R. (1980). Social and emotional needs of culturally diverse children. *Exceptional Children, 46*(8), 598-605.

Herbert, C.H. (1979). *Basic Inventory of Natural Language* (rev. ed.). San Bernadino, CA: CHECpoint Systems, Inc.

Krashen, S. (1981). Bilingual education and second language acquisition theory. In California State Department of Education, *Schooling and language minority students: A theoretical framework* (pp. 51-79). Los Angeles, CA: Evaluation, Dissemination and Assessment Center.

Krashen, S. (1982). *Principles and practice in second language acquisition.* New York: Pergamon Press.

Krashen, S., & Terrell, T. (1983). *The natural approach: Language acquisition in the classroom.* Oxford, England: Pergamon Press.

Langer, J. (1986). *Children reading and writing: Structures and strategies.* Norwood, NJ: Ablex.

Mattes, L., & Omark, D. (1984). *Speech and language assessment for the bilingual handicapped.* San Diego, CA: College-Hill Press.

McCollum, P.A. (1981). Concepts in bilingualism and their relationship to language assessment. In J.G. Erickson & D.R. Omark (Eds.), *Communication assessment of the bilingual bicultural child: Issues and guidelines* (pp. 25-41). Baltimore: University Park Press.

McConnell, B. (1981). *IBI (Individualized Bilingual Instruction): A validated program model effective with bilingual handicapped children.* Paper presented at the Council of Exceptional Children Conference on the Exceptional Bilingual Child, New Orleans, LA.

Newcomer, P.L., & Hammill, D. (1977). *Test of Oral Language Development.* Austin, TX: Pro-ed.

Oller, J.W., Jr. (1979). *Language tests at school: A pragmatic approach.* London: Longman Group Limited.

Oller, J.W., Jr. (1983). Testing proficiencies and diagnosing language disorders in bilingual children. In D.R. Omark & J.G. Erickson (Eds.), *The bilingual exceptional child* (pp. 69-88). San Diego, CA: College-Hill Press.

Ortiz, A.A. (1984). Choosing the language of instruction for exceptional bilingual children. *Teaching Exceptional Children, 16,* 208-212.

Ortiz, A.A., & Garcia, S.B. (1988). A prereferral process for preventing inappropriate referrals of Hispanic students to special education. In A.A. Ortiz & B.A. Ramirez (Eds.), *Schools and the culturally diverse exceptional student: Promising practices and future directions* (pp. 6-18). Reston, VA: Council for Exceptional Children.

Ortiz, A.A., Garcia, S.B., Holtzman, W.H., Jr., Polyzoi, E., Snell, W.E., Jr., Wilkinson, C.Y., & Willig, A.C. (1985). *Characteristics of limited English proficient Hispanic students in programs for the learning disabled: Impli-*

cations for policy, practice, and research. Austin, TX: The University of Texas, Handicapped Minority Research Institute on Language Proficiency.

Ortiz, A.A., & Maldonado-Colon, E. (1986). Recognizing learning disabilities in bilingual children: How to lessen inappropriate referrals of language minority students to special education. *Journal of Reading, Writing, and Learning Disabilities International, 1* (1), 47–56.

Ortiz, A.A., & Yates, J.R. (1989). Staffing and the development of individualized educational programs for the bilingual exceptional student. In L. Baca & H.T. Cervantes (Eds.), *The bilingual special education interface* (2nd eds. pp. 183–203). Columbus, OH: Merrill Publishing Company.

Paris, S.G., & Oka, E.R. (1986). Self-regulated learning among exceptional children. *Exceptional Children, 53* (2), 103–108.

Payan, R. (1984). Language assessment for bilingual exceptional children. In L.M. Baca & H.T. Cervantes (Eds.), *The bilingual special education interface* (pp. 125–137). St. Louis: Times Mirror/Mosby.

Ramirez, M., & Castaneda, A. (1974). *Cultural democracy, bicognitive development, and education.* New York: Academic Press.

Rosenshine, B.V. (1983). Teaching functions in instructional programs. *Elementary School Journal, 83,* 335–352.

Tucker, J. (Ed.) (1985). Curriculum-based assessment. *Exceptional Children* (special issue), *52*(3).

U.S. Bureau of the Census. (1983). *Statistical abstract of the United States, 1984* (104th ed.). Washington, DC: U.S. Government Printing Office.

Weiss, R. (1980). *Efficacy and cost effectiveness of an early intervention program for young handicapped children.* Paper presented at the meeting of the Handicapped Children's Early Education Program (HCEEP) Project Directors, Washington, DC.

Westby, C.E. (in press). Cultural variation in storytelling. In L. Cole & V. Deal (Eds.), *Communication disorders in multicultural populations.* Washington, DC: American Speech-Language-Hearing Association.

Willig, A.C., & Ortiz, A.A. (in press). Linking assessment to instruction for exceptional language minority children. In E. Hamayan & J. Damico (Eds.), *Nonbiased assessment of limited English proficient special education students.* San Diego, CA: College-Hill Press.

chapter **3**

An Overview of Issues on the Development and Implementation of Bilingual Special Education Programs

Nivia Zavala

INTRODUCTION

For many years, bilingual education and special education had separate regulations, funds, and research projects in the educational arena (Podell & Kaminsky, 1988). Therefore, it can be stated that as a merged field, bilingual special education is relatively new. Attention to this new hybrid is demonstrated by the increased number of participating students, regulations, court cases, funding, and recent publications and research.

New York City, as well as the New York State Department of Education, have formulated policy documents that combine bilingual and special education guidelines for identification, assessment, and placement of limited-English-proficient (LEP) students with special needs. Revision of current practices and interpretation of existing regulations have produced numerous changes in the educational system. For instance, efforts have been devoted to ensure nonbiased assessment and the placement of students in appropriate educational programs (New York State Education Department, 1988).

The trend toward better practices in the assessment and education of bilingual handicapped students calls for more research in this area. Experts are confronted with complex questions related to the second language acquisition of LEP handicapped students. In particular the research questions of what it means to know English and what are the linguistic characteristics which make a student ready to learn in an English-only classroom setting (Shuy, 1978; Spolsky, 1973) are essential to any initiative in developing educational programs for LEP students.

School districts across the nation have initiated bilingual programs for students who are speakers of other than English languages in an attempt to satisfy their educational needs and to enable them to learn the mainstream language (Hakuta & Gould, 1987). In New York City, for example, the Aspira Consent Decree requires the placement of LEP Hispanic children into bilingual education programs. A language proficiency test, Language Assessment Battery (LAB), has been developed to assess students' relative language proficiency (Abbott, 1985; Tilis, Weichun, & Cumbo, 1978). Thus, limited-English-proficient students are entitled to bilingual education as a result of these activities.

On the basis of this identification process, an accurate and valid assessment of language proficiency is basic to the design of educational programs for bilingual handicapped students. In special education the use of multiple assessments raises additional questions about the validity of a single proficiency instrument versus multiple indicators. A multidisciplinary assessment team must collect data to develop a child-specific language profile with information about English and Spanish. This profile is essential to the design of a language-specific, individualized educational program (IEP) for LEP students (Willig, 1986).

This chapter presents an overview of critical issues related to the development of bilingual special education programs. The first section reviews traditional methods of assessment and discusses their impact on the design of individualized educational programs for limited English proficient students. The second section describes the need for bilingual special education programs and anticipated changes, and concludes with a discussion of the features of an effective bilingual special education program.

ASSESSMENT OF THE SPECIAL NEEDS OF LIMITED ENGLISH PROFICIENT STUDENTS

Since the early 1930s, school personnel have concerned themselves with the appropriateness of procedures, measures, and techniques used in assessing linguistically different students (Mendoza, 1983). A number of surveys and research studies undertaken in California in the 1960s clearly demonstrated the overrepresentation of Spanish-surnamed and black children in special education classes of that state (Baca & Cervantes, 1984; Mercer, 1973). In the 35 counties involved, the percentage of these minority children in special classes was often two to three times what it was in the total school population (Mercer, 1973; Sarason & Doris, 1979).

Historically, testing has legitimized the disability of minority students (Bailey & Harbin, 1980; Cummins, 1981; Oakland, 1977). The conceptual base for assessment was scientific measurement and appraisal, a test-based process rather than a functional evaluation of an individual's strengths and weaknesses. Consequently, because of lower scores obtained by minority group members, incorrect interpretations were made about the abilities of these individuals, resulting in a denial of their emotional, technical, and vocational opportunities, (Cummins, 1986; MacMillan & Meyers, 1977). Due to increased public awareness, the testing industry found itself in the position as creators of "subtle, mistaken and all-pervading judgement of races, classes, and sexes" (Gould, 1981, p. 2).

In response to this testing dilemma, Public Law 94-142 mandated team decision making in 1975. School systems across the nation have put into operation procedures for teams of educators to meet in making eligibility decisions and in writing individualized educational plans for students (Ysseldyke & Algozzine, 1979). This law stressed the need for a multifactor and multisource assessment, that is:

[A]n assessment should be made on the child's educational functioning in relation to the academic program of the school; and the results of this assessment should be expressed in terms of both the child's strengths and weaknesses. The assessment should be comprehensive, using a full range of available instrumentation and observations, including diagnostic tests and other appropriate formal and informal measurements. (Bureau of Education for the Handicapped, 1974, p. 27)

As noted by the text of the law and as suggested by Glaser (1963), assessment should be used primarily for educational and instructional purposes regarding the student's progress. Acquiring information should be one main purpose for instruction, regardless of a child's sociocultural background. Rather than emphasizing, categorizing, and sorting students for program placement, information from assessment should also enhance the development and evaluation of programs and students (Baca & Cervantes, 1984).

Educational planning, then, has become a consensual form of decision making characterized by specification of goals and the nonspecialized participation by all team members, who will implement the program. It is predicted that this consensual planning will lead to maximum satisfaction and the likelihood that the plan will be carried out (Fenton, Yoshida, Maxwell, & Kaufman, 1979; Ysseldyke, Algozzine, & Mitchell, 1982). When a team is engaged in educational planning, the individual disciplines should only operate toward the effective development of an appropriate educational plan. In this process, the multisource quality of the assessment comes together for a unified purpose which is the development of the IEP. Thus, specialists firmly believe that the cooperative involvement of a team is one of the most effective ways of collecting more comprehensive, adaptive, and accurate diagnostic information about a student's functioning.

However, Trachtman (1981) has cautioned that the expansion of the information in team assessments may not provide a guarantee as to its validity. Cummins, Huebner, and McLeskey (1986) have suggested that the validity of the data might greatly affect the decision making. If the information collected is not an accurate reflection of the student's strengths and weaknesses, or if the information is not interpreted accurately, the assessment can end up not being valid.

EDUCATIONAL DECISION MAKING AND THE LIMITED ENGLISH PROFICIENT STUDENT

In the 1970s, interest focused on the role of language in learning when the judicial court system mandated remedies about the incorporation of language and cultural variables in the education of other than English-speaking students (*Aspira v. N.Y.C. Board of Education*, 1974; *Lau v. Nichols*, 1974). Renewed interest in the role of language testing was brought about as a result of the need to comply with court stipulations requiring the identification of limited-English-proficient students for the mandatory delivery of bilingual instructional services.

Shuy (1978) points out that the Aspira Consent Decree "requires that the placement of children in programs using English and Spanish as the medium of instruction be determined by their ability to effectively participate in instruction" (p. 377). This quote promotes the process of assessment instead of testing. For example, observations of children's ability to seek clarification from the teacher when they do not understand could be as important as the results from any grammar test. Consequently, the study of the learning activity becomes indispensable for the decision making necessary for appropriate placement in bilingual classrooms.

Given the numerous tests available, nevertheless, the relationship of these tests with functional language competencies required in the educational setting is seldom encountered (McCollum, 1981). Even when there is an important educational decision depending on reliable and valid data, language testing alone cannot be the solution because the results from existing instruments have been shown to be severely limited in their capacity to produce the necessary information for adequate decision making. Placement into special programs, based solely on relative levels of English and Spanish proficiency as defined by these tests, should not be undertaken (Merino & Spencer, 1983).

Integrative tests are a good example of the type of tests Shuy (1978) and Cummins (1984) suggest that educational systems adopt for placement decision making. Integrative tests are not isolated from natural context. Classroom activities are the focus of the assessment from such instruments. The problem now is to determine first just exactly what behaviors are important and valued and then to decide exactly how to measure them. Integrative tests do not appeal to policy makers because they are more time consuming from an administrative viewpoint.

Traditional methods of measuring students' abilities and academic performance rely heavily on bureaucratic procedures and funding requirements rather than students' academic performance in the classroom (Cummins, 1986). A test score can facilitate a process that needs to justify the provision of funds for services to children in a systematic and expeditious way. Regulations from the federal government are not clear as to what type of tests are sensitive to the other than English-proficient child. The regulations only specify that the child should be tested in his or her native language.

Cummins (1986) has alerted professionals to the need for changes on the area of assessment. He has proposed a new role for the assessment professional by which the assessor becomes an advocate for the child, giving as much credit to the child's potential as possible and providing opportunities at the time of the assessment for the child to perform. Under this new position the potential of the child is not in doubt; the responsibility for school failure is shifted away from the individual child and moved toward the educational system in charge of effective services.

According to this new trend, the relationship between assessment and services for LEP students needs to be redefined. The changing role of the assessment professional needs to be characterized by clarity of goals (Ysseldyke et al., 1982). The goal behind the multiple source assessment has been to share information for educational planning; educational planning for the LEP child needs to follow a clear notion of what it means to be able to function adequately in an all-English curriculum setting.

A BILINGUAL CONTINUUM OF LANGUAGE AND A STUDENT'S EDUCATIONAL PROGRAM

The construct of language proficiency has caused much controversy in the assessment field. Traditionally, having proficiency in a language was viewed as possessing mastery of the grammatical rules and vocabulary of that language (Ingram, 1985). Language testing therefore responded to the definition by measuring the different components of language; the components of phonology, morphology, syntax, and lexicon needed to be tested to determine proficiency. The publication of Lado's language testing in 1961 marked the beginning of a period recognized for language testing. The psychometric-structuralist period was primarily concerned with constructing tests which measured knowledge of discrete linguistic structure and rules and doing so with demonstrable statistical reliability and validity (Cziko & Lin, 1984).

More recently, there has been a reaction against this approach, resulting in what Spolsky (1973) has termed the integration-sociolinguistic approach to language testing. This approach, while not discounting the importance of psychometric reliability and validity, places major emphasis on testing language as a functional, communicative tool which is used in genuine communicative settings (Cziko & Lin, 1984). The LEP student in Special Education may benefit from this new approach.

Ortiz (1984) has noted that a wide variation exists in the communication skills of linguistic minorities. Frequently, these skills are stereotyped and generalized as homogeneous in nature. As a result, assessment may not lead to the necessary differentiated instructional planning because of inaccurate or incomplete collection of data; faulty judgments about language abilities and needs will be wrongly established (Ortiz, 1984).

The linguistic skills of minority children must be viewed as a continuum. This continuum represents varying degrees of bilingualism or usage of the two languages along the way (Ortiz, 1984). At one extreme of the continuum, students can be located who are proficient only in a language other than English. Moving along the continuum, proficiency into the English language is increased at the same time as native language fluency is assumed to be maintained to a point of bilingualism; the increase of English fluency continues to progress until the child reaches full proficiency in English which is represented by the other extreme of the continuum (Baca & Cervantes, 1984; Ortiz, 1984).

Along with the idea of a continuum of language skills, frequently the literature in this area cites the fact that bilingual students are a heterogeneous group. Among the most prominent studies in the field was the one conducted by Dulay and Burt (1980). They surveyed a population of 3,000 bilingual students in California. Their findings demonstrated that since the language needs of the students were different within the groups labeled bilingual, educational programs needed to respond with a variety of adaptations according to the particular language needs of each student.

Unfortunately, research has shown that administrators do not always follow the rule of developing programs specifically geared to satisfy the individual's language needs as promoted by Dulay and Burt, and Ortiz (Thonis, 1988). According to a study conducted by Development Associates for the U.S. Department of Education, the amount of native language and English in bilingual programs encompasses a great variety to the extent to which the native language is used for instruction (Development Associates, Inc. and Research Triangle Institute, 1984; Thonis, 1988). Hakuta and Gould (1987) point out that while these programs differ substantially in the role of the first language, they differ significantly less in terms of their goals. They make note of the fact that in the Development Associates' study, every district surveyed listed as a goal the development of English to the level of participation in all-English classrooms; 91 percent listed as a goal the development of other academic skills concurrently with the student's language development; and only 15 percent listed as a goal the maintenance of the student's first language.

These findings are very similar in special education. Frequently, the amount of native language versus second language is not adjusted to the language characteristics of the student, but to a district formula controlled by availability of qualified personnel and the attitudes of local administrators toward bilingualism (Garcia & Yates, 1986; Metis Associates, Inc., 1988; Ortiz & Yates, 1983). Bilingual Education is a political subject across the nation (Hakuta & Gould, 1987; Toch, 1984). They reflect the politics in education defined by the way the schools are organized, the way materials are allocated, and by the relationship between power and personal opinion, and professional values and responsibilities (Heather, 1983).

DEVELOPMENT OF EDUCATIONAL PROGRAMS
FOR LEP-HANDICAPPED STUDENTS

On the basis of the National Research Council Report of 1982 (Finn & Resnick, 1984; Messick, 1984; Reschly, 1984) in reference to minority overrepresentation in special education and research on bilingual special education (Rodriguez, Prieto, & Rueda, 1984; Wilkinson & Ortiz, 1986), children's achievement in special education classrooms has not improved to the extent warranted. This lack of improvement on the part of specialized instruction has not led to favorable opinions about the purpose of special education. As a result, serious questions are currently being raised by researchers and practitioners (Hagerty & Abramson, 1987), such as: (a) What kind of programs can meet the needs of limited-English-proficient, special education students?; (b) Do programs actually meet their special needs?; (c) Are the programs effective in producing desirable outcomes?; and (d) What is the effectiveness of these programs in relation to other programs in the mainstream?

As demonstrated by these questions, the focus of attention has shifted from assessment to instructional services (Messick, 1984; Reschly, 1984). The issue of overrepresentation of minority children in services for the mentally retarded is no longer a question of the validity of assessment as an isolated issue; rather attention has now shifted to the linkage between assessment and instruction. The quality of the IEP and how it is implemented depends greatly on the analysis of what is needed for the student to perform (Tikunoff, 1987).

A school district is obligated to provide each handicapped child with a planned program which takes into account the specific deficiencies in the child's functioning and designs a special curriculum with particular goals for improvement (Zigmond & Miller, 1986). The instructional opportunities need to be individualized, intensive, and systematic, with frequent evaluation (Reschly, 1988). In a continuous effort to educate the students as close as possible to the mainstream, the setting and the curriculum must be as similar as possible to those provided to nonhandicapped students.

In the case of the bilingual special education student, there are additional requirements for program design. New developments in the implementation of services have been a natural reaction to the nature of the students, although at times forced by legislative and court mandates. In either case, the innovations and educational changes necessary in special education require extensive planning, strong leadership, and collaboration among different and well-informed practitioners.

Students coming from culturally and linguistically diverse backgrounds are different with respect to such important educational variables as preferred learning styles, personality configurations, perceptual-cognitive patterns, family structure, attitude toward the educational process, sex role development, maternal teaching strategies, and linguistic development. The linguistic development variable is the one around which most program development efforts are operated. Satisfying the needs of the linguistically different child and therefore complying with regulations on bilingual education as well as special education is indeed a very complex process.

In spite of its complexity (Audette, Brown, & Olson, 1983), bilingual special education programs now exist in California, New York, Massachusetts, Texas (Rodriguez et al., 1984), Illinois, and Florida. Many of these cities have experienced aid to continue to experience an influx of immigrant families, causing the educational system to change. Failure to provide appropriate services has placed some states under critical review and legal conflicts (Fradd & Vega, 1987; Slater & Franse, 1987). Litigation has focused much attention on the adaptations a system needs to initiate for the effective instruction of linguistically diverse students. It is clear that policy makers can be held responsible for failing to comply with the needs of the bilingual handicapped child (Benavides, 1985).

It is important to realize that a school system cannot accept or even survive with continual reports describing its failures, particularly within the context of taking into account the impact that the issue of special education will have on the life of children and society in general. There seems a point when it is no longer possible to recognize institutional failure, and policy has to be proposed to overcome these failures. Ochoa, Pacheco, and Omark (1983) reviewed 16 policy considerations that a school system must consider in an effort to ensure that LEP learning disabled students received equal access to appropriate learning opportunities. They concurred that major changes are necessary, concluding that schools have both an obligation to provide equality of educational opportunity and also diversity of opportunity.

Cummins and McNeely (1987) point out that enough data about bilingual education exist to facilitate some policy decisions on the education of these students. But having a general direction for intervention may not always imply that the intervention will take place. Even when the information and data are present for the improvement of the system, the changes may not always happen. Knowledge of what to do and the power to actually make changes are necessary for programs to develop (Sue & Padilla, 1986).

Once the challenge of this new trend is accepted, the leadership qualities of the administrator will be under scrutiny. Administrators need to have a vision (Benavidez, 1985) of the future to attempt to mold it, and to program the efforts needed to carry out innovations with responsible planning. Planning includes an analysis of the issues and a commitment (Tikunoff, 1987) to invest in organizing and allocating resources to action. The action needed in special education implies the need for a total reform. Therefore, the administrator needs to be a risk taker with an experimental attitude (Benavidez, 1985) to face the challenge of solving problems even when there might not be any previous research to offer a direction.

Cummins and McNeely (1987) remind us that administrators have a crucial leadership role to play in communicating with special educators and other professionals. Braden and Fradd (1987) go farther explaining the need and types of collaboration that should exist for bilingual special education programs to succeed. Benavidez (1985) explains that freedom to disagree is extremely important for effective educational change. Thus, it is psychologically and educationally basic that for policy in bilingual special education to occur, the administrator will need to address the concerns of a variety of groups and to orchestrate efforts for the empowerment of children.

Changes in beliefs and attitudes can be enhanced by demonstration projects carrying out different approaches (Cummins, 1984). The evidence can persuade other teachers as well as administrators of the academic gains of students they considered underachieving. Programs such as Carpinteria, an early childhood program with high utilization of the native language, and Descubrimiento, teaching math and science with a bilingual approach rich in comprehensible input, have served as springboards for other innovative approaches in many school districts.

Research on bilingual education and their outcomes leave no doubt. One implication has been that there is no reason to assume that the special education student will actually do better in an all-English setting, particularly if English is not the child's stronger language (Cummins, 1984). Contrary to the research findings, many special educators persist in recommending English-only instruction to LEP handicapped students. Garcia and Yates (1986) and Willig (1986) consider that not identifying the language of instruction and not utilizing the contribution of bilingual professionals in the design of the IEP for the LEP student constitutes a serious problem.

Choosing the language of instruction is one of the most conflicting decisions in the development of an IEP for bilingual students. In most cases, the dilemma is resolved by assuming a transitional model of intervention, where the first language is utilized until the English language is learned. Moving students out of native language instruction as soon as possible is a risk for special education students who may need extra help for a gradual transition.

New York City functions under a transitional model of bilingual education, with a unique design for handicapped LEP students. The basic components of the New York City model program include these elements: (a) English as a second language; (b) subject area instruction in the native language or English; and (c) native language arts. The New York City Board of Education (1985) publication, *Educational Services for Children with Handicapping Conditions,* describes the instructional elements that must be integrated within each component, as follows:

Intensive instruction in English as a second language (ESL) is a specific educational approach designed to develop English language skills in speakers of other languages. It presumes that students have learned the basic elements of language and assists in the transference of these skills to English. Instruction follows the first language acquisition sequence: listening, speaking, reading, and writing are presented in that order. Students develop basic interpersonal communicative skills (e.g., ability to give names, age, address, ask directions, etc.), pre-academic language skills (e.g., ability to follow directions for instructions in English), and academic language skills (i.e., ability to learn academic subject matter in English) while progressing in academic instruction in English. (p. 22)

Instruction in subject areas in the student's native language. The term substantive subject areas is a concise term which includes, but is not limited to, science and social studies. The teaching of these subject areas in the native language allows students to maintain academic gains while learning English. (p. 23)

Reinforcement and development of native language arts skills. This element provides students with the language skills necessary to continue to make academic gains in subject areas. These same skills will later be transferred to English and will provide the language base necessary for development. (p. 23)

The New York City programs adopted the concept of a continuum of language needs in its design of bilingual instructional programs for the handicapped. Indeed, for the student who is more fluent in the native language than in English, and whose native language skills may assist in learning new concepts in the classroom, instruction will be delivered using more native language than English. Therefore the program will include language arts in the native language, specialized and intensive English as a second language instruction, and subject areas in the native language of the student. In the case of a student who is advanced in the second language, which means that learning in English is not difficult—particularly the gaining of new concepts and higher-level cognitive skills through English—instruction will consider the progress the student has demonstrated in English. Consequently, the program for this student will include some subject areas in the second language, advanced English as a second language, and language arts in the native language.

THE ROLE OF THE NATIVE LANGUAGE IN THE EDUCATION OF LEP-HANDICAPPED STUDENTS

To understand the basic elements of a bilingual program for special education students, it is important to discuss the important role native language has in their instruction. Primary language instruction is necessary at all grade levels to achieve the proficiency necessary for academic work. The benefits from effective primary language instruction are best explained by Cummins (1981, 1984) who found that while children may acquire oral proficiency in as little as two years, it may take five to seven years to master the decontextualized language skills necessary to function successfully in an all-English classroom. Effective bilingual programs that developed the child's primary language to adequate threshold levels of Cognitive Academic Language Proficiency (CALP) enable children to master English and to succeed in our schools (Lagarreta-Marcaida, 1981).

Children who are not instructed in their native language, who are behind in subject matter, and who are weak in the second language face the most negative penalties provided by a school system. Their failure to understand will not only cause them to fall further behind, but will also prevent them from making progress in second language acquisition. As a result, students may not refine their native language, may not learn English well, and also may become nonachievers in subject areas.

Available studies indicate that, for language minority students to achieve high levels of primary language proficiency, they must receive substantial amounts of instruction in and through that language, at least until they are able to achieve at age level norms on English measures of academic skills. Community background factors, such as the extent to which and the manner in which the primary language is used outside the school, should be considered when determining the amount of time to be allocated to primary language development. Language minority students should receive their initial reading instruction in the native language, with English reading introduced after literacy skills are well established. Other subject areas, especially those in which the content is cognitively demanding and the presentation provides little contextual support, should also be taught in the primary language (Cummins, 1980, 1983, 1984; Krashen, 1981a; Legarreta-Marcaida, 1981).

Second Language Acquisition

A main objective of bilingual education is to effectively promote the acquisition of a second language. Special education students acquire English through similar stages as their nonhandicapped peers. There is a need to include ESL objectives in the development of IEPs for special education students. Assessment personnel as well as teachers need to be informed as to what English language acquisition and learning are to be able to effectively plan for it.

There is a close relationship between the development of the native language and the second language. Cummins (1980) describes his theory in terms of the child's needs: "There may be threshold levels of linguistic competency which a bilingual child must attain both in order to avoid cognitive disadvantages and to allow the potential beneficial aspect of bilingualism to influence his or her cognitive and academic functioning" (p. 222). According to Cummins, children whose greater competence is in the native language but are asked to learn to perform in English prematurely will not only suffer a cognitive disadvantage in the learning process, but whatever potential benefits are to be had from their abilities in the native language will be lost (Fishground, 1982). Cummins' theory constitutes the basis for most of today's recommendations for teaching native language first and gradually introducing the second language after the student shows cognitive academic skills in the native language. His theory can be divided into three basic parts: (a) the interdependence hypothesis, which differentiates between basic interpersonal communicative skills and cognitive academic language skills; (b) his classification of classroom activities into context-embedded and context-reduced forms; and (c) threshold levels of development.

It is also important to know that the transfer from one language to another should be done cautiously and systematically. Cummins' classification of classroom activities into contest-embedded and context-reduced can assist the teacher in analyzing the classroom setting in search for effective strategies. In general, context-embedded communication refers to interpersonal involvement in a shared reality that reduces the need for explicit linguistic elaboration of the message. Meanwhile context-reduced communication implies that there are times when the communication needs elaboration to avoid misinterpretation. In a context-reduced communication, the parties involved have no cues as to the meaning of the words; therefore they depend solely on the words for the mediation of meaning (Cummins, 1986). This theory provides direction for the teacher in the planning of instruction and the creation of an effective learning environment.

Furthermore, Krashen and Terrell (1983) maintain that a second language can be best acquired when it is presented in "comprehensible input" activities. According to Krashen (1981b, 1982), comprehensible input situations are those which utilize the child's interactions and experiences in the classroom, that is, providing a here-and-now orientation to language development. Additionally, second language acquisition activities should build on those already acquired linguistic structures and the student's personal experiences. A meaningful experience at a level the child may understand and the provision of clear, concrete experiences is what makes up comprehensible input.

Assessment professionals and teachers need to be aware of the different stages of second language acquisition to be able to monitor the progress of the acquisition and adapt the instructional program accordingly. Ortiz and Yates (1988) alert practitioners to the fact that recommendations of assessment committees, often and with very few exceptions, assume that LEP students profit from instruction delivered totally in English. Their findings in reviewing IEPs of language minority students demonstrate that the selection of goals and objectives was not done based on the linguistic characteristics of children.

CONCLUSION

Every administrator needs to analyze and evaluate the various questions derived from the process of program development and set a plan of action. The important principles discussed in this chapter can offer a guide for the administrator to accomplish this difficult and challenging endeavor.

The assessment of students suspected of handicapping conditions must be done by gathering data from a variety of sources. New directions on integrative measures are extremely relevant to the assessment of the LEP student and therefore should be evaluated. The development of the child's IEP is the core of the assessment process. Accountability on the improvement of the child's education will rest on a well-designed IEP reflecting both of the child's languages.

The concept of a continuum of language skills can assist professionals to view bilingual students as a heterogeneous population. Development of programs to reflect the specific linguistic characteristics of students as well as their special needs is a basic rule for organizing the educational setting. In addition to a program design matching the students' needs, the assessment professional must have a clear set of techniques and activities related to the educational setting to which they are referring students.

Bilingual Special Education is a relatively new field. Administrators and other practitioners are facing an enormous responsibility. This analysis has been made to encourage a continuous effort for improvement.

REFERENCES

Abbott, M.M. (1985). *Theoretical considerations in the measurement of the English language proficiency of limited English proficient students.* Paper presented at the annual meeting of the National Council of Measurement in Education, Chicago, IL.

Aspira of New York et al. v. Board of Education of New York City et al. Southern District of New York. 72, Civ. 4002 S.D. N.Y. (MEFN). Consent Decree, August 29, 1974 (1974).

Audette, R., Brown, G., & Olson, D. (1983). *A study of some factors which influence the educational decisions regarding individual placement of students from cultural-racial minorities.* Syracuse, NY: Special Education Resource Center, Syracuse University.

Baca, L.M., & Cervantes, H.T. (1984). *The bilingual special education interface.* St. Louis, MI: Times Mirror/Mosby College.

Bailey, D.B., Jr., & Harbin, G. (1980). Nondiscriminatory evaluation. *Exceptional Children, 46*(8), 590-596.

Benavidez, A. (1985). Planning effective special education for exceptional language minorities. *Teaching Exceptional Children, 17*(2), 127-134.

Braden, J.P., & Fradd, S.H. (1987). Proactive school organization: Identifying and meeting special population needs. In S.H. Fradd & W.J. Tikunoff (Eds.), *Bilingual education and bilingual special education: A guide for administrators* (pp. 211-229). Boston: College-Hill Press.

Bureau of Education for the Handicapped, U.S. Department of Health, Education, and Welfare, Office of Education. (1974). *State plan amendment for fiscal year 1975 under part 8, Education of the Handicapped Act, as amended by section 614 of P.L. 93-380: Basic content areas required by the act and suggested guidelines and principles for inclusion under each area.* (Draft). Washington, DC: Author.

Cummins, J. (1980). The construct of language proficiency in bilingual education. In J. Alatis (Ed.), *Georgetown University Round Table on Languages and Linguistics: Current issues in bilingual education* (pp. 81-103). Washington, DC: Georgetown University Press.

Cummins, J. (1981). The role of primary language development in promoting educational success for language minority students. In California State Department of Education, Bilingual Education Office, *Schooling and language minority students: A theoretical framework* (pp. 3-49). Los Angeles: Evaluation, Dissemination and Assessment Center, California State University, Los Angeles.

Cummins, J. (1983). Bilingualism and special education: Program and pedagogical issues. *Learning Disability Quarterly, 6,* 373-388.

Cummins, J. (1984). *Bilingualism and special education: Issues in assessment and pedagogy.* San Diego, CA: College-Hill Press.

Cummins, J. (1986). Empowering minority students: A framework for intervention. *Harvard Educational Review, 56*(1), 18-36.

Cummins, J.A., Huebner, S.E., & McLeskey, J. (1986). Psychoeducational decision making: Reason for referral versus test data. *Professional School Psychology, 1*(4), 249-256.

Cummins, J., & McNeely, S.N. (1987). Language development, academic learning, and empowering minority students. In S.H. Fradd & W.J. Tikunoff

(Eds.), *Bilingual education and bilingual special education: A guide for administrators* (pp. 75-97). Boston: College-Hill Press.

Cziko, G.A., & Lin, N.H.J. (1984). The construction and analysis of short scales of language proficiency: Classical psychometric latent trait and nonparametric approaches. *TESOL Quarterly, 18*(4), 627-647.

Development Associates, Inc., & Research Triangle Institute. (1984). *The national longitudinal evaluation of the effectiveness of services for language minority limited-English-proficient students.* Roslyn, VA: National Clearinghouse for Bilingual Education.

Dulay, H., & Burt, M. (1980). The relative proficiency of limited English proficient students. In J. Alatis (Ed.), *Georgetown University Round Table on Languages and Linguistics: Current issues in bilingual education* (pp. 181-200). Washington, DC: Georgetown University Press.

Fenton, K.S., Yoshida, R.K., Maxwell, J.P., & Kaufman, M.J. (1979). Recognition of team goals: An essential step towards rational decision making. *Exceptional Children, 45,* 639-644.

Finn, J.D., & Resnick, L.B. (1984). Issues in the instruction of mildly mentally retarded children. *Educational Researcher, 13*(3), 9-11.

Fishground, J.E. (1982). Language intervention for hearing impaired children from linguistically and culturally diverse backgrounds. *Topics in Language Disorders, 2*(3), 57-66.

Fradd, S.H., & Vega, J.E. (1987). Legal considerations. In S.H. Fradd & W.J. Tikunoff (Eds.), *Bilingual education and bilingual special education: A guide for administrators* (pp. 45-74). Boston: College-Hill Press.

Garcia, S.B., & Yates, J.R. (1986). Policy issues associated with serving bilingual exceptional children. In A. Willig & H.F. Greenberg (Eds.), *Bilingualism and learning disabilities: Policies and practices for teachers and administrators* (pp. 113-134). New York: American Library Publishing Company, Inc.

Glaser, R. (1963). Instructional technology and the measurement of learning outcomes: Some questions. *American Psychologist, 18*(5), 519-521.

Gould, S.J. (1981). *The mismeasure of man.* New York: W.W. Norton & Company, Inc.

Hagerty, G.J., & Abramson, M. (1987). Impediments to implementing national policy change for mildly handicapped students. *Exceptional Children, 53*(4), 315-323.

Hakuta, K., & Gould, L.J. (1987). Synthesis on research on bilingual education. *Educational Leadership, 44*(6), 38-45.

Heather, N. (1983, February). *The politics of psychotherapy: Themes, dilemmas and possibilities.* Paper presented at International Conference on Psychotherapy, Bogota, Columbia.

Ingram, D.E. (1985). Assessing proficiency: An overview on some aspects of testing. In K. Hyltenstam & M. Pienemann (Eds.), *Modelling and assessing second language acquisition* (pp. 215-276). San Diego, CA: College-Hill Press.

Krashen, S.D. (1981a). Bilingual education and second language acquisition theory. In California State Department of Education, Bilingual Education Office, *Schooling and language minority students: A theoretical framework* (pp. 51-79). Los Angeles: Evaluation, Dissemination an Assessment Center, California State University, Los Angeles.

Krashen, S.D. (1981b). *Second language acquisition and second language learning.* New York: Pergamon Press.

Krashen, S.D. (1982). *Principles and practice in second language acquisition.* New York: Pergamon Press.

Krashen, S.D., & Terrel, T.D. (1983). *The natural approach: Language acquisition in the classroom.* San Francisco: Alemany Press.

Lau vs. Nichols, 414 U.S. 563 (1974).

Legarreta-Marcaida, D. (1981). Effective use of the primary language in the classroom. In California State Department of Education, Bilingual Education Office, *Schooling and language minority students: A theoretical framework* (pp. 83-116). Los Angeles: Evaluation, Dissemination and Assessment Center, California State University, Los Angeles.

Macmillan, D.L., & Meyers, C.E. (1977). The nondiscriminatory testing provision of PL 94-142. *Viewpoints, 53*(2), 38-56.

McCollum, P.A. (1981). Issues and procedures in the analysis of syntax and semantics. In J.G. Erickson & D.R. Omark, *Communication assessment of the bilingual bicultural child: Issues and guidelines* (pp. 25-42). Baltimore, MD: University Park Press.

Mendoza, P. (1983). The role of language in psychological assessment of students. *Bilingual Special Education Newsletter, University of Texas at Austin, 11*(2), 1-5.

Mercer, J.R. (1973). *Labeling the mentally retarded: Clinical and social system perspective on mental retardation.* Berkeley: University of California Press.

Merino, B.J., & Spencer, M. (1983). The comparability of English and Spanish versions of oral language proficiency. *NABE Journal, 7*(2), 1-31.

Messick, S. (1984). Assessment in context: Appraising students performance in relation to instructional quality. *Educational Research, 13*(3), 3-8.

Metis Associates, Inc. (1988). *Evaluation for the control of clinical assessment personnel and units* (Final Report). New York: Board of Education.

New York City Board of Education, Division of Special Education & Division of High Schools. (1985). *Educational services for students with handicapping conditions.* New York: Author.

New York City Board of Education, Division of Special Education. (1988). *Bilingual special education program models.* New York: Author.

New York State Education Department. (1988). *Guidelines for services to students with limited English proficiency and special education needs in New York State.* Albany, NY: Author.

Oakland, T.M. (1977). *Psychological and educational assessment of minority children.* New York: Brunner/Mazel, Inc.

Ochoa, A.M., Pacheco, R., & Omark, D.R. (1983). Addressing the learning disability needs of limited English proficient students: Beyond language and race issues. *Learning Disability Quarterly, 6,* 416-423.

Ortiz, A.A. (1984). Choosing the language of instruction for exceptional bilingual children. *Teaching Exceptional Children, 16*(3), 218-222.

Ortiz, A.A., & Yates, J.R. (1983). Incidence of exceptionality among Hispanics: Implications for manpower planning. *NABE, 7*(3), 41-53.

Ortiz, A.A., & Yates, J.R. (1988). Characteristics of learning disabled, mentally retarded, and speech-language handicapped Hispanic students at initial evaluation and reevaluation. In A.A. Ortiz & B.A. Ramirez (Eds.), *Schools and the culturally diverse exceptional students: Promising practices and future directions* (pp. 51-62). Reston, VA: ERIC Clearinghouse on Handicapped and Gifted Children, Council for Exceptional Children.

Podell, D.M., & Kaminsky, S. (1988). *Bilingual special education: Developing an approach to assessment and instruction.* Unpublished manuscript.

Reschly, D.J. (1984). Beyond IQ test bias: The National Academy Panel's analysis of minority EMM overrepresentation. *Educational Researcher, 13*(3), 15-19.

Reschly, D.J. (1988). Special education reform: School psychology revolution. *School Psychology Review, 17*(3), 459-475.

Rodriguez, R.F., Prieto, A.G., & Rueda, R.S. (1984, Spring). Issues in bilingual/multicultural special education. *NABE Journal, 8*(3), 55-65.

Sarason, S.B., & Doris, J. (1979). *Educational handicap, public policy an social history: A broadened perspective on mental retardation.* New York: Free Press.

Shuy, R.W. (1978). Problems in assessing language ability in bilingual education programs. In H. Lafontaine, B. Persky, & L. Galubchick (Eds.), *Bilingual education* (pp. 376-380). Wayne, NJ: Avery Ground, Inc.

Slater, G.M., & Franse, S.R. (1987). High school bilingual education. *NABE News, 10*(3), 1-5.

Spolsky, B. (1973). What does it mean to know a language, or how do you get someone to perform his competence? In J.W. Oller & J.C. Richards (Eds.), *Advances in language testing.* Arlington, VA: Center for Applied Linguistics.

Sue, S., & Padilla, A. (1986). Ethnic minority students: A contextual interaction model. In California State Department of Education, Bilingual Education Office, *Beyond language: Social and cultural factors in schooling language minority students* (pp. 35-72). Los Angeles: Evaluation, Dissemination and Assessment Center, California State University, Los Angeles.

Thonis, E.W. (1988). *Beyond language: The other needs of culturally diverse students.* New York: Santillana Publishing Company.

Tikunoff, W.J. (1987). Providing instructional leadership: The key to effectiveness. In S.H. Fradd & W.J. Tikunoff (Eds.), *Bilingual education and bilingual special education: A guide for administrators.* Boston: College-Hill Press.

Tilis, H.S., Weichum, W., & Cumbo, R.F. (1978). On language testing: The development of the language assessment battery. In H. Lafontaine, B. Persky, & L. Galubchick (Eds.), *Bilingual education* (pp. 385-390). Wayne, NJ: Avery Ground, Inc.

Toch, T. (1984). The emerging politics of language. *Education Week, 3*(20), 1–18.

Trachtman, G.M. (1981). On such a full sea. *School Psychology Review, 10*(2), 182–187.

Wilkinson, C.Y., & Ortiz, A.A. (1986). Reevaluation of learning disabled Hispanic students: Changes over three years. *Bilingual Special Education Newsletter, 5,* 1–6.

Willig, A. (1986). Special education and the culturally and linguistically different child: An overview of issues and challenges. In A. Willig & H.F. Greenberg (Eds.), *Bilingualism and learning disabilities: Policies and practices for teachers and administrators* (pp. 191–209). New York: American Library Publishing Company, Inc.

Ysseldyke, J.E., & Algozzine, B. (1979). Perspectives on assessment of learning disabled students. *Learning Disability Quarterly, 2*(4), 3–11.

Ysseldyke, J.E., Algozzine, B., & Mitchell, J. (1982). Special education team decision making: An analysis of current practices. *Personnel and Guidance Journal, 60,* 308–313.

Zigmond, N., & Miller, S.E. (1986). Assessment for instructional planning. *Exceptional Children, 52*(6), 501–509.

chapter 4

Teaching a Second Language to Limited-English-Proficient Learning-Disabled Students

Angela L. Carrasquillo
Maria A. Reyes Bonilla

In the United States, a growing number of minority language students, both limited-English-proficient (LEP) and non-English speakers, are enrolled in the public schools and are learning English through bilingual or English as a Second Language (ESL) programs. The fact that a significant number of these language minority students are placed in special education and are learning English as a second language justifies the need for discussing the rationale for teaching a second language.

Learning disabilities are one of the areas with more representation of LEP students. For example, federal data indicate that 44 percent of all Hispanics in special education are in programs for the learning disabled followed by 30.2 percent in speech classes (McNett, 1983). The most frequent reasons for referral are problems in language and reading, indicating that the language characteristics of learning disabled students play an important role not only in the placement of such students, but also in the design of the instructional program. For LEP students, this means that they not only need language, reading, or speech development in the primary language, but also in a second language (Garcia & Yates, 1986). Acquiring a second language and learning through that language are important aspects of language minority students enrolled in special education programs.

This chapter focuses on the assumption that learning-disabled children can learn a second language at the same time that they are developing their first language. Although there is very little literature dealing with the teaching of a second language to children who have language deficits in their primary language, the authors attempt to match literature from both disciplines in presenting this theoretical overview. This overview serves to present a general language profile of learning-disabled students. This profile is followed by identification of key issues that one must consider in teaching a second language: (a) the need to learn the second language, (b) when the second language should be introduced, and (c) recommended programmatic and methodological practices.

LEARNING-DISABLED CHILDREN'S LANGUAGE

An important question is raised when adding the learning of a second language to learning-disabled children: Should another burden be placed on these students when they have not been able to develop primary language skills to their appropriate developmental level? Common sense might say that they should be instructed in only one language in order to maximize academic development. On the other hand, in an era of equal educational opportunities and a need for knowledge of more than one language, one can argue that by not exposing these children to a second language, they might have been excluded from an educational right. Also, there is no evidence to show that the addition of a second language has negative effects on the cognitive and academic development of students participating in special education programs.

The literature on learning disabilities is unclear in defining learning disabilities. Rather than a definite definition, authorities tend to enumerate characteristics often associated with students with learning disabilities. Back in 1971, Kirk and Kirk (1972) described these children as those "who have disorders in development in language, speech, reading, and associated communication skills" (pp. 2–3). Their definition, as cited by Bryan and Bryan (1986), agrees in part with the 1981 National Joint Committee of Learning Disabilities that described learning disabilities as a "generic term that refers to a heterogeneous group of disorders manifested by significant difficulties in the acquisition and use of listening, speaking, reading, writing, reasoning, and mathematical abilities" (p. 336). These are children who show delays in learning to talk, using language well, in developing normal visual or auditory perception, reading, spelling, writing, or calculating (Kirk & Chalfant, 1984). And as these authorities maintain, some of these children do not understand language, but are not deaf, they are not able to perceive visually but are not blind; and some cannot learn by ordinary methods of instruction though they are not mentally retarded. These are long-standing disabilities, neither temporary nor situational, and most are subject to improvement or remediation.

One characteristic is common to all definitions of learning disabilities. Learning-disabled students manifest severe discrepancy between achievement and intellectual ability in some areas such as oral expression, written expression, listening comprehension, reading comprehension, and mathematics (Gearheart, 1985). When children appear to have the potential to learn, have had the opportunity to learn in school, and fail to learn after adequate instruction, these children can be considered learning disabled (Kirk & Chalfant, 1984).

Language disabilities are severe discrepancies in educational performance—usually in a language-related area—between apparent ability to perform and actual level of performance (Gearheart, 1985). Impaired language abilities are one of the prevalent conditions among children with learning disabilities. Kirk and Chalfant (1984), Stark and Wallach (1980), and Vellutino (1979) have noted that it is difficult to distinguish learning disabilities from language disorders. Learning disabilities involve specific disorders in perceiving, thinking, talking, reading, writing, spelling, arithmetic, and related disabilities, that is, primarily in the communication process (Kirk & Kirk, 1972). Many learning-disabled children show language deficits or language disorders. This was the reason why Stark and Wallach (1980) proposed a joint category called "language learning disability" since cognitive, academic, and language functioning overlap.

Language disorders have long been linked to learning disabilities. Delayed spoken language development appears to be common to students with learning disabilities. Hammill, Leigh, McNutt, and Larsen (1981) reported that the most prevalent condition to be found among children with learning disabilities is impaired language abilities. It has been estimated that a high percentage of all learning-disabled children have severe language deficits and these deficits have pervasive and negative effects on school adjustment and achievement (Bryan & Bryan, 1986; Feagans, 1983). A language disorder can manifest itself solely in the production of language at the phonological or grammatical level or both. It may also be reflected in the comprehension of specific concepts of language structures (Langdon, 1983). This may include characteristics such as limited vocabulary, an unusually large number of grammatical errors, difficulty in relating ideas in logical sequence, and regular "groping" for words (Gearheart, 1985). A language disability exists when children's comprehension and/or expression does not compare favorably with the language used by their peers (Linares, 1981).

Today, much information is available about the language acquisition process of normal children, the ages and stages by which children learn to combine words into meaningful sentences (syntax) to develop vocabulary (semantics) and to use this vocabulary and sentences for meaningful purposes (communicative competence). There are different theories about how children acquire language. The three most common theories postulate that:

1. Language and thought are intertwined. In other words, to develop language, individuals need to make use of thinking processes, and to process thought, individuals need to make use of communication skills (McNeill, 1970).
2. Children learn by reinforcement. Children learn language, among other things, by listening to language and repeating it in meaningful contexts in which it is appropriately reinforced (Skinner, 1968).
3. Children have innate capacities to generate and produce language. Children are born with the potential to learn language and to deduce a grammatical theory that helps their understanding and production of language (Chomsky, 1965).

Despite these varying theories, it is widely accepted that the development of language is tied to the development of comprehension and the acquisition of concepts. Language does not operate without meaning or function; it assists cognitive and affective development. Comprehension exceeds production and it precedes production in the child's linguistic ability. The acquisition of meanings and concepts is a process that continues beyond the primary years and is not simply the learning of the categories and organization of a rule system. The acquisition of the phonological and syntactical system seems to be automatic and mature, but the acquisition of meaning requires many experiences, trials and corrections of errors, and direct teaching by adults. Children normally show phonemic development—the production of single sounds and the rules whereby sounds are combined in sequences appropriate to the language. By age 3, most children's utterances can be interpreted by the adult listener; by the age of 4, children have an adequate vocabulary repertoire. Children, however, do not merely speak isolated words when they begin to acquire a vocabulary, but instead, their utterances reflect unspoken and perhaps clear sentences (Chomsky, 1965). Children make the same combinations of words as adults, but in the early stages of language development they fail to verbalize the whole message. Children's language, although imperfect in terms of adult grammar, focuses on the critical element of the message that the child desires to communicate. Young children show a rapid expansion of syntactic development such as verb forms, use of questions, negatives, and inflections. While children are acquiring semantic and syntactic skills, they are also learning how to use these skills appropriately in social contexts.

Recent research has not answered questions related to the nature of learning disabilities or learning deficits in children. There are many unanswered questions in terms of what specifically causes these observable disorders. In relation to language, theories exist that link the nature of disabled children's language problems to brain damage, genetic influences, and other nonphysiological conditions. For reasons of its relationship to language development and language performance, these theories are mentioned in the following paragraphs. Most of the information below was summarized by Bryan and Bryan (1986).

One theory states that brain damage, whether genetic or not, has an effect on language speech development (Lennenberg, 1967). According to Lennenberg, the child who suffers a lesion will experience delayed, but normal, development of language if the child is younger than about 20 months of age at the time of the trauma. During 21–36 months, brain damage to the language areas of the brain will produce greater debilitation. Children who suffer damage between the ages of 3 through 10 will demonstrate aphasic (partial or complete loss of the ability to use spoken language) symptoms, but recuperation is possible. Thus, it is possible that a significant number of students who have been labeled "learning-disabled" suffered a lesion in the brain and thus show a delayed language development.

Another theory maintains that there are genetic influences on language and learning. Not all children who have language problems suffer from brain damage. According to Pennington and Smith (1983), there are two general conceptual perspectives in the study of genetic influences on language and learning. One view holds that both language and learning problems represent the tail end of a normal distribution. On any given skill there are people who excel and people who do very poorly, with the majority somewhere in between these two extremes. Thus, learning-disabled children could be at the tail end of the normal population on measures of achievement. Because genes contribute to where on this continuum of skills a person happens to fall, it is claimed that learning disabilities may have a genetic basis. Another perspective within this theory is that language and learning deficits represent genetic accidents and that specific genetic mechanisms generate specific learning problems. These children's language skills are not consistent with chronological age or developmental norms for native speakers of the language.

Other children without physical evidence of brain damage or genetic influences may show delayed language development or language deficits. These are children whose speech production is different in quality and quantity from that of their peers (Lee, 1974; Menyuck, 1969). A language deficit may be the result of both known and unknown causes and it is a language behavior that is not on a par with age peers in the linguistic community (Menyuck, 1971). In other words, the syntactic, semantic, and communicative competence behaviors of language-delayed children at any age level do not match those employed by normal children.

Research on the language characteristics of learning-disabled children indicates that these students show deficits in areas such as syntax, semantics, and communicative competence. In the area of syntax (the arrangement of words into meaningful phrases/sentences and of the means by which such relationships are shown), the literature shows that these children are less capable than comparison students at detecting semantic structures, and they demonstrate significant delays in the acquisition of syntax. If children have difficulty in the acquisition or use of syntactic rules, it is likely that oral language development will be disorganized and difficult to understand. Researchers (Feagans, 1983; Feagans & Short, 1985; Idol-Maestes, 1980; Moran & Byrne, 1977; Vogel, 1977) have identified these common syntactical difficulties among learning-disabled children such as: (a) determining if a sentence is a statement of information or a question, (b) filling in deleted words in spoken paragraphs, (c) completing morphological tests and exercises, (d) oral retelling or restating information, (e) repeating sentences, (f) appropriate use of verb-tense markers (whether the action is present, past, or future), and (g) incorrect use of past tense responses. Hence, limited facility with syntax appears to depress their performance in reading and listening to academic material. It has also been found that children's syntax used in speech was less complex than that employed by their nondisabled peers, and even if the syntax was correct and complex, it was found to be limited (Bryan & Bryan, 1986).

Learning-disabled children are often found deficient in semantics (the understanding and production of words) when compared with normal age children. Research (Ceci, 1983; Donahue & Bryan, 1983; Pearl, Donahue, & Bryan, 1981) has identified specific language deficits in: (a) expressive language, (b) language comprehension, (c) generating or recalling stories, (d) naming verbal opposites, (e) defining words, (f) retrieving words from memory, (g) responding with words, and (h) formulating sentences.

The areas of communicative competence (language usage in a variety of social contexts) has recently been researched with learning-disabled children. Research tends to indicate that some learning-disabled children are less likely than their normal peers to make speech changes, depending on the audience (Bryan, Donahue, & Pearl, 1981; Donahue, 1981; Perlmutter & Bryan, 1984). These children lack the pragmatic skills of asking questions, persuading, responding to messages, and supporting an argument. Also, these children have difficulties in constructing messages that allow listeners to make correct interpretations (Bryan & Bryan, 1986; Pearl et al., 1981). In another area of communciative competence, the relationship of language and social relationships (Bryan & Bryan, 1986; Pearl et al., 1981) has indicated that many of these children have difficulties in eliciting positive responses from others and are less skillful than developmental/normal achievers in using language in a variety of social contexts.

ISSUES IN IDENTIFYING LANGUAGE MINORITY LD STUDENTS

The literature reviewed in the previous section suggests that many students participating in LD classes are students who show language, reading, or speech disabilities. Many of those students come from language minority backgrounds and are limited in English. A significant number of those students participating in LD classrooms show language deficits, deficits that are the basis for placing them in classrooms for the learning disabled. However, many of these students do not belong in special education classrooms because their language and learning disabilities are more related to the normal stages of second language acquisition than developmental learning deficits (Ortiz, 1984; Willig, 1986).

Children and adults learning a language, first or second, make syntactical, semantic, and articulation errors. One of the reasons these children are placed in classrooms for the learning disabled (LD) is that, when they are being tested for learning disabilities and the tester does not know the process of second language acquisition, the tester may indicate that these normal stages of language development are communication disorders. Willig (1986) mentions other examples of incorrect referrals such as distractibility, lack of attention, poor comprehension, or inability to follow directions, not necessarily meaning disability, but simply lack of understanding of the English language. When testing limited-English-proficient students to determine that indeed they have an educational handicap, it requires that students be tested in their strongest language, or better, that students be tested in both languages. If the disability is apparent in the stronger and weaker language or in the strongest language only, it may indicate that students show a learning disability. If students are non-English speakers or are limited in English, it is recommended that students receive most of the instruction in the primary language and receive daily regular instruction in English as a second language. Another instructional alternative, although not the best, might be to receive instruction in the second language, in this case English, and daily instruction in English as a second language.

A significant group of these students live in a dual language environment showing a great deal of variety in their patterns of language usage. As Willig (1986) states, certain topics of conversation with certain types of individuals in certain kinds of settings may call for another language. A student's home language may not be parallel with the school language. Language proficiency in the different domains will vary and affect their linguistic and academic development.

Students may show variety in oral proficiency and academic language proficiency. They may manifest a certain high degree of proficiency in oral interpersonal contexts, but very low proficiency in the language they need to understand, speak, read, and write in the different subject areas of the curriculum. These students may need proficiency in the English language to deal with abstract language and vocabulary development (Cummins, 1981, 1984). Students need time to learn the language and to learn through the language; language proficiency for academic purposes is not learned or acquired in one year. Cummins explained that for oral proficiency, students with normal learning abilities can learn the language in about two years. However, students need between five and seven years to learn the language for academic success. Many times program planners assume that limited-English-proficient students will learn in one year the necessary English to function in a monolingual English-speaking classroom.

CHARACTERISTICS OF A SUCCESSFUL SECOND LANGUAGE PROGRAM

This section summarizes theories and research on the characteristics of a successful second language program. In this article, a second language is defined as the language that students are learning other than the native language or mother tongue and which is the language of the community at large and the school where students live. It is an activity undertaken when students have already nearly or fully acquired the basic structure and vocabulary of the first language. Second language learners are influenced by the setting in which they learn a language and by the people with whom they have contact while they are learning the language.

Most of the research on children's second language acquisition tends to indicate that the cognitive structure which children possess and the way that the second language is introduced play a major role in the way the children learn the language (Cummins, 1983; Dulay & Burt, 1980; Garcia, 1980). In other words, the student's own disposition and ability to learn the language and the way it is being taught are important variables in the successful acquisition of the second language. The following paragraphs identify principles of second language teaching that need to be considered in designing a second language program for students participating in special education classrooms.

1. Language is acquired in social situations and children are always ready and able to learn provided they can make sense of the situation they are in. Learning a second language requires the use of cognitive, linguistic, and social strategies. Students need to use the target language in social, academic, and linguistic situations. Students need to see a reason or purpose to use the second language so that they begin to use the language in meaningful situations. Children learn through experimentation, and they are learning all the time using social and cognitive strategies. Keller-Cohen (1980) stressed that prior experience with language contributes to a child's second language learning by providing the child with heuristic for searching and organizing linguistic data and knowledge about language (both general and specific). The simultaneous use of linguistic, social, and cognitive strategies allows the learner to acquire the second language.

Second language learning is most efficient when it is highly motivated by communication needs and when it is a medium for meaningful content. It is a creative construction in which a significant part of the language comes from natural communication experiences to allow learners to use their creative construction abilities (Dulay & Burt, 1980). Children do not begin by "learning a second language"; they are never engaged in a purely linguistic exercise. The language they hear and use always has a function: to satisfy needs, express feelings, explore ideas, ask questions, obtain answers, and maintain interpersonal relations. In other words, language acquisition is not essentially habit formation, but inductive generalization and hypothesis testing in a variety of communication contexts. The focus of both—the speaker and the listener— is on the message being conveyed, on information about the real world that they receive and use depending on the linguistic and cognitive structures that they possess.

2. First and second language learners apply strategies that are similar to the first language acquisition process. Research on second language indicates that the process of children's second language acquisition is similar in many ways to the general process described by Brown (1979, 1980) and Cazden (1972) for first language acquisition. Some of these strategies are: (a) the use of simple structures when constructing sentences (e.g., following a construction order of subject plus verb plus object), (b) the use of simple structures before more complex ones (e.g., "Me no go" for "I don't want to go"), (c) the use of overextending the meanings of words (e.g., using the word "want" instead of "like"), (d) disregarding past tenses (e.g., "I walk two miles yesterday" instead of

"I walked two miles yesterday"), and (e) overgeneralization of rules (e.g., "You doed" instead of "You did").

Children begin to express their meaning through an interlanguage which is an approximation of the adult or native speaker model and which contains many omissions, overgeneralizations, and errors in grammar. This implies, among other things, that second language learners are making the same kinds of errors that first language learners make (Dulay & Burt, 1980; Wode, 1978).

3. Academic skills learned in the first language exercise a major role in the acquisition and development of the second language. A second language is mostly introduced to students after these students have been exposed for several years to their native language. These students have developed, to a certain extent, first language semantic, syntactical, and grammatical knowledge. These students have an adequate receptive and expressive knowledge of their first language which is primarily used for functional communication. Cummins (1983) stated that the first and second language skills are interdependent, which he refers to as "common underlying proficiency." According to Cummins, if the learning disabled student has acquired a basic level of proficiency in the first language, this proficiency can be transferred in the second language provided there is adequate exposure to the second language. The learning-disabled student may manifest delays in the use of expressive language, but may demonstrate strengths in visual perception which are showed in first language reading skills. This proficiency in first language literacy is manifested in second language literacy skills. Bruck (cited in Cummins, 1983), in a study on the performance of children with learning disabilities in early French immersion programs, found that first language cognitive/academic skills were predictive of the development of academic skills in French. Learning-disabled children's language development was similar to the control group. The French learning disabled students did very well in listening comprehension and poorly in oral production skills. The program's success, according to Bruck and Cummins, was based on the meaningful strategies and experiences presented by the teacher where there was authentic communication and not isolated language drills.

Perozzi (1985) conducted a pilot study of six participants to explore the facilitation of conversational skills, especially vocabulary, from native language to the second language. Three of the subjects were Spanish-speaking categorized as mild language delay, a language-disabled, and a normal language participant and three English-speaking subjects. The treatment consisted of teaching receptive vocabulary in the second language followed by teaching receptive vocabulary in the first language. Although the study consisted of a small population, the results supported the practice of initial language intervention in the first language to facilitate transference in the second language. In other words, in a special education program where instruction is conducted in the native language (for example, in Spanish), if the students are being taught conversational skills in Spanish, this program is not merely developing Spanish conversational skills, but also a deeper conceptual and linguistic proficiency which is strongly related to the development of second language literacy and general academic skills (Cummins, 1983, 1984).

Language development is acquired gradually. At the beginning, learning-disabled children's second language development may be very slow, since they will be progressing through their individual developmental stages. For some students the preproduction or production stages will take longer due to the severity of the learning or language disorder. At any stage it is very important to assess the native language of the individual and to identify areas of deficits and language strengths. There are linguistic patterns that are typical of language development and there are transitional linguistic patterns that are typical of second language learners. Additionally, there are dialectical patterns of community and individual patterns from stress, lack of motivation, or fatigue. When second language-disabled students are enrolled in a second language program, the question to ask is not what their problems are, but what their language/academic strengths in the first language are, such as ability to communicate and extensive receptive vocabulary. These strengths are later used in the second language as a source of instructional motivation and initiation. A second language program should build on the first language experiences and background brought to the classroom. The learning disabled children can learn the language at a slower rate when compared to normal peers.

A good second language program should be designed in close contact with the first language program. It should be based on the language development program that promotes first-language literacy in the initial grades. The students add a second language to their repertoire of skills at no cost to first-language proficiency (Cummins, 1983). Continued development of the first language is important. Children with learning disabilities require an individualized method of instruction designed specifically for the individual child's disorder. The second language class is a good opportunity to group them as a whole to develop creativity and opportunities to express themselves. Learning disabled children should participate in second language instruction as long as they have a level of first-language proficiency to base the second language acquisition (Garcia, 1980; Langdon, 1983). It is recommended that specific learning be given first in language skills in the native language when feasible. Their level of first language development varies as well as characteristics of language use. The second language needs to be not beyond the grasp of children experiencing developmental disabilities.

4. Second-language students need some form of input for the learner in which to understand the message being conveyed regardless of the level of proficiency in the second language. Second-language theorists (Cummins, 1983, 1984; Krashen, 1982; Long, 1983; Wong-Fillmore, 1983) endorse some form of stimulus or "comprehensible input" for the development of meaning and communication. This input is the learning understanding of the message being conveyed regardless of the level of proficiency in the second language. One aspect of this input is the subject matter content and literacy skills acquired in the first language which play a major role in making input in second language comprehension. Cummins (1983) stated: "The acquisition of a second language is not necessarily too difficult for students with learning problems in the first language" (p. 379). It might not be difficult if the students' success will depend on the extent to which the instruction is meaningful and motivates them to become intrinsically involved in the learning process.

5. Motivation influences the speed and ease of acquiring a second language. Research indicates that the more interest students show in learning the second language, the easier and faster they will learn the language. Positive attitudes toward the second language allow the acquirer to be open to input so it can be utilized for acquisition (Gardner, 1980). For example, the desire to be similar to valued members of the community, that speak a second language, and the desire to achieve proficiency in the target language for utilitarian or practical reasons are aspects that have been related to second language acquisition.

6. Errors are a natural part of language learning. Language acquisition is not based solely on grammatical structure but on meaning. Communication does not have to be grammatically correct, but just beyond the learner's current ability (Krashen, 1982). When speakers have something to communicate, listeners will make every effort to understand, and this very effort will advance the second language acquisition process.

Errors are reflections of a provisional grammar that learners are creating. Learners are constructing their new language in much the same way that children learn their first language. Errors are helpful to students in providing opportunities to test their ideas about language. Teachers need to be more tolerant of errors in second language acquisition production to help students improve without overcorrection, using strategies such as expansions and restatement of students' deviant utterances. Correction of speech patterns in communicative or expressive contexts can strongly inhibit the development of language skills.

7. Second language learners undergo a silent period before they begin to orally produce the language. Since children acquire language in meaningful situations, speech emerges in natural stages. For instance, second language learners go through a preproduction period in which they begin to comprehend but say very little (Terrell, 1977). This silent stage helps students concentrate on the message that is being conveyed to them. In this initial stage, students concentrate on the receptive skills of listening for comprehension and perhaps reading.

Children have been shown to benefit from initial periods of silence and active listening (Asher, 1977; Krashen, 1981). The fact that children do not verbally interact very much does not necessarily mean that their knowledge of the language is inferior to more verbally active children. Children's nonverbal clues are evidence that they are actively listening and are not merely silent and withdrawn. Second language learners, and especially LD students, do little talking in class for some time. They listen a great deal and begin to listen and use familiar words and phrases. Children should not be put on the spot by being asked to answer questions that they are not able to understand (Krashen, 1982; Krashen & Terrell, 1984).

8. Students vary in the strategies that they use in acquiring a second language. Flexibility should be built into any program to allow for differences in learning styles, both cognitive and social, as well as differences from the input and material to be mastered.

The language teacher plays a significant role in directing language-learning activities in the classroom. The teacher needs to use different teaching strategies to account for language differences in the classroom. Peer interaction student-centered language activities and individualized activities have had a positive effect on second language acquisition (Ramirez, 1985).

NEEDS OF STUDENTS TO LEARN THE SECOND LANGUAGE

Many children in the United States go through the process of acquiring English as a second language. Some learn it for enrichment purposes, others for survival purposes. When the second language is needed for survival, it becomes an urgent need and in many cases, it is argued, the second language must be learned as soon as possible. For students with learning disorders in their first language, the acquisition of the second language might be more difficult, but it can be learned. It is not too difficult or inappropriate (Cummins, 1983, p. 379). Their success will depend on the extent to which the instruction is meaningful and motivates them to become involved in the learning process.

Bruck (1978) identifies another need for learning-disabled students to learn a second language: development of their self-concept. These children in whom everyone is identifying deficits, disorders, or deficiencies are learning a second language that parents, siblings, or neighbors may not have and thus they tend to feel better about themselves and about school. The acquisition of a second language is a special achievement to be valued and developed.

WHEN SHOULD CHILDREN BE EXPOSED TO THE SECOND LANGUAGE?

The question of when to introduce the second language to learning disabled children is a relevant one. It is assumed that children have been raised at home using only one language. When children come to school, the question of which language to use as part of instruction becomes critical. The answer depends on the students' need for the second language. The place of residence, the values that the community places on the learning of a second language, as well as the role that second language plays in the academic life of the children, will determine when and how fast the children should learn a second language. The following is a list of hypothetical cases showing academic and social considerations in answering the question of when to introduce the second language:

1. *A learning disabled child living in New York City in which only Spanish is spoken at home.* Spanish has been used throughout the child's early developmental years. English is an unknown language and, when introduced, will be learned as a second language. There is an immediate need to learn this second language since it is the language of academic survival.

2. *A learning-disabled child, born and raised in Los Angeles, incidentally in contact with two languages, Spanish and English.* The child's family appears to use both languages for communication without a complete mastery of the structure of either language. Which language is considered the primary and developmental language? Which language will be used to develop academic proficiency? It appears that the language to develop academic proficiency might be the language most often used in communicating with the child and which is used to develop the child's speech. The language of less emphasis might be considered the second language (Ortiz & Garcia, 1988).

3. *A learning-disabled child living in Puerto Rico where most students are enrolled in classes of English as a second language.* Would the child feel "left out" if the second language was not part of the curriculum? Would second language instruction be based on the proficiency developed in the first language? The child should participate in second language instruction as long as the child has a level of first-language proficiency to base his second language acquisition (Cummins, 1984).

4. *An English-speaking, learning-disabled child whose parents want the child to learn a second language, such as French.* The second language is not needed for survival purposes, but for enrichment purposes.

Once the child's need for the second language and the time for its introduction are identified, how much participation the children will need in the second language will depend on: (a) child's first language competencies, (b) the linguistic and social environments in which the language is based and used, (c) cognitive factors that the second language will contribute to the child's language development, and (d) the semantic, grammatical, and pragmatic differences between the two languages under consideration. An analysis of all these variables will determine how useful or effective the introduction of the second language will be in enriching the language of this learning-disabled child.

RECOMMENDED INSTRUCTIONAL AND METHODOLOGICAL STRATEGIES

In planning a second language program for the learning-disabled student, the current practices of teaching a second language apply. Recent literature tends to suggest that:

1. Children will participate in cognitive and linguistic tasks as best they can from the beginning so long as they are interested in what is going on in the classroom. Children must be active learners to have the ability to map their own language-learning strategies. Language skills are emphasized as part of the job that has to be done in which there are instrumental values for listening, speaking, reading, and writing in the second language. Children have a need to understand concepts through active and motivated learning. The teacher's role is to help students learn and verbalize concepts, not to correct their grammar or punctuation. In special education classrooms, motivating activities play a key role in how much cognitive involvement students put into what they do. Second language activity tasks need to maintain students' interest from the beginning to the end, and if the teacher recognizes that students are losing interest, that is the time to move them into another learning task.

2. For language-disabled students, language instruction should not be broken into parts (phonic or grammar rules) but into meaningful tasks. The instructional focus of the task should be on the message (communication and understanding), not on the form. Language is a natural creative process rather than one of habit formation. Teachers should provide guidance and practice in thinking in the language rather than mere repetitive drills. Cummins (1983) suggests a second language program which is embedded in a meaningful concrete context and supported by a wide range of paralinguistic cues which allow students to infer the intended meaning and simultaneously acquire the second language. Second language learning must occur as part of a meaningful communication; teaching makes language learning more enjoyable for students since they will focus on language as a means of accomplishing a cognitive activity. Students need to see the second language classroom as one where they go to acquire knowledge about the world as well as about the language being learned. Every activity in the classroom is a cognitive and linguistic learning experience from lining up in the yard (learning about structure and organization) to discussing the lunchroom menu of the day (learning about what is considered a balanced diet).

3. Provide for diversity of classroom interactions for students' participation in challenging activities. The second language classroom has to provide for a variety of classroom interactions to allow students to participate in cognitively challenging activities. Also, some language tasks require specific classroom organizations. For example, in any given time period, opportunities need to be provided for whole class instruction, small group interactions, and one-to-one interaction. Second language students can benefit from whole class instruction at the initial stage when they are just beginning to get acquainted with the language and they are going through the silent period. Choral activities and pattern drills may also be guided using a whole class format. But students also need to work in small groups encouraging them to talk, learn together and provide opportunities to listen, speak, read, and write in the second language. Children need various opportunities for sustained one-to-one interaction which involves an almost equal number of turns attuned to the children's language development. One-to-one situations are more conducive to attempts at talking.

4. The language of the classroom should be simplified. The language of the classroom needs to be meaningful and comprehensible. In other words, students must be able to understand its content although they might not understand every word included in the sentence. For this reason, the language being used needs to be simple and understandable. This does not mean that the teacher has to change the tone of voice or speed in posing a sentence, thinking that this oral approach will

provide for greater student understanding. However, the teacher needs to understand that these second language learners have a limited vocabulary, and limited syntactical and grammatical structure. At the beginning, sentences need to be syntactically and grammatically simple and short.

One way of simplifying language is through the simplification of the vocabulary. The amount of new vocabulary words or phrases needs to be limited to the level of student understanding. Also, knowing isolated words without a context has little meaning to the students. This by no means suggests that vocabulary will be kept to a minimum. It means that new words will be used in meaningful contexts. Vocabulary will be emphasized through the use of repetition and expansion. Vocabulary should be selected for immediate need or usefulness (family, home, TV programs) and should be within the students' experience.

Syntax and grammar should be presented in small structured units, systematically progressing from concepts that have been learned, moving up to the next level of difficulty. The teacher can relate previously learned knowledge and skills to new tasks, simplifying to a certain extent the mechanical aspects of the language and facilitating communication through nonverbal gestures and body language and relying on motor activities.

5. Classroom instructional activities should integrate the four areas of listening, speaking, reading, and writing. There was a popular misconception in English as a second language that oral skills must be mastered before written skills. But in the last decade, the focus has been on the interactions in which learners engage to develop language, reading, and writing skills. Recent literature suggests that it is not necessary for young learners to achieve complete fluency in the spoken language before moving to written language (Krashen & Terrell, 1984). Listening and reading are receptive skills, which always exceed the productive skills of speaking and writing. Language proficiency is balanced between the two receptive processes of listening and reading, and the two productive processes of speaking and writing. Students can comprehend through listening and reading and can communicate through speaking and writing tasks. From the beginning, students learn to use language in meaningful contexts as part of an attempt to understand and relate to the world around them. Language is a process of thought and production that must be used by second language learners if both processes are to be mastered.

The integration of language in classroom activities includes auditory processing, oral language development, reading-related activities, and creative writing. Children can comprehend a great deal more (through listening and reading) than they demonstrate on speaking and writing tasks (Cummins, 1980).

6. Provide for the development of literacy skills (reading). Literacy skills develop written comprehension. When students are reading in a second language, they need to fully utilize their experiences and knowledge to acquire immediate comprehension. There will be times when students, due to their own cultural and linguistic backgrounds, have little or no background on a given topic. Activities to generate background knowledge need to be provided in the classroom and need to be of a more concrete nature. These activities may include viewing a film, working with concrete objects, prior reading, prior discussion on the topics through pictures, or any other concrete material.

In order to help students develop literacy in English, the following strategies are recommended: (a) continually reinforce the development of the oral language, (b) expand students' vocabulary, (c) use strategies that involve figuring out word or phrase meanings, and (d) expose students to a variety of reading selections.

7. Provide for creative communicative writing. Writing is viewed as a creative medium of communication. It is a difficult and abstract form of verbal thinking. Creative as well as practical writing needs to be functional and require creativity and knowledge of writing skills. Students react differently to assigned writing tasks because of differences in developmental stages, home classroom environments, and their interests. Writing, as well as speaking, is almost always directed toward an audience whose expectations shape the form and content of the message.

Students need to listen to stories as well as create their own. Experience, getting in touch with one's feelings, and having many opportunities to write are necessary ingredients of writing. Students need a rich and varied literacy environment to which they can add their first-hand knowledge and experiences and communicate using the second language.

8. Provide for a variety of language instructional techniques. The field of English as a second language has been enriched with literature on successful language methodologies. It is recommended that a variety of strategies be used, such as problem solving, role playing, total physical response, story telling, experience charts, dialogues, content-based language emphasis, semantic mapping (especially for the development of vocabulary), language experience approach, and natural approaches (for oral communication). A brief description of these strategies is included in the following paragraphs.

Strategies for the Development of Communication Skills

Language acquisition is a process which involves interactions among the four language areas and interactions of different manipulative strategies to move students from nonverbal communication to the development of advanced cognitive and linguistic skills. A brief description of a selected group of communication strategies is included in the following section with the purpose of identifying them as recommended approaches to be used in the second language classroom.

Role playing. The role play technique creates a dramatic situation in the classroom, in part by simply acting out dialogues or relabeling objects and people in the teaching setting. The interest is in oral material which synthesizes useful vocabulary, realistic context, and social and psycholinguistic features. Role playing releases inhibitions and, in so doing, encourages humor. It allows students to express themselves while it exposes them to English and the American culture.

Problem solving. Through problem solving, students work on topics, information, or opinions which are meaningful to them. Students are given the mechanism to share facts and information with the class in small or large group settings using oral and written language. Again, because students are using the language for a cognitive task, they feel free enough to use English to express themselves without seriously thinking that they are making mistakes in the second language.

Content-based language tasks. The literature is prolific on how the language classroom can use content in the classroom. There exists a long list of activities in which language is used to fulfill communicative purposes. The following are some of these activities: (a) to seek information on a given topic (i.e., earth's gravity), (b) to give information on a specific area (i.e., fertilization of plants), (c) to express reactions in a particular topic (i.e., to a TV program, to a movie, to a controversial issue, such as the Vietnam War), (d) to solve a problem (i.e., the need to provide solar energy to plants), and (e) to display one's achievement (i.e., demonstrating computer literacy).

Total physical response. It is a good strategy in the early stages of second language learning. The teacher gives a command and models the physical movement to carry out the command. At first, students focus only on listening comprehension by responding to the commands with the appropriate physical movement. In the production stage, they begin speaking, and eventually move to reading and writing.

Natural approach techniques. These strategies focus on providing a context in the classroom for natural language acquisition to occur, with acquirers receiving maximum comprehensible input and providing opportunities in the classroom to feel less anxious toward the second language. Language content is based on the students' interests, lack of initial correction, avoidance of initial production, and acceptance of the native language for communicative purposes. The students' knowledge or background in their native language, activities focusing on nonverbal and auditory processing, are strategies used in the preproduction stage to facilitate students' comprehension and ease of the target language.

Semantic mapping. Research in vocabulary development indicates that the larger the number of words that language learners have, the better their auditory and written comprehension. Word meaning is not acquired in isolation, but within a conceptual framework. Vocabulary acquisition is an interactive process that focuses on the contributions of the learners' prior knowledge to the new concept. Semantic mapping is a strategy of structuring information in graphic form by displaying related words in categories. Although this is a strategy recommended for a prereading activity, it has its place in oral development too, in which case the teacher may show pictures to the words of the graphic form.

SUMMARY

Public schools in the United States receive a significant number of learning-disabled students for whom English is not their native language. Learning-disabled students need to learn English for survival and enrichment purposes. They need proficiency in the English language to deal with challenging cognitive classroom activities. But language proficiency for academic purposes is not learned or acquired in a short period of time. It requires sufficient time, motivation, and students' positive attitudes toward the language.

A successful second language program provides students with cognitive, linguistic, and social strategies to use the language in social, academic, and linguistic situations. A good second language program is designed in class contact with the first language program. An affective second language classroom is one where students are highly motivated by communication needs and is a medium for meaningful content. Students need to be active learners to be able to understand and communicate concepts through speaking and writing tasks. Language is a process in thought and production that needs to be used and mastered by second language learning-disabled students.

REFERENCES

Asher, J.J. (1977). *Learning another language through actions: The complete teachers' guide.* Los Gatos, CA: Sky Oaks Productions.

Brown, D. (1979). *Mother tongue to English.* Cambridge, MA: University Press.

Brown, D. (1980). *Principles of language learning and teaching.* Englewood Cliffs, NJ: Prentice-Hall.

Bruck, M. (1978). The suitability of early French immersion programs for the language-disabled child. *Canadian Journal of Education, 3,* 51–72.

Bryan, T.H., & Bryan, J.H. (1986). *Understanding learning disabilities.* Palo Alto, CA: Mayfield Publishing.

Bryan, T., Donahue, M., & Pearl, R. (1981). Learning disabled children's communicative competence on referential communication tasks. *Journal of Pediatry Psychology, 6,* 383–393.

Cazden, C.B. (1972). *Child language and education.* New York: Holt, Rinehart, & Winston.

Ceci, D.J. (1983). Automatic and purposive semantic processing characteristics of normal and language/learning disabled children. *Developmental Psychology, 19,* 427–439.

Chomsky, N. (1965). *Aspects of a theory of syntax.* Cambridge, MA: MIT Press.

Cummins, J. (1980). The exit and entry fallacy in bilingual education. *NABE Journal, 4,* 25–60.

Cummins, J. (1981). The role of language development in promoting educational success for language minority students. In California State Department of Education (Ed.), *Schooling and language minority students: A theoretical framework* (pp. 3–49). Los Angeles, CA: Evaluating, Dissemination and Assessment Center.

Cummins, J. (1983, Fall). Bilingualism and special education: Program and pedagogical issues. *Learning Disability Quarterly, 6,* 373–386.

Cummins, J. (1984). *Bilingualism and special education: Issues in assessment and pedagogy.* San Diego, CA: College Hill Press.

Donahue, M. (1981). Requesting strategies of learning disabled children. *Applied Psycholinguistics, 2,* 213–234.

Donahue, M., & Bryan, T. (1983). Conversational skills and modeling in learning disabled children. *Journal of Applied Psycholinguistics, 4,* 251–278.

Dulay, H., & Burt, M. (1980). *Testing and teaching communicatively handicapped Hispanic children.* San Francisco: Bloonsbury, West, Inc.

Feagans, L. (1983). Discourse processes in learning disabled children. In J.D. McKinney & L. Feagas (Eds.), *Current topics in learning disabilities* (Vol. 1, pp. 87–115). Norwood, NJ: Ablex.

Feagans, L., & Short, E.S. (1985). *Referential communication and reading performance in learning disabled children over a three year period.* Chapel Hill, NC: Frank Porter Graham Child Development Center.

Garcia, E. (1980). Bilingualism in early childhood. *Young Children, 5,* 52–66.

Garcia, S.B., & Yates, J.R. (1986). Policy issues associated with serving bilingual exceptional children. *Journal of Reading, Writing and Learning Disabilities, 2,* 123-137.

Gardner, R.C. (1980). On the validity of affective variables in second language acquisition: Conceptual, contextual and statistical considerations. *Language Learning, 30,* 255-277.

Gearheart, B.R. (1985). *Learning disabilities educational strategies.* St. Louis, MO: Times Mirror/Mosly.

Hammill, D., Leigh, J., McNutt, J.G., & Larsen, S. (1981). A new definition of learning disabilities. *Learning Disability Quarterly, 4,* 336-342.

Idol-Maestes, L. (1980). Auditory perceptual ability of normal children aged five through eight. *Journal of Genetic Psychology, 3,* 289-294.

Keller-Cohen, D. (1980). *A review of child second language learning: Using experience with language to learn language.* Paper presented at the Fifth Annual Conference on Language Development, Boston University, Boston, MA.

Kirk, S.A., & Chalfant, J.C. (1984). *Academic and developmental learning disabilities.* Denver, CO: Love Publishing Company.

Kirk, S.A., & Kirk, W.P. (1972). *Psycholinguistic learning disabilities: Diagnosis and remediation.* Urbana: University of Illinois Press.

Krashen, S. (1981). *Second language acquisition and second language learning.* Oxford: Pergamon Press.

Krashen, S. (1982). *Principles and practice in second language acquisition.* Oxford: Pergamon Press.

Krashen, S., & Terrell, T.D. (1984). *The natural approach: Language acquisition in the classroom.* London: Pergamon Press.

Langdon, H.W. (1983). Assessment and intervention strategies for the bilingual language disordered student. *Exceptional Children, 50,* 37-46.

Lee, L.L. (1974). *Developmental sentence analysis.* Evanston, IL: Northwestern University Press.

Lennenberg, E. (1967). *Biological foundations of language.* New York: Wiley.

Linares, N. (1981). Management of communicatively handicapped Hispanic American children. In J. Erickson & D.R. Omark (Eds.), *Communication assessment of the bilingual, bicultural child: Issues and guidelines* (pp. 145-162). Baltimore, MD: University Park.

Long, M.H. (1983). *Process and production in ESL program evaluation.* Paper presented at the 5th Annual TESOL Summer Meeting, Toronto.

McNeill, D. (1970). *The acquisition of language: The study of developmental linguistics.* New York: Harper and Row.

McNett, I. (1983). *Demographic imperatives: Implications for educational policy.* Washington, DC: American Council on Education, Forum of Educational Organization Leaders, Institute for Educational Leadership.

Menyuck, P. (1969). *Sentences children use* (Research Monograph, No. 52). Cambridge, MA: MIT Press.

Menyuck, P. (1971). *The acquisition and development of language.* Englewood Cliffs, NJ: Prentice-Hall.

Moran, M.R., & Byrne, M.C. (1977). Mystery of verb tense markers by normal and learning disabled children. *Journal of Speech and Hearing Research, 20*, 529-542.

Ortiz, A.A. (1984). Choosing the language of instruction for exceptional bilingual children. *Teaching Exceptional Children, 16*, 208-212.

Ortiz, A.A., & Garcia, S. (1988). A prereferral success for preventing inappropriate referrals of Hispanic students to special education. In A.A. Ortiz & B.A. Ramirez (Eds.), *Schools and the culturally diverse ,exceptional student: Promising practices and future decisions* (pp. 6-18). Reston, VA: The Council for Exceptional Children.

Pearl, R., Donahue, M., & Bryan, T. (1981). Children's responses to non-explicit requests for clarification. *Perceptual and Motor Skills, 53*, 919-925.

Pennington, B.F., & Smith, S.D. (1983). Genetic influences on learning disabilities and speech and language disorders. *Child Development, 54*, 369-387.

Perlmutter, B., & Bryan, J. (1984). First impressions, ingratiation, and the learning disabled child. *Journal of Learning Disabilities, 3*, 157-161.

Perozzi, J.A. (1985). A pilot study on language facilitation for bilingual, language-handicapped children: Theoretical and intervention applications. *American Speech-Language Hearing Association, 50*, 403-406.

Ramirez, A.G. (1985). *Bilingualism through schooling: Cross-cultural education for minority and majority students.* Albany, NY: SUNY Press.

Skinner, B.F. (1968). *Science and human behavior.* New York: MacMillan.

Stark, I., & Wallach, G.P. (1980). The path to a concept of language learning disabilities. *Topics in Language Disorders, 1*, 1-14.

Terrell, T.D. (1977). A natural approach to second language acquisition and learning. *Modern Language Journal, 6*, 325-337.

Vellutino, F.R. (1979). *Dyslexia: Theory and research.* Cambridge, MA: MIT Press.

Vogel, S.A. (1977). Morphological ability in normal and dyslexic children. *Journal of Learning Disabilities, 7*, 103-109.

Willig, A.C. (1986). Special education and the culturally and linguistically different child: An overview of issues and challenges. *Journal of Reading, Writing and Learning Disabilities, 2*, 161-173.

Wode, H. (1978). Developmental sequences in naturalistic L2 acquisition. In E. Hatch (Ed.), *Second language acquisition* (pp. 101-117). Rowley, MA: Newbury House.

Wong-Fillmore, L. (1983). The language learner as an individual: Implications of research on individual differences for the ESL teacher. In M.A. Clarke & J. Handscombe (Eds.), *On TESOL '82: Pacific perspectives on language learning and teaching.* Washington, DC: TESOL.

chapter 5

Instructional Language Preferences of Bilingual Elementary Learning-Disabled Students*

Angela L. Carrasquillo

THE PROBLEM

This chapter explores the instructional language characteristics of bilingual (English and Spanish) students in special education. Its tentative conclusions are based on data collected through observations, audiotapes, and interviews conducted in a bilingual special education classroom with the specific aim of investigating the language patterns of handicapped students in instructional settings. Given the dearth of empirical data describing the instructional practices of bilingual handicapped students or their language characteristics in the classroom, the investigation is exploratory and descriptive in nature.

One basic premise of the study is that language functions as the major medium of instruction and learning. The language characteristics of these students and how they are reflected in the classroom play an important role in the academic, cognitive, and linguistic development of such students. Classroom language use provides numerous opportunities to understand content information while promoting communication and language development. Language provides the mechanism for active intellectual and cognitive involvement required by the communication task in which speakers are engaged (Holdaway, 1979; Smith, 1979; Stevick, 1985; Vygotsky, 1962). The language used in a bilingual special education classroom, in particular, needs special consideration due to the learning and linguistic characteristics of these students. Two related issues are: (a) bilingual special education students reflect differences in the use of both languages, and (b) not all students partic-

* This study was sponsored by the Office of Research Services of Fordham University, New York, New York 10023.

ipating in special education programs show language or learning disorders.

Bilingual handicapped students reflect different language characteristics; wide variation in the communication skills of language minority students is evident (Cummins, 1984; Oller, 1983; Ortiz, 1984). Frequently, however, students' language skills are sterotyped in comments such as: "Spanish is the first language of Hispanics"; "All Hispanics speak Spanish"; and "The child who is Spanish-dominant is proficient in that language" (Ortiz, 1984). The language dominance of minority children varies as a result of several factors such as the speech community in which they are reared, the language environment, and linguistic interactions with other people. Many times, educators assume that students have equal mastery of both languages, and that they are able to understand the communication of others and can communicate and achieve goals in both languages. But rarely are students consulted in terms of their language preferences and their demonstrated language behaviors for instructional purposes. Students need to feel that they are active members in the classroom. By asking students about their opinions and feelings about the languages being used in the classroom, they would feel that their opinions are seriously considered in planning instruction in the classroom.

Not all bilingual students participating in special education programs reflect language or learning disorders. Behaviors directly or indirectly related to linguistic proficiency constitute the most frequent reason for referral of language minority students (Carpenter, 1983; Garcia, 1985; Ortiz & Yates, 1983). The identification of language disorders of a bilingual child consider: (a) competencies of the child in both languages; (b) the semantic, pragmatic, and programmatic differences between the two languages; (c) the linguistic and social environment of students at home and at school; and (d) contributing individual cognitive factors. There are bilingual students who demonstrate deficiencies of language not because of their language limitations, especially in the second language, but because they are subject to the same factors, i.e., environmental home-related factors that cause language disorders in the monolingual child. All the more reason that in interpreting assessment data for the culturally and linguistically different child, an effort is made to relate the features of the second language acquisition process and their overlap with features of language disorders.

Some assessment personnel treat bilingual students as pathological cases regardless of the language background which reflects exposure to different linguistic conditions (Garcia, 1985). Maldonado-Colon (1986) suggests that due to the impact that language proficiency has on the outcomes of educational assessment and classroom settings, it is necessary to collect as much information as possible in the assessment phase. She enumerates various sources of information. One is the child's linguistic preference by setting (e.g., home, classroom, play area) which can only be identified by observing formal and informal settings and by asking students about their language preferences in instructional activities. Students' own perceptions of how they contribute in the process of language development is another source of significant information in their instructional development.

Affective variables, such as attitudes, motivation, and personality traits, also play a role in "who learns languages and how well they learn them" (Gardner, 1985; Krahonke & Christison, 1983). Gardner and Lambert (1972) have established the importance of attitude and motivation in relation to learning outcomes in second language acquisition. They found that a high level of drive by the student to acquire the language of a valued second language community, or an identification with this community, combined with sincere interest in the group, underlines the motivation needed to master a second language. One main hypothesis of the role of affective variables in second language acquisition is that the learners who have highly positive attitudes will have increased motivation and, thus, attain greater proficiency in a second language. Genesee, Rogers, and Holobow (1983) also contend that positive attitudes and motivation toward the second language learning situation may be necessary for learning to occur. These researchers indicate that both motivation and attitudes are important factors which help to determine the level of proficiency achieved by different learners.

Studies in the area of language attitudes and preferences of the learning disabled bilingual child are almost nonexistent. The studies which are found are mostly related to bilingual students in mainstream settings and address the characteristics of classrooms as settings for language learning (Wong-Fillmore, 1985). This study intended to identify the bilingual learning-disabled students' instructional language behaviors that were observable in the classroom, including their perceptions of and preferences for both languages as well as their perceived language strengths and weaknesses. Through classroom observations, audiotaped materials, and student interviews, these research questions were addressed:

1. What is the language classroom environment of bilingual disabled students? Is it a Spanish-dominant or English-dominant environment?
2. What role do students play in the process of language development? For example, do they use more Spanish or more English? What

language do they predominantly use in talking to the bilingual teacher? What language do they mostly use when they talk to one another? When the teacher asks a question in English/Spanish, do they always answer it in the language used in the question?

3. What classroom situations promote second language use? What relationship exists between a student's language preference and actual language use in the classroom?

4. What are students' attitudes toward the native and second language?

5. What are students' perceptions of their specific strengths and weaknesses in both languages?

6. Do students' language characteristics reveal language disorders or language differences?

METHOD

Subjects

For the purposes of this study, a learning-disabled student was defined as presenting a disparity between some measure of potential and another one of performance, that is, an assumption of some underlying dysfunctional learning process (McIntire, Keeton, & Agard, 1980). The term "bilingual" was defined as the ability to engage in communication in more than one language.

This study was conducted in a bilingual special education class for the learning disabled. The sample consisted of 12 male students enrolled in a public school in New York City in a low-income neighborhood. The school served about 600 students with three bilingual special education classes; the ethnic composition of the school was 60 percent Hispanic and 40 percent black. The subjects were 5 fourth-grade, 4 fifth-grade, and 3 sixth-grade Hispanic students. Ninety percent of the students spoke Spanish at home and were identified in school as limited-English-proficient (LEP). Students' mean age was 11 and their mean years in the United States was 5.3. The subjects were in a self-contained classroom with a certified bilingual teacher who was fully bilingual and possessed a master's degree in bilingual special education.

The criteria used to identify the subjects included: (a) learning-disabled students with Spanish surnames; (b) students who had already been tested, evaluated, and placed in bilingual instruction services; (c) subjects who were matched for grade, age (11–13), low socioeconomic status, and level of English proficiency in which the students scored less on the English version of the Language Assessment Battery test than on the Spanish version; (d) subjects who manifested the ability to participate in instruction presented in the primary language (Spanish); and (e) subjects who showed limited ability to participate in instruction presented in English only.

Data Sources

Data for this study were derived from classroom observations and audiotapes collected over a period of three weeks. The entire bilingual class was observed for three weeks in which time the researcher kept detailed observational records of their daily school experiences. Students were observed and audiotaped three times a week for three hours for a total of nine days, or 27 hours. Observations, conducted in the morning and afternoon, consisted of notes and recordings of audiotapes of language behaviors that students showed in English and Spanish. Each student was interviewed two times, at the beginning and end of the study, to identify their perceptions, strengths, and weaknesses toward both languages. Reading, language arts, and mathematics were the subject areas observed.

RESULTS AND DISCUSSION

Being exploratory with tentative conclusions, the examination of student classroom language characteristics provided an excellent opportunity to describe those activities suggestive of successful language instructional strategies for bilingual pupils participating in special education.

Language Environment of the Classroom

The school environment was mostly an English one since the school's policy was to promote the development of English. This was observed through announcements made over the loudspeaker (only in English); bulletin board materials were mostly in English; information from the principal's office was mostly written in English except when communication was sent to the parents. However, the specific classroom environment was bilingual. The teacher used various techniques to promote language in the classroom and tended to use Spanish when addressing affective aspects such as discipline and personal matters. Spanish was used mostly to keep students quiet, to stay on line, and to start assigned tasks. Students used Spanish for permission to go to the bathroom and to request intervention in a fight or discussion among themselves. Every time that students addressed the teacher, they called him "maestro," indicating some degree of respect.

The classroom had materials in both languages. Directions for the day were given in English and Spanish. The schedule was always written in Spanish: "Horario: 8:30–9:15, Lectura, 9:15–9:50—Matematicas." The class was organized into two groups—the more English-proficient group and the less English-proficient group. Grouping was mostly for the follow-up activities of the lesson. Lessons followed a structure in which the whole class lesson was done in English or Spanish, and individualized activities were done in small groups in English and/or Spanish. In the small group, students were asked questions or were given specific tasks to do based on the material read or discussed in the group presentation. The teacher was always concerned about the English limitations of the students; he used translations and code switching to clarify material for students. For instance, "The story que vamos a leer hoy es muy interesante. Let's open the books. Abran los libros."

One behavior observed throughout the study was the large amount of talking, especially Spanish, that was going on in the classroom. The teacher motivated students to talk by posing a question or thought:

T (teacher):	The story that we read yesterday presented a child with a problem. ¿ Cual fue el problema que vimos en el cuento de ayer?
S (student):	Maestro, yo creo que tenia que ver con perder a su perro.
T:	Yes, the dog, the dog.
S:	Eso es malo perder un perro.
S:	It is sad.

And the discussion went on concerning the sadness of losing an animal.

In conclusion, the language environment of the classroom was bilingual, students using Spanish and English in the classroom to the extent that they understood the content being presented, especially if it was related to their prior experiences and meaningful to them.

Classroom Situations that Promote Language Development

Students felt comfortable in using the Spanish language in the instructional setting. It was observed that when the instructional task was in Spanish, students tended to attend longer than when it was presented in English (the Spanish average was 15 minutes; English averaged 6 minutes). When the conversation was in English, students tended not to participate. On many occasions, they were unable to expand their thoughts due to their English language limitations. In general, observations showed that students showed preferences for using Spanish over

English. Nevertheless, when the teacher asked questions in English, students tried to answer in English, although their answers were mostly one- or two-word responses. However, whenever they had time to speak freely without the pressure of "speaking to practice and learn English," they used Spanish, especially among themselves.

The major sources of language input came from other students and from the teacher. Students spent about 65 percent of their time in the classroom talking about themselves and listening or talking to the teacher. The teacher asked questions for students to respond to or to expand on the question. Although the teacher asked many questions, students seemed to enjoy that type of activity. Examples included: T: "Who wants to tell the class what we learned yesterday in mathematics? Uds creen que aprendimos algo en la clase de ayer? What do you remember? ¿ Quien quiere ser el primero?"

When students gave an improper grammatical answer, the teacher continued with the conversation and at some point in the discussion repeated the same expression correctly. It was observed that on several occasions he asked the students to repeat the expression after him. One phrase that the teacher used frequently was: "Estamos aprendiendo ingles y para eso tenemos que aprender a oir y a repetir."

Vocabulary was introduced through pictures, use of students' background knowledge, and the dictionary. Once students were able to get the meaning of the word, the teacher engaged them in a series of related activities such as using the words in sentences, matching the word with phrases, pictures, or sentences, and making comparisons and locating the word in structured charts. Students' language responses were very creative. For example, students reacted creatively in language solutions that presented a challenge to them.

T: What is the girl doing?
S: Many things, she is looking, thinking, meditating.
    I see something else, maestro.

Students were able to identify different actions in a picture of a girl by concentrating on the position of her eyes and head.

Students' Role in the Process of Language Development

Students were able to follow the instruction in the classroom. Effective activities that were observed included those that encouraged expression of their experiences, language background, and interests. The following sections explain how students saw themselves in the process of language development.

Students' language development. Student participation in instructional activities contributed to their language development. These findings are based on the most frequent observations.

1. In general, students used more Spanish than English. When students were in the Spanish class their thoughts were clearer and more precise; they demonstrated more academic language proficiency. For example,

T: ¿ Que piensas despues de haber leido el cuento?
S: Maestro, parece como si uno estuviera viendo un retrato de Neuva York.
T: A veces uno se abochorna, ¿ saben lo que es abochornarse?
S: Es algo asi como ponerse rojo y pensativo.
Yo me abochorno cuando hablo ingles.
Maestro, ¿ ha Ud. le ha pasado eso alguna vez?

It was observed that during activities in Spanish, the emphasis was on oral communication and comprehension, while in the English class the emphasis was only on oral communication. In Spanish, students applied their prior knowledge and experiences. On one occasion in mathematics while students were using multiplication tables, when the time to do the calculation came, they preferred to mentally do the process in Spanish (many of the students did the mental process orally). The teacher had instructed them to do the mental process in Spanish if necessary. After the process was completed, they expressed the result in English. Most of the time mathematics was done in Spanish, but the teacher stated to the researcher that sometimes he used an ESL approach to teach mathematics to familiarize students with the vocabulary and mental process in English. This approach was characterized by introducing the vocabulary, presenting the content orally, writing the problem on the board, reading it, and then explaining the steps in the solution of the problem.

2. Most of the conversation produced by the students in English was nonacademic language. Students were able to express ideas or ask questions in English that were more related to daily experiences than to academic work, for example, reciting the days of the week or the months of the year, answering the question, "how are you?" One frequent observation during mathematics, reading, and language arts concerned the use of English in that students appeared not to know what was expected of them. Observed lessons indicated that students followed the lessons in English, sometimes without knowing what was happening in

the lesson, not because of their learning disability, but because of their limitations with the English language.

T: What is a story teller?
S: Story teller is that telling the story.
T: What is the definition of the word "made"?
S: Something that you made.

If challenged, students were able to use impersonal language to move into some cognitive activities.

T: When you say "story teller" you are thinking of someone, right?
S: Yes, maestro, do you remember the story you said yesterday?
        yes, a man tell the story.
        Yes, it was something that happen to him, verdad, Maestro?

Another behavior frequently observed was that when the teacher made a statement in English, students tended to internalize it by repeating it. For example:

T: Let's do it right.
S: Let's do it right.
T: We need to follow the steps.
T: We need to follow the steps.

3. Most of the time when students talked to the teacher they used Spanish. This observation was consistent in all of the frequency count data. Students felt comfortable speaking in Spanish since the teacher was also Hispanic and the students knew that the teacher spoke both languages very well. It was observed that students felt close to the teacher when he was speaking to them in Spanish and were able to communicate their ideas better. However, when the teacher asked a question in English, the students tended to answer the question in English.

T: Who can do the multiplication in this problem?
S: I can, maestro.

4. Students used Spanish in talking to one another. Students spoke among themselves in Spanish (90 percent of the time) in all classes observed and in all activities. It was seen as the natural way to communicate with one another. When students used Spanish, they showed "normal language speech" in their conversations. For example,

they used complete sentences, answered content asked in the question, and followed a particular topic in a conversation.

Student Attitudes Toward English and Spanish

Data for this component were obtained through interviewing students twice, at the beginning and at the end of the study. Table 5.1 summarizes the responses of students to interview questions.

Students expressed satisfaction with being in a bilingual class with a teacher who knew their primary language and who could teach them English. When students were asked the question: "Do you like people talking to you in Spanish?," all students responded in the affirmative. When asked: "Do you think you speak good Spanish?," all of them responded in the affirmative. Only one student admitted that he gets "mixed up" with the two languages. It appeared that these students had an overall positive attitude toward their native language and that they viewed their language as being very much tied up with their family and place of birth. One student put it concisely: "I love Spanish."

Students perceived that they were forced to use more English in the

Table 5.1. Distribution of 12 LEP Student Responses About Their Perceptions Toward English and Spanish.

Responses	n
1. Satisfied being in a bilingual program	12
2. Speak "good" Spanish	12
3. Use Spanish when speaking to the teacher	12
4. Like people talking to them in Spanish	10
5. Use Spanish when speaking to friends	9
6. Prefer that the teacher use Spanish	9
7. Express strengths in Spanish	8
8. Use Spanish and English when speaking to the teacher	6
9. Express weaknesses in understanding and orally communicating in English	7
10. Like people talking to them in English	5
11. Express weakness in understanding and communicating in Spanish	5
12. Speak "fair" English	5
13. Use English when speaking to friends	4
14. Use English when speaking to teacher	4
15. Use English and Spanish when speaking to friends	3
16. Express strengths in understanding and orally communicating in English	3
17. Express weaknesses in understanding and orally communicating in English and Spanish	3
18. Prefer that the teacher use English	1
19. Speak "good" English	1

classroom than Spanish. When asked the question: "Do you like people talking to you in English?," the group's answers varied. Five students did not like people talking to them in English. From those who answered in the affirmative, a common reason was that they could learn more English. The students who responded negatively stated that they did not understand English very well, and that when they spoke English they were unsure of what they were saying. Two students stated that they could learn English from their friends and that they could teach them Spanish. Overall, it appears that these students accepted the fact that they have to learn and use English in school. Students were aware of the school pressure to learn English, and they accepted the idea of the importance of learning English.

Student perceptions of language strengths. Student interviews revealed that students perceived themselves as having "good Spanish" skills and "fair" to "not good" English skills. They did not complain about not having enough instruction in Spanish. They perceived English as the language to be learned as soon and as well as possible. Four students said that by forcing them to learn English it had given them the opportunity to practice more and to get better at speaking English. Seven students saw Spanish as a strength in translating for their parents and being able to communicate with their relatives. Three students said: "I am proud to speak two languages."

Student perceptions of language weaknesses. In general, students viewed their English language development as "needing some improvement," especially the skills of speaking and pronunciation. Three students mentioned that reading was very difficult, especially when answering the teacher's questions. Two students said that they had some problems in remembering what was read. When asked, "when the teacher is helping you to understand a word or problem, do you understand what he is saying?," most students said "yes" if it is in Spanish or if he says it in English but explains it in Spanish. Thus, student weaknesses seem to be related to being unfamiliar with the English language.

Language Differences or Learning Disorders?

This question was not completely addressed in the study. It is a concern that the researcher had throughout the study and would like to share with the reader. The literature suggests that identification of speech and language handicaps has been based on students' ability to use surface forms of speech, especially the morphological and syntactical forms of language (Oller, 1983; Ortiz, 1988b; Stevick, 1985). These authorities claim that identification of communication disorders can only be made by comparing the child's ability to communicate in both languages. To be truly handicapped, students must be handicapped in their dominant language and not only in the English language.

Audiotape transcripts of the classroom language interactions and student interviews revealed that these students were able to communicate in Spanish. It was observed that these students were able to manipulate language to the extent that it was challenging and related to their background and experiences. Observations also revealed that students had limited vocabulary in English. In many instances, this limitation did not prevent them from expanding on a particular topic in conversation. Their Spanish vocabulary, although not extensive, was more complete (related to specific content and variety of words used) than their English vocabulary. Students manipulated the Spanish language to express ideas and follow up on conversations.

Transcripts showed that the Spanish language of these students may be as "complete" as other fourth-, fifth-, or sixth-grade "normal" students from the same socioeconomic and parental background. Then, why are these students labeled as "disabled"? Perhaps because these students made language mistakes in English that are normal to children learning a second language. The following were English language deficiencies consistently observed in 80 percent of the sample.

1. The use of the past tense as present tense, e.g., "made" for "make"; "had-have"; "came"-"come," and "did"-"do"
2. The use of simple structures when constructing sentences. One common structure linked subject plus verb plus object, e.g., "Me drink the milk" for "I need to drink the milk"
3. Disregard of past tenses, e.g., "I write (wrote) the story yesterday," "I do (for did) the homework, maestro"
4. Overgeneralization of rules, e.g., "I goed to lunch" for "I went to lunch."

Language disorders observed in both languages among these students are listed below. These language behaviors (or language deficiencies or mistakes) were not consistent across all students. In other words, students did not make or repeat these mistakes all of the time. They were present but not on a frequent basis. Three students made them more often than all the students.

1. On several occasions, their oral language was disorganized and difficult to understand. When students spoke, their content was not clear (sentences were not complete; words used did not relate to the concept being expressed). When students tried to answer the teacher's

questions, they used sentences that were not cognitively and grammatically understandable.

2. Students had difficulty in determining if a sentence was a statement of information or a question. This observation occurred when students were using academic language (e.g., in a discussion in the mathematics class or answering questions of a story read). Several times they did not understand if the teacher was expressing a sentence or posing a question. Also, when the teacher told them to ask a question, they gave a sentence.

3. Orally retelling or restating information. This observation was a linguistic strategy used by the students to cognitively process what was being heard. It was a technique mostly observed in the English class with the exception of three students.

4. Retrieving words from memory. Data indicated that five of the students had difficulties in stating specific ideas or using words previously taught.

5. Formulating sentences. Data indicate that three of the students had difficulty in phrasing their thoughts in sentences. Students showed very limited vocabulary and had insufficient words to state ideas clearly. Again, this linguistic deficiency was mostly observed when students were using the English language.

Half of the students showed the above learning deficits in English. It is not clear to the researcher if these language behaviors are true disorders related to dysfunctional learning or normal reflections of individuals learning a new language. These observations alone are not sufficient evidence to conclude that the students are learning-disordered. Many language minority students are referred to special education because educators are unable to distinguish individual differences among handicapping conditions. As Ortiz (1988a) says, "a child should be judged to have speech and language deficits only if presenting behaviors which are atypical of peers from the same cultural group who speak the same dialect and who have had similar opportunities to hear and use language" (p. 54). These problems could be associated with handicapping conditions, but they could also reflect a lack of English proficiency.

CONCLUSIONS AND RECOMMENDATIONS

This was a short descriptive study with a very limited population. Only 12 students participating in a bilingual special education class were observed. This in itself is a limitation and the results are primarily exploratory. The identification of students' instructional language, the situations that promote language development, and the role of students in the process of that development will require more formal study in the future. The relationship of second language acquisition, language and learning disorders, and language deficits need careful research attention. The conclusions and recommendations derived from these data can only be applied to this particular classroom. Analysis of the data on this bilingual special education classroom led to these tentative conclusions.

1. Students showed mastery of basic Spanish vocabulary, concepts and grammatical structures, and reading comprehension. They also showed an affective attachment to Spanish. Instruction should be consistent with what is known about language acquisition and about the interrelationship between first and second language development (Cummins, 1984; Krashen, 1982; Ortiz, 1988a). Authorities have indicated that the native language provides the foundation for acquiring English as a second language skills. Promotion of conceptual native language skills will be more effective in providing a basis for English literacy. A recommendation for the teacher is to mediate instruction using both the first and the second language and integrate English development with subject matter instruction.

2. Participants showed limited proficiency in English basic skills, especially in vocabulary, sentence construction, elaborating on a topic, and reading comprehension. Students benefited more when Spanish was used to develop cognitive and academic skills. There is a need for a strong English as a Second Language component to help students feel more comfortable in using English. The English as a Second Language (ESL) program needs to provide a low-anxiety environment for students in which mistakes are not immediately corrected and in which meaningful communication is provided through "comprehensible" input. Comprehensible input can be provided through the understanding of the content of the subject matter and through literacy skills in the native language.

3. Student attitudes toward both languages were very positive. Spanish was seen as attached to family and cultural ties; English was seen as an important language to be learned well and quickly. Students were concerned about the need to learn English. Students need to be relaxed in the classroom and they need not be told that the more immersed they are in English, the more English they will learn.

4. Students' language may be labeled as language in the process of development or expansion. Students used language to communicate and to learn. There is a need to expand their Spanish language, especially to move to the academic proficiency level. At the same time, this academic knowledge will help them in acquiring proficiency in English.

The development of both languages needs to be seen together and not as one language affecting the other.

5. The teacher is a very important factor in the process of student learning and language development. The teacher in this study was critical. Students felt comfortable with the teacher. The aspect of demonstrating bilingual proficiency was a very important factor in providing bilingual instruction to these students. Classroom observations, however, indicated that students would have benefited more if the teacher would have provided more challenging instructional activities in both languages in large and small teaching instructional settings. It is recommended that more inservice teacher training be provided to bilingual special education teachers, especially in the area of effective instructional practices.

REFERENCES

Carpenter, L. (1983). *Communication disorders in limited and non-English proficient children.* Los Alamitos, CA: National Center for Bilingual Research.

Cummins, J. (1984). *Bilingualism and special education: Issues in assessment and pedagogy.* San Diego, CA: College-Hill Press.

Garcia, S.B. (1985). *Effects of student characteristics, school program and organization on decision-making for the placement of Hispanic students in classes for the learning disabled.* Unpublished doctoral dissertation, University of Texas of Austin.

Gardner, R.C. (1985). *Social psychology and second language learning: The role of attitudes and motivation.* Baltimore, MD: Edward Arnold Publishers Ltd.

Gardner, R.C., & Lambert, W.E. (1972). *Attitudes and motivation in second language learning.* Rowley, MA: Newbury House.

Genesee, F., Rogers, P., & Holobow, N. (1983). The social-psychology of second language learning: Another point of view. *Language Learning, 33,* 209-224.

Holdaway, D. (1979). *The foundations of literacy.* Sydney: Ashton Scholastic.

Krahonke, K., & Christison, M.A. (1983). Recent language research and some language teaching principles. *TESOL Quarterly, 17,* 4625-4645.

Krashen, S. (1982). *Principles and practices in second language.* Oxford: Pergamon Press.

Maldonado-Colon, E. (1986). Assessment: Considerations upon interpreting data of linguistically/culturally different students referred for disabilities or disorders. In A. Willig & H. Greenberg (Eds.), *Bilingualism and learning disabilities.* New York: American Library Publishing Company, Inc.

McIntyre, R.B., Keeton, A., & Agard, R. (1980). *Identification of learning disabilities in Ontario: A validity study.* Toronto: Ministry of Education, Ontario.

Oller, J.W. (1983). Testing proficiencies and diagnosing language disorders in bilingual children. In D.R. Omark & J.G. Erickson (Eds.), *The bilingual exceptional child.* San Diego, CA: College-Hill Press.

Ortiz, A.A. (1984). Choosing the language of instruction for exceptional bilingual children. *Teaching Exceptional Children, 16,* 208-212.

Ortiz, A.A. (1988a). Characteristics of learning disabled, mentally retarded, and speech-language handicapped Hispanic students at initial evaluation and reevaluation. In A.A. Ortiz & B.A. Ramirez (Eds.), *Schools and the culturally diverse exceptional student: Promising practices and future directions* (pp. 51-62). Reston, VA: The Council for Exceptional Children.

Ortiz, A.A. (1988b). A pre-referral process of preventing inappropriate referrals of Hispanic students to special education. In A.A. Ortiz & B.A. Ramirez (Eds.), *Schools and the culturally diverse exceptional student: Promising practices and future directions* (pp. 6-18). Reston, VA: The Council for Exceptional Children.

Ortiz, A.A., & Yates, J.R. (1983). Incidence of exceptionality among Hispanics: Implications for manpower planning. *NABE Journal, 7*(3), 41-53.

Smith, F. (1979). *Essays into literacy.* Exeter, England: Heineman.

Stevick, E. (1985). *Teaching languages: A way and ways.* Rowley, MA: Newbury House.

Vygotsky, L. (1962). *Thought and language* (E. Hanfman & G. Vikar, Trans.). Cambridge, MA: MIT Press.

Wilner, R. (1985). *Ten years of neglect: The failure to serve language-minority students in the New York City public schools.* New York: The Educational Priorities Panel.

Wong-Fillmore, L. (1985). When does teacher talk work as input? In R. Scarcella & M. Long (Eds.), *Input in second language acquisition* (pp. 17-50). Rowley, MA: Newbury House Publishers, Inc.

chapter 6
Planning and Implementing an English as a Second Language Program

Nancy Cloud

In the 25 largest city school systems, where the majority of students are minority ("Here they come . . .," May 14, 1986), overenrollment of minority students in special education has been a continuing and increasing problem, although the categorical programs within special education in which over-representation occurs has shifted over time from programs for the mentally retarded to programs for the learning disabled and speech impaired (Dew, 1984; Willig, 1986). While there are no accurate national figures disaggregating the number of limited-English-proficient (LEP) students enrolled in special education settings from among the sizable minority population, Baca and Cervantes (1984) have recently estimated the number of school-aged LEP exceptional children to be over half a million.

Because of more stringent requirements to identify LEP students receiving special education services in urban school systems, more accurate figures are becoming available for the LEP special education population. For example, in New York City, it is currently estimated that there are some 10,000 to 15,000 students with limited English proficiency in special education programs in the city's schools ("New York City agrees. . ." September 7, 1988). A growing awareness of the presence of LEP students in special education settings has prompted many concerns, several related to ESL service delivery: (a) that teachers not refer LEP students to special education without having provided adequate second language programming as a part of regular education services (Ortiz & Maldonado-Colon, 1986); (b) that, if referred, the team conducting psychological testing account for the student's second language status in the selection of measures and approaches for the assessment process and carefully interpret results accounting for the influence of the second language (Nuttal, Landurand, & Goldman, 1984); and (c) that LEP students appropriately placed in special education receive specialized instructional services that account for their linguistic and cultural characteristics (Dew, 1983; Plata, 1986), as well as their identified disabilities.

This volume is designed to address the educational needs of exceptional LEP students. In designing comprehensive special education programs for such students, educators will have to take into account their complex learning needs, including their need for specialized English as a Second Language (ESL) services. This chapter focuses on the process of planning and implementing ESL services in a special education context, based on a well-articulated, integrated knowledge base from special education and bilingual/ESL education.

DEFINITIONS

In this section essential program definitions related to English as a Second Language and Special Education are provided so that readers of various professional backgrounds can have equal access to the concepts to be presented.

English as a Second Language (ESL) is a specialized approach to language instruction designed for those whose primary language is other than English. ESL is not limited to oral language instruction; rather it involves the total spectrum of English communication skills (listening, speaking, reading, and writing). In general, when English instruction is provided to speakers of other languages in their own countries prior to emigration, it is referred to as English as a Foreign Language (EFL). ESL refers to instruction provided in an English-speaking country to speakers of other languages. ESL can be provided as a component of a bilingual education program, as an independent course of instruction taught on a pullout basis, or as an integrated component of an intensive instructional program in which all subjects are taught using ESL methods, such as in Sheltered English, High Intensity Language Training (HILT), or Immersion Programs (McKeon, 1987). ESL instruction is not the same as English instruction for native speakers (English Language Arts) with all of the psycholinguistic, sociological, and cultural assumptions that encompasses. The delivery of ESL requires specially trained teachers using methodologies, techniques, and materials designed to meet the particular needs of limited-English-proficient students, who are in the process of acquiring English as their second language. The ESL teacher's role is to provide the student with an environment conducive to acquiring English by analyzing their current instructional needs (stage of acquisition, skills profile, motivational status, language needs, language learning style, etc.). Because ESL instruction can be offered to students of all achievement and age levels, methods and materials should differ accordingly.

Many states do not require teachers providing ESL services to be certified in this area and some teachers who provide ESL instruction do so without the necessary professional preparation to insure effective ESL program delivery. In 1980–1981, the Teacher's Language Skills Survey (TLSS), a study conducted by InterAmerica Research Associates, Inc. for the U.S. Department of Education under the research authority of the Bilingual Education Act (O'Malley, 1983), estimated that half of all public school teachers have immediate or previous experience with LEP students in their classes. At the same time, teachers teaching ESL to their LEP students are not professionally prepared to do so. Only 40 percent of the ESL teachers and 6 percent of teachers in general had taken even *one* academic or nonacademic course to learn how to teach English as a second language (O'Malley, 1983). In the 1980–1981 school year, only 1 teacher in 17 had been adequately prepared to teach English to his/her LEP students (fewer than 4 percent). Preparation for teachers who provide such instruction is available at the preservice level by colleges and universities with TESOL (Teaching English to Speakers of Other Languages) departments and at the in-service level by ESL specialists.

Over the last 20 years, second language teaching techniques have changed a great deal. In the 1950s and 1960s, ESL and foreign language instruction were influenced by contrastive linguistics and behavioral psychology. Methodologies concentrated heavily on rote learning of language forms (grammar, vocabulary, pronunciation). As a result, the techniques used by teachers were often mechanical (e.g., choral repetition, minimal pair drills, grammar translation exercises). Currently ESL and foreign language instruction are influenced by psycholinguistics, sociolinguistics, and cognitive psychology, and ESL methods have changed to reflect this. Current methods and materials are designed to stimulate and foster the natural development or acquisition of English language skills, related to the functional needs of the learner, in a particular social context.

Because a larger goal of second language instruction in the United States is to facilitate acculturation into U.S. society, ESL curriculum materials are often designed to contrast aspects of the culture of the United States with those of the student's native culture and to facilitate cross-cultural understanding and accommodation to the host culture's customs and values. Thus, ESL instruction is specially designed instruction provided to speakers of other languages which recognizes and accommodates their second language status and acculturation needs.

Special Education is instruction designed for students who require some degree of modification in their educational programs because they have intellectual, emotional, sensory, or physical impairments (Glass, Christiansen, & Christiansen, 1982). Modifications might include use of special curriculum materials, specialized teaching strategies or behavioral management techniques, and specially designed equipment and/ or facilities. Some students' disabilities are mild and they can succeed with modifications in mainstream classrooms; other students' disabilities are moderate or severe in nature, requiring placement in special settings. Exceptional students are most often categorized as mentally retarded, emotionally disturbed, learning disabled, speech impaired, hearing impaired, visually impaired, or physically and health impaired. Despite the considerable diversity in the special education student population, there are certain commonalities underlying effective programs for these students. All special students, regardless of the type or degree of disability, share certain rights and needs, including: (a) the right to a free and *appropriate* public education; (b) the right to an Individualized Educational Program (IEP), specifying the student's unique needs and the special education and related services the student is to receive; and (c) the need to have cognitive, linguistic, academic, and social/emotional characteristics considered and appropriate environmental modifications or adaptations made.

In keeping with these features, educational programs for exceptional LEP students would individualize instruction to account for basic educational needs, including the need for English as a Second Language (ESL) instruction. Regarding the provision of ESL services, LEP students enrolled in special education will require what is most appropriately labeled *Special Education-ESL (SE-ESL)*.

Special Education-ESL (SE-ESL) is a special ESL program designed for LEP students with identified disabilities. The use of a special term is required to emphasize the need to simultaneously account for a particular LEP student's disability needs and second language status. SE-ESL differs in two important ways from traditional ESL programs. First, it is an individualized instructional program, rather than a program designed for a group of learners at a particular stage of development in the second language (e.g., beginner, intermediate, advanced). Here ESL goals and objectives, methods, and materials would all be specified *individually*, as a part of the student's comprehensive IEP (Individualized Educational Program). Second, knowledge of the effect of disability on second language acquisition is required to plan effective programs. For example, in planning an ESL program for a LEP mentally retarded youngster, knowledge of the educational, emotional, and physical needs of mentally retarded youngsters must be integrated with knowledge of the second language acquisition process in order for the

ESL program to be effective for the learner with identified cognitive deficits.

Special Education as a field has benefitted very much from and has contributed much to the advancement of our knowledge base regarding attributes of the learner that affect instructional outcomes. Cognition, strategic behavior, motivation, and learning style preferences are just a few learner attributes studied to improve instruction for exceptional students. Learner attributes are also crucial to understanding the process of second language (L2) learning. Oxford-Carpenter (1986) lists five critical learner attributes for L2 learning: aptitude, attitudes/motivation, personality, learning style, and learning strategies. In planning individualized ESL services, analysis of learner attributes would be essential to the formulation of appropriate goals and objectives.

The reader is referred to Spolsky (1989, 1988) for an excellent discussion of theoretical considerations in planning a second language program for all types of LEP students, including students with disabilities. Spolsky proposes that for any given individual, the amount and nature of second language learned will depend on the totality of the conditions under which the second language is being acquired. For Spolsky, linguistic and nonlinguistic oucomes for the learner are explained by the interaction and integration of a large number of factors, some essential and others having a graded effect (the more the condition is present, the more its effect on language learning). Based on the work of Oxford-Carpenter and Spolsky, it is logical to conclude that the more factors accounted for and responded to in planning second language instruction, the more successful the SE-ESL program would be for a particular individual.

Clearly there is a need to understand the characteristics of exceptional LEP students in order to plan appropriate programs; however, in addition practitioners will need a rich knowledge of ESL methods and materials to propose appropriate goals and objectives, and to select effective strategies and materials for each student's IEP (Dew, 1985).

ESL PROGRAM PLANNING THROUGH THE IEP PROCESS

As has been noted above, SE-ESL is a service provided to students with disabilities through the IEP process. This section will describe the following aspects of ESL program planning which are governed through the IEP process: (a) assessment, (b) team planning, (c) service delivery arrangements, (d) selecting appropriate goals and objectives based on nature and degree of disability, (e) monitoring progress, and (f) home support and involvement.

Assessment

Two types of assessment are included in the IEP planning process. The first type of assessment *identifies* students; the second *diagnoses* instructional needs. LEP special education students are assessed two ways during the identification phase of assessment. They are identified as LEP by some type of language proficiency assessment procedure and they are identified as handicapped by a multidisciplinary team assessment process. It is important to remember that a student's second language status should be considered in planning the psychoeducational testing to be conducted and that the student's suspected disability issues should be considered in planning the language proficiency testing to be conducted. For example, in conducting psychological testing, procedures will have to be selected that are as nondiscriminatory as possible given the student's language and cultural characteristics. In selecting language proficiency testing procedures and interpreting results, the sensorial, neurological, cognitive, and emotional status of learners will have to be considered. In both cases, testing modifications may be required and caution is urged in the selection and interpretation phases.

Federal and state regulations distinguish the identification process as a first phase in special education service provision. In this phase, students are qualified to receive special education and related services, a placement is recommended, and broad educational goals are written. It would be appropriate at this level to specify the need for SE-ESL on a student's IEP, signaling the fact that the student has been identified as having limited English proficiency and a particular handicapping condition. Broad goals would be written for the SE-ESL program, based on the needs of the student and the particular SE-ESL curriculum model selected. It would also be appropriate to specify the service delivery arrangement at this time. SE-ESL curriculum models and service delivery arrangements will be discussed in more detail later in the chapter.

The second type of assessment to be conducted as a part of the ESL program planning process would be diagnostic in nature. Here the SE-ESL short-term instructional objectives would be formulated based on an in-depth analysis of the learner and SE-ESL teaching strategies and curriculum materials would be suggested. The goal of this type of assessment would be to understand the learner's current stage of second language acquisition, the learner's profile of strengths and weaknesses in particular skill areas (listening, speaking, reading, and writing), the emotional and motivational status of the learner, the language learning style, personality characteristics, interests and needs of the learner, and the amount and type of opportunities (formal and informal) the learner has to engage in the second language. All of this information would be useful in planning short-term objectives for the SE-ESL program in the student's IEP.

Team Planning

Team planning is an essential part of the IEP planning process. In the case of an exceptional LEP student, a bilingual/ESL specialist would be an integral part of the team. The bilingual/ESL specialist would be familiar with formal and informal second language assessment procedures for both assessment phases previously mentioned (identification and instructional diagnosis) and with the predominant SE-ESL curriculum models, related instructional strategies and curriculum materials. The role of the bilingual/ESL specialist would be to oversee the assessment and program planning process for exceptional LEP students and to actively collaborate with the other team members to improve clinical and instructional services for LEP special education students.

Effective teams would be those in which all team members have the basic knowledge required to serve exceptional LEP students, while at the same time, depending on their area of specialization, each member would accept responsibility to extend the group's knowledge of clinical and/or instructional practice for LEP students by concentrating on particular aspects related to their discipline.

Service Delivery Arrangements

Special education services can consist of: (a) special education services delivered in regular education classes (consulting teacher models), (b) transitional support services (following declassification), (c) related services, (d) resource room instruction, (e) special class instruction, (f) home and hospital instruction, and (g) private school instruction. SE-ESL instruction must be available in all of these varied service delivery arrangements. SE-ESL can be delivered as a separate component of instruction by a teacher designated as the SE-ESL teacher for a specified time period each day, or it can be integrated into all aspects of intervention by the student's primary interventionist. This distinction is represented in Figure 6.1.

In order to determine the optimal service delivery arrangement the

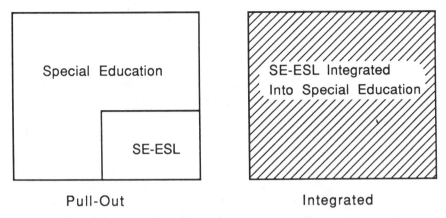

Figure 6.1   **Pull-Out and Integrated SE-ESL Service Delivery Arrangements.**

following aspects will have to be considered: relative expertise of the available service providers, the proficiency level of the student, the nature and extent of SE-ESL goals and objectives written for a particular student, the student's need for a separate period of formal instruction, and the potential for integrating SE-ESL instruction into the other curricular areas specified on the IEP. While SE-ESL instruction can be delivered by an ESL specialist or by a special educator, the service provider selected will have much to learn from both fields of ESL and Special Education, respectively, to bring coordinated services to students. An integrated program accounting for a complex of student factors is required. Several of these factors will be discussed in the sections that follow.

Selecting Appropriate Goals and Objectives Based on the Nature and Degree of Disability

A major factor to consider in designing SE-ESL programs is the nature and extent of the student's disability(ies). A primary distinction is made in designing special education services between students with *mild* disabilities and those with *moderate* or *severe* disabilities. Typically such knowledge directs both the program focus and the need for specialized knowledge in order to appropriately deliver instruction and modify the instructional environment.

In designing SE-ESL programs for mildly handicapped students the emphasis would most likely remain on delivering the mainstream ESL program, where a focus is placed on both oral language development and literacy development in the second language. Here the instructor would modify instruction to account for the student's disability issues, for example, by using a multisensory teaching approach, employing positive reinforcement and behavior management techniques, matching teaching strategies to the student's learning style, providing more practice, or attending to self-concept concerns.

For moderately or severely handicapped students the focus might shift dramatically to a program which develops functional skills (basic communication skills around daily routines) and later prepares the student for future life environments, concentrating on community living skills (shopping, using public transportation, getting along with neighbors). SE-ESL for these students might be developmental for younger students in an attempt to establish basic or self-help communication skills in the second language (requesting assistance, giving personal information, interacting with friends), while at the later grades it might have a life-skill focus, concentrating on functional communication skills needed by the particular individual being served at home, in the workplace, and in the community.

While the need for specialized knowledge of teaching techniques, adaptive equipment or prostheses exists for both groups of special education students (the mildly handicapped and moderately/severely handicapped), the need for such knowledge would increase incrementally as the degree of disability increases.

Monitoring Progress

Best practice in instructional service delivery suggests ongoing monitoring of student performance. In special education, such monitoring of student progress is required to measure the attainment of instructional objectives.

For this reason, in delivering SE-ESL services, informal assessment procedures will be an integral part of instruction. Such assessment would consider the validity of short-term objectives written, the success of methods selected, the efficacy of curriculum materials being employed, the adequacy of feedback provided to the student, and the effectiveness of behavior management programs instituted to support the intervention. Diagnostic teaching or process approaches provide for this type of ongoing analysis of student performance and are highly recommended. Examples would include: shared book (big book) approach to reading instruction, and Graves writing workshop (Garcia & Ortiz, 1988).

Home Support and Involvement

Irrespective of the English proficiency of family members, service providers are urged to view each student as part of a larger family system which both affects and is affected by the educational intervention provided to the student. Parents should participate in the development of SE-ESL annual goals and short-term objectives so that they are actively involved in determining the nature and extent of ESL programming to be provided. Service providers should explain the various programming options to parents and request their viewpoint regarding what they perceive as potentially of most benefit to their youngster. In each case, school personnel should explain ways in which the family can support the goals that are collaboratively established.

In some cases, school districts are under court mandates that specify the nature and extent of language services to be provided to exceptional LEP students. In such cases, parents should be fully informed as to the rationale behind the mandated services. Even in cases where the amount of services is prescribed or the qualifications of the service provider are specified, considerable flexibility exists as to the actual methods and materials that will be employed and the ways in which family members can provide support at home. Therefore, there is always room for meaningful parental involvement.

An important aspect for family members to understand is that their child must be given the opportunity to use the second language in formal (e.g., school-based) and informal (e.g., community-based) settings in order to successfully acquire the desired skills. Where parents have the requisite level of proficiency to offer such opportunity for practice they should be urged to do so and provided with any necessary supports (materials, ideas, encouragement). In cases where parents are limited-English-proficient, they should be encouraged to continue to provide high-quality language interactions in their native language, while at the same time they may be able to provide opportunities for their youngster to practice English in creative ways, such as enrolling their child in school-based activities or clubs, encouraging out-of-school friendships with English-proficient youngsters, or the viewing of educational television programs in English.

It is not beneficial or desirable to prematurely encourage the use of English by parents whose proficiency is so limited that it would reduce the quantity and quality of linguistic interactions in the home. Such misguided efforts can create a feeling of inadequacy among LEP parents and reduce their efforts to provide mediated learning experiences to their children; the foundation of adequate cognitive, social/emotional, and linguistic development (Feuerstein, 1980).

SE-ESL CURRICULUM MODELS

Since curriculum is the *content* of instruction, specified in terms of the *broad skill areas* to be taught, the *organization* or *sequencing* of these broad skill areas and the *steps* or *tasks* within each skill area (Van Etten, Arkell, & Van Etten, 1980), the ESL curriculum model selected would have a great impact on the actual content of instruction provided to the learner. It would determine which language skills are taught, how the ESL course is organized, and what types of activities or tasks are engaged in by the learners. In large part, the curriculum model selected would determine the end product or outcome of instruction.

In designing ESL programs for special education students, it is important to select an appropriate and applicable curriculum paradigm from among the major curriculum paradigms in ESL and special education. A promising means of doing this is by identifying those paradigms that exist concurrently in both fields. Five major curriculum models emerge from this search which can be useful in designing SE-ESL programs: (a) Developmental ESL, (b) Content-based ESL, (c) Cognitive/Learning Strategies ESL, (d) Functional/Life Skills ESL, and (e) Career-based/Vocational ESL. Each of these models is described in the next section of this chapter.

Developmental ESL

In a developmental ESL paradigm, the second language learner would be viewed as evolving through a set hierarchy of stages of language development. The teacher's role would be to facilitate this natural growth process. According to a developmental paradigm, students with disabilities would be expected to pass through the same stages of development as their nondisabled counterparts; however, it would be expected that they would require more support to do so and that growth would not be as spontaneous or rapid due to the identified disability issues.

An example of a developmental ESL curriculum model is the Natural Approach (Krashen & Terrell, 1983), which generally subsumes the Total Physical Response Approach (Asher, 1982), particularly at the early stages. According to this model of language development, second language learners are viewed as passing through four stages of development, on their way to becoming fully proficient in English: preproduction, early production, speech emergence, and intermediate fluency (Krashen & Terrell, 1983). According to a developmental ESL paradigm, analysis of the learner's stage of development in English is critical to providing an appropriately structured program and to selecting activities that would promote development from one stage to the next.

In accordance with this paradigm, while exceptional second language learners are expected to move through the same sequence of stages, they would be expected to require specialized instruction (e.g., the use of multisensory strategies, the provision of carefully sequenced instruction, active teaching for generalization) or the use of adaptive devices (e.g., amplification, large print materials) in order to do so.

Content-based ESL

Content-based ESL is a paradigm not unlike that of the *functional academic paradigm* in special education (Bilsky & Blackman, in press), where a compensatory/remedial emphasis is present, implying that the student cannot "fit" into the mainstream class without special assistance. However, it is also maintained that the student's special learning needs *can* be met, allowing access to the regular education curriculum, with appropriate modifications.

In content-based ESL, the standard, which determines the content of the language instruction program, is the mainstream academic program (social studies, mathematics, science). A content-based ESL curriculum is based on both the *language* and *content* demands of mainstream curriculum materials. Typically, great emphasis is placed on functional reading and writing skills in a content-based ESL program. Another term applied to this type of ESL instruction is Sheltered English, indicating that content area lessons are modified to account for the linguistic needs of second language learners. The concept of sheltered instruction for LEP students with identified disabilities should be expanded to account for not only language and content demands, but also for the routines or procedural demands of mainstream classes. Thus, sheltered instruction for exceptional LEP students might involve the teaching of requisite study skills, self-management strategies, or other support strategies (e.g., testing modifications) to promote and maintain successful functioning in mainstream classes.

Cognitive/Learning Strategies ESL

The training of cognitive strategies has been advocated in special education settings by those who believe that if a student's deficient cognitive functions can be identified and remediated, more efficient, automatic learning will result. This approach is sometimes referred to as a process-training approach, wherein remediating underlying processes are seen as more important than teaching specific content to learners (Bilsky & Blackman, in press). Examples of process-training approaches are Feuerstein's (1980) Instrumental Enrichment Program and Deshler's Strategies Intervention Model (Deshler & Schumaker, 1986).

In a cognitive/learning strategies ESL program, the primary emphasis is on understanding and advancing the learner's current repertoire of learning strategies to facilitate independent second language learning. In this type of approach, learners are made consciously aware of the types of cognitive, metacognitive, and social strategies that can assist them in acquiring the target language.

Oxford-Carpenter (1985) has designed a taxonomy of second language learning strategies in which she divides strategies into *direct* or primary strategies for second language learning and *indirect* or support strategies for second language learning. Examples of direct strategies would be native language to second language transfer strategies (e.g., contrastive analysis) and mnemonic strategies (e.g., use of flash cards). Examples of indirect strategies would be attention-enhancing strategies (e.g., use of advance organizers) or self-management strategies (e.g., self-rein-forcement). In all, Oxford-Carpenter lists some 64 strategies used by second language learners to acquire their second language. Recently (Oxford, 1990), she wrote a comprehensive volume on the topic in which she provides an eight-step model, suggested assessment tools, and teaching activities for second language learning strategy training.

Chamot and O'Malley (1987) have elaborated a learning strategies ESL curriculum model: the Cognitive Academic Language Learning Approach (CALLA). In their approach, metacognitive strategies are distinguished from cognitive and both of these are distinguished from social-affective strategies. For Chamot and O'Malley a metacognitive strategy might be self-monitoring (checking one's comprehension during listening or reading); a cognitive strategy might be resourcing (using reference materials such as dictionaries or textbooks); and a social/affective strategy might be self-talk (reducing anxiety by using mental techniques that make one feel competent to do the learning task). The CALLA approach can also be categorized as a content-based ESL model, described above, as it is referenced to academic content areas. (See Chapters 10 and 11 for more information on this model.)

A cognitive/learning strategies ESL paradigm makes the assumption that language-learning strategies must be taught because the learner has not acquired them naturally, or has not acquired efficiency in their use. Once the strategies are internalized, it is envisioned that language learning will become more automatic and efficient.

Functional/Life-Skills ESL

A functional curriculum model in special education can be characterized as a model which teaches functional, age-appropriate skills in natural environments (Bilsky & Blackman, in press). In this model, the curriculum is highly individualized to each particular learner's needs across domestic, academic or vocational, and recreational areas. An excellent source of such practical skills is the *Community Living Skills Taxonomy* published by the American Association on Mental Retardation (Dever, 1988) which specifies community referenced skills in the personal maintenance and development, homemaking, vocational, leisure and travel areas.

A functional/life skills ESL curriculum model is a community-referenced paradigm. Here essential, practical language skills required by individuals for survival in their natural environments (home, job or school, neighborhood) are identified and the ESL curriculum is organized to facilitate their development. In designing a functional/life skills ESL curriculum, a notional/functional type of approach to curriculum design is recommended since it is ideal for such a practical language development program. A notional/functional syllabus is based on a semantic and pragmatic theory of language, which contends that speakers use language to accomplish different communicative tasks, and hence that instructional programs should focus on building an individual's communicative competence by emphasizing the content and purpose of language communication (Van Ek, 1977; Wilkins, 1976).

An example of a functional/life skills ESL approach is Community Language Learning (Curran, 1976), where the needs of individual students determine the aspects of language to be taught. In Community Language Learning, the course of study centers on functional routines or daily language needs, social interaction or personal language needs, and academic or occupational language demands.

Career-based and Vocational ESL

This model can actually be considered to be a part of the Life Skills model presented above. However, because there are cases where other aspects of an individual's life are ignored and the career/vocational needs are the exclusive focus of language programming efforts, it is presented here as a separate model. In a career-based or vocational paradigm the focus is on essential, practical skills needed on the job or in preparation for a particular career. While personal-social skills are included, this is done only in relation to the particular vocation or career in question (e.g., communicative needs of a nurse, mechanic, airline worker). An excellent overview of vocational ESL program design is provided by Friedenberg and Bradley (1984).

This model of second language programming is often referred to as English for Special Purposes (ESP), where language instruction is integrated with occupational or vocational training to produce an individual who has the occupational and linguistic competence to succeed on a particular job. Each job would be analyzed to determine the linguistic demands (e.g., type and amount of literacy required) as well as other skills required to function effectively on the job (e.g., keyboarding skills). In the case of a disabled second language learner, job sites would be selected because of their potential as successful work environments for the particular student in question. The instructor would also consider the effect of the student's disability in designing the vocational ESL instruction (e.g., establishing an attainable scope and sequence of skills to be taught, implementing strategies to insure generalization from the classroom to the job site, providing sufficient practice under different conditions).

Each model presented above has special potential for application to exceptional LEP students. Some models are more appropriate with younger students (e.g., developmental), some with older (e.g., vocational). Some models are better applied to students with mild handicaps (e.g., content-based), others to students whose disabilities are more moderate or severe (e.g., life-skills); however, it is wise not to think restrictively of any particular model as limited on an a priori basis. The reader is encouraged to learn more about each of the models which have been briefly described in this section in order to select the best curriculum model for each student in question and thereby write appropriate SE-ESL goals and objectives for the IEP.

SE-ESL INSTRUCTIONAL STRATEGIES

Whereas curriculum has previously been defined as the "ends" of instruction, instructional strategies are "the means" of reaching the desired end (Bilsky & Blackman, in press). Instructional strategies include: (a) teaching methods, (b) behavior management techniques, and (c) environmental arrangements in which instruction takes place. Instructional strategies are not restricted to a particular curriculum model. For example, cooperative learning strategies might be used in any of the models mentioned above; a token economy might be implemented under any of the curriculum models to provide the external reinforcement required to enhance motivation. So, too, a teacher might change the lighting, seating arrangements, or mode of presentation of a lesson in order to enhance learning under any of the models described.

With this caveat in mind, several ESL instructional strategies are mentioned here because they hold special promise for LEP students with disabilities. They are: (a) computer-based instruction; (b) peer tutoring/cooperative learning instruction; (c) learning style-based instruction; and (d) whole language instruction.

Computer-based Instruction

The use of technology (computer, video, and audio) as an aid to learning is becoming increasingly important in the fields of Special Education and TESOL. Subdivisions currently exist in both fields to which professionals specializing in the use of technology belong. In special education, applications include: (a) *Computer-Assisted Instruction* (CAI); the use of tutorials, drill and practice, simulations, games, learner-centered software; (b) *computers as adaptive devices* for physically handicapped students, hearing or visually impaired students, and severely handicapped students; (c) *computer-managed instruction* or programmed learning; and (d) *computer assisted management* or data-based management systems. The reader is referred to Bailey and Raimondi (1984) and Behrmann (1984) for more information on the topic. In ESL education, the field is known as Computer-Assisted Language Learning (CALL). Applications parallel those listed above. The reader is referred to Higgins and Johns (1984), Johnson (1988), and McCahill (1984) for further information on the topic.

In both cases, the use of computers allows for more efficient, individualized, and interactive programming, which enhances program success. Because of advances being made in both fields, it holds special promise for teachers delivering SE-ESL programs.

Peer Tutoring/Cooperative Learning

Cooperative learning approaches are currently in favor in both special education and second language programs. According to Schniedewind and Salend (1987), using this strategy, teachers structure the class so that students work together in an atmosphere of positive interdependence to achieve a shared academic goal. Students are accountable for not only their own achievement, but also the performance of other group members, since the group's evaluation is based on its product. According to these authors, cooperative learning is valuable for heterogeneous populations because it encourages liking and learning among students of various abilities and backgrounds. Johnson, Johnson, Holubec, and Roy (1984) summarized both the theory and research findings related to this approach and have specialized in its application to students with disabilities. The research they summarize indicates that exceptional students prefer cooperatively structured classrooms and that cooperatively structured classrooms promote higher achievement and self-esteem than those that are structured competitively.

Cooperative language learning approaches have also been recommended for use in ESL classrooms. Dyad or paired activities provide the type of interaction which is required to promote language acquisition. By moving away from teacher-centered instruction, more opportunity is provided to each learner to engage in the target language. By structuring activities such as "information-gap" activities, where each partner possesses some of the information required, but they most work together and pool their knowledge to complete a task, a communicative need is created. Such cooperative learning strategies predominate in communicative (Savignon, 1983) and counseling learning (Curran, 1976) approaches to language teaching.

Learning Style-Based Instruction

Both the TESOL and Special Education fields have recognized the importance of matching teaching methods to predominant learning styles of individual students.

Reid (1987) summarizes the literature on the learning styles of native and non-native speakers of English in a study on the perceptual learning styles of second language learners. She found that LEP students' learning style preferences often differ significantly from those of native speakers of English, that LEP students from different language backgrounds sometimes differ from one another in their learning style preferences, and that other student-specific variables (level of acculturation, gender, age) are related to differences in learning styles. She concludes that while learning style preferences of students cannot be the sole basis for designing instruction, LEP students' learning style preferences should be identified; instruction that respects those preferences should be employed, at least initially; and students should be given opportunities to diversify their learning style preferences.

Another author who focuses attention on this topic is Ventriglia (1982). She has observed three predominant language learning styles in LEP children: *beading,* a style of learning based on the individual's need to learn a word at a time, a style in which meaning or semantics is of the utmost importance; *braiding,* a style which utilizes chunking, in which the learner attends to the context of phrases and to the relationships among them; and *orchestrating*, a style in which sounds and the repetition of those sounds are the individual's key to language. Ventriglia states that the styles are not mutually exclusive and that each style is an equally valid way of approaching the language learning task. From the work of Reid and Ventriglia we can see that it is possible to identify students' preferred learning styles and accordingly plan our instruction to improve instructional outcomes.

In compensatory educational settings, a system often applied to matching teaching and learning styles is that of Dunn and Dunn. They have identified 21 learning style characteristics which can be accommodated in instruction to improve learner performance (Carbo, Dunn, & Dunn, 1986). These characteristics fall into five major categories of stimuli: (a) environmental (sound, light, temperature, and design); (b) emotional (motivation, persistence, responsibility, and structure); (c) sociological (peers, self, pair, team, adult, varied); (d) physical (modality preference, intake demands, time, and mobility); and (e) psychological (analytic/global, cerebral preference, and reflective/impulsive). According to Dunn and Dunn, among the 21 characteristics there are some for which each individual will demonstrate strong preferences. They assert that if these strong preferences are accommodated in instruction, improved learning outcomes will result. An excellent reference book which defines multiple systems for analyzing and accommodating learning styles is *Marching to Different Drummers* by Burke-Guild and Garger (1985) and the reader is encouraged to explore the range of possibilities that exist in this area to improve instructional outcomes for students.

Whole Language Approaches

Whole language approaches are those approaches that integrate the teaching of listening, speaking, reading, and writing in a meaningful learning context. Grammar, spelling, handwriting, and vocabulary are taught in an integrated fashion. Whole language teaching usually centers around thematic units, teacher demonstrations, and shared or collaborative learning activities. Language experience, shared literacy, and writing process approaches are whole language approaches. Whole language approaches hold special promise for SE-ESL classrooms because they are reciprocal teaching models, actively engage learners in a process, provide ongoing feedback, and are developmental in nature.

Cummins (1984) contrasts transmission models of teaching with reciprocal interaction models. The former place emphasis on imparting presequenced, context-reduced knowledge and skills to students, assign them a passive and dependent role, and inhibit motivation and active involvement, whereas reciprocal interaction models stress active learner participation, genuine dialogue between student and teacher in oral and written modalities, guidance and facilitation of student learning (mentoring), encouragement in a collaborative learning context, and a focus on intrinsic motivation. Cummins maintains that reciprocal interaction models are beneficial to cognitive and linguistic development while transmission models increase the academic problems of "at risk" students.

A FRAMEWORK FOR RESPONSIVE SECOND LANGUAGE INSTRUCTIONAL PLANNING

A model (Figure 6.2) is provided which demonstrates the instructional planning process related to language development for exceptional LEP youngsters.

In the shaded area, the reader will note that two aspects are listed which will have considerable impact on instruction: (a) service delivery factors (instructional philosophy of the school, staff expertise, fiscal/logistical constraints), and (b) support factors (reinforcement potential in mainstream classes and the home). These aspects must be considered in setting goals and objectives for individual students' SE-ESL programs

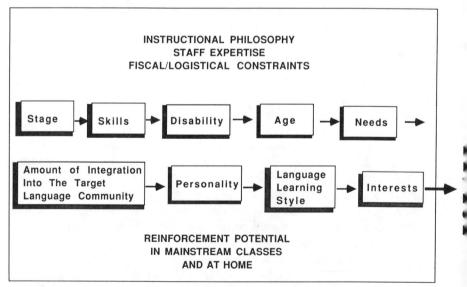

Figure 6.2 Selection of Method/Activities for Language Development in Culturally and Linguistically Diverse Exceptional Children.

and in selecting a curriculum model, instructional strategies, and materials for individual students. For example, in terms of service delivery factors, in order to deliver effective computer-based instruction, staff expertise, fiscal and logistical constraints must be considered. Computer-based ESL cannot be delivered without providing teachers with needed training in computer use and care and in CALL teaching methods. Furthermore, computer-based ESL cannot be delivered without considering how hardware and software will be funded and where equipment will be housed to provide access to LEP students with disabilities. In terms of support factors, methods should be selected that interface well with other student-specific programming efforts and because reinforcement will naturally occur outside of the ESL classroom.

At the core of the model are primary and secondary learner attributes to consider in setting up instructional programs for ESL students with disabilities in order to insure their effectiveness.

As has been previously mentioned in this chapter, and is now represented in Figure 6.2, primary learner attributes essential to consider when designing SE-ESL programs would include: (a) the disability(ies) of the learner, (b) the learner's current stage of second language acquisition (both oral and literacy levels), and (c) the particular skills of the learner by area (strengths and weaknesses in listening, speaking, reading, and writing).

The ESL teacher must match the instruction to the stage of second language acquisition of the learner (e.g., preproduction, early production, speech emergence, intermediate fluency), and should place emphasis on particular skill areas that have been identified as weak areas for the student (e.g., vocabulary, listening comprehension, etc.). However, without modifying instruction for the student's disability(ies), instruction may fail. In this regard it is important to distinguish the need to design "comprehensible input" (Krashen, 1982) from insuring that the language input becomes "intake" for the learner. If a student is hearing impaired, mentally retarded, or neurologically impaired, the teacher will have to modify instruction to insure that well-structured "input" becomes "intake." This means that the mode of presentation of instruction, pace of instruction, amount of practice provided, type of teaching approach, and instructional activities selected, as well as the nature and extent of feedback and reinforcement provided to the learner will all be dimensions that the teacher will actively manipulate. Figure 6.3 portrays this distinction between input and intake.

Secondary learner attributes to consider which would be expected to enhance program success if accommodated would include: (a) the age of the learner, (b) the communication needs of the learner in the second language, (c) the amount of integration into the target language com-

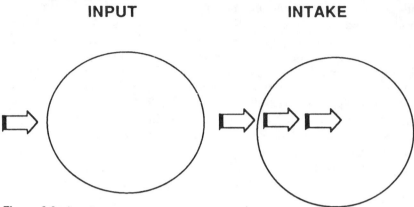

Figure 6.3 Input versus Intake.

munity, (d) personality factors, (e) language learning style, and (f) interests of the learner. These are also depicted in Figure 6.2.

Teachers of SE-ESL students must actively motivate students by capitalizing on identified needs and interests, selecting instructional techniques based on learning style and personality variables, and structuring additional opportunities to use English in formal and informal settings if needed, based on an analysis of the actual amount of interaction the student has with the target language community.

In selecting an appropriate focus for each student's SE-ESL program, an analysis of primary and secondary learner attributes should guide the selection of promising methods and materials, while consideration of service delivery and support factors would determine the respective viability of each of the potential methods selected. At a minimum, SE-ESL programs must be designed to account for and respond to the primary learner characteristics enumerated in this section, for without such basic consideration of student characteristics they have little chance of success.

CURRENT ISSUES AND FUTURE CHALLENGES

Expanding Mainstream ESL Options

Currently, overreferral of LEP students to special education is a topic of concern (National Coalition of Advocates for Students, 1988) and correspondingly there is a focus on preferral strategies which can prevent such overreferral (Benavides, 1987; Ortiz & Maldonado-Colon, 1986). Designing mainstream ESL services to be as flexible as possible in order to prevent unnecessary referrals to special education is a major challenge facing ESL educators. For example, more substantive efforts are needed through intensive ESL programs to adequately meet the needs of special populations of LEP children present in U.S. schools today (e.g., pre-literate students, underschooled students, highly mobile students, and refugee students). Such efforts might reduce the well-documented risk of inappropriate referral to special education among these groups who have unique educational needs, but are not properly served in special education settings.

Providing Crossover Training to ESL and Special Educators

A second challenge is equipping Special Educators and ESL educators with the crossover training required to deliver integrated services that account for children's second language and disability characteristics. Currently there is a paucity of TESOL programs which provide crossover training in special education, or Special Education programs that encourage specializations in TESOL. Because of this, professionals are left to find their own training opportunities at conferences and workshops and from these fortuitous events to piece together the elements that would formulate appropriate practice. Responsive Special Education/TESOL teacher training programs would create a well-formulated and comprehensive sequence of new course offerings for personnel wishing to specialize in this important area, covering both the theoretical and practical issues in serving LEP students with disabilities.

Research-based SE-ESL Demonstration Programs

In this chapter it was suggested that particular ESL curriculum models and particular ESL instructional strategies hold promise for exceptional bilingual students. However, to date, extremely limited research has been conducted to validate the effectiveness of these models and methods with exceptional LEP students. Recently the Office of Bilingual Education and Minority Languages Affairs (OBEMLA) sponsored research to strengthen the effectiveness of instructional programs for LEP students. The Innovative Approaches Research Project included a study entitled "Effective Practices in Assessment and Instruction of Language Minority Students: An Intervention Model." Directed by Dr. Alba Ortiz at the University of Texas at Austin's College of Education, the study involved Hispanic students in grades K–5 and included three major interventions: (a) Teacher Assistance Teams, (b) Curriculum Based Assessment, and (c) Effective Instructional Practices Workshops (*NCBE*

Forum, November–December 1988). This type of research is desperately needed and must be expanded to include other language minority populations, grade levels, and aspects of special education programming.

SE-ESL Materials Development

A third challenge is to develop materials for this special population of ESL students. ESL materials must be developed for both populations of students with disabilities, the mildly handicapped, and the moderately/severely handicapped. Some efforts have been initiated by individual practitioners and school districts (Division of Special Education, New York City Board of Education, 1985; Duran, 1985; Fairfax County Schools, 1986); however, commercial publishers have been remiss in addressing this special need. Diverse materials must be developed that adjust the pace of instruction, amount of practice provided, teaching approach and instructional activities recommended, as well as feedback and reinforcement strategies suggested. Materials for oral language development and literacy development are needed; materials that focus on the needs of LEP hearing impaired, visually impaired, learning disabled, mentally retarded, and emotionally disturbed youngsters are needed. Having appropriate materials is a key to unlocking the potential of exceptional children for whom English is a second language and insuring their fullest participation in society. Such full participation is their civil right, but it cannot become a reality without effective educational supports. This will take the combined talents of ESL and Special Educators currently charged with serving these special children.

SUMMARY

In this chapter, essential program definitions were provided; an explanation of how to plan ESL programs through the IEP process was given; SE-ESL curriculum models were explored; promising instructional strategies were identified; and a framework for responsive second language instructional planning was outlined. While there are still many issues to be resolved and future challenges await educators serving LEP students with disabilities, it is hoped that this chapter has provided the reader with a starting place for designing responsive programs for this important group of language minority youngsters.

REFERENCES

Asher, J.J. (1982). *Learning another language through actions: The complete teachers guidebook.* Los Gatos, CA: Sky Oaks Productions.

Baca, L.M., & Cervantes, H.T. (1984). *The bilingual special education interface.* St. Louis: Times Mirror/Mosby.

Bailey, M.N., & Raimondi, S.L. (1984). Technology and special education: A resource guide. *Teaching Exceptional Children, 16*(4), 273–277.

Behrmann, M. (1984). *Handbook of microcomputers in special education.* San Diego: College-Hill Press.

Benavides, A. (1987, May 21). *High risk predictors and prereferral screening for language minority students.* (ERIC Document Reproduction Service No. ED 291 175). Paper presented at the Annual Children with Exceptional Needs Conference, Los Angeles, CA.

Bilsky, L.H., & Blackman, L.S. (in press). *Education for all persons with mental retardation.* Englewood Cliffs, NJ: Prentice-Hall.

Burke-Guild, P., & Garger, S. (1985). *Marching to different drummers.* Alexandria, VA: Association for Supervision and Curriculum Development.

Carbo, M., Dunn, R., & Dunn, K. (1986). *Teaching students to read through their individual learning styles.* Englewood Cliffs, NJ: Prentice-Hall.

Chamot, A.U., & O'Malley, M.O. (1987). The Cognitive Academic Language Learning Approach: A bridge to the mainstream. *TESOL Quarterly, 21*(2), 227–249.

Cummins, J. (1984). *Bilingualism and special education: Issues in assessment and pedagogy.* San Diego: College-Hill Press.

Curran, C. (1976). *Counseling-learning in second languages.* Dubuque, IA: Counseling Learning Publications.

Deshler, D.D., & Schumaker, J.B. (1986). Learning strategies: An instructional alternative for low-achieving adolescents: *Exceptional Children, 52*(6), 583–590.

Dever, R. (1988). *Community living skills: A taxonomy.* Washington, DC: American Association on Mental Retardation.

Dew, N. (1983). Criteria for selecting instructional materials for CLDE students. *Learning disability Quarterly, 6*(4), 497–505.

Dew, N. (1984). The exceptional bilingual child: Demography. In P. Chinn (Ed.), *Education of culturally and linguistically different exceptional children* (pp. 1–41). Reston, VA: The Council for Exceptional Children.

Dew, N. (1985). Delivering ESL instruction to handicapped LEP children. *Elementary TESOL Education News, 7*(2), 10.

Division of Special Education, New York City Board of Education. (1985). *Project ESL-SEDAC, 1983-84. ESEA Title VII annual evaluation report.* (ERIC Document Reproduction Service No. ED 262 147). Brooklyn, NY: New York City Board of Education, Office of Educational Evaluation.

Duran, E. (1985). Teaching functional reading in context to severely retarded and severely retarded autistic adolescents of limited English proficiency. *Adolescence, 20*(78), 433–440.

Fairfax County Schools. (1986). *Driver education. Supplemental lessons and activities for use with limited English proficient (LEP) students enrolled in ESL or special education classes.* (ERIC Document Reproduction Service No. ED 279 159. See related documents ED 279 158, ED 279 157, ED 279 156). Washington, DC: Office of Bilingual Education and Minority Languages Affairs (Grant # G008525195).

Feuerstein, R. (1980). *Instrumental enrichment: An intervention program for cognitive modifiability.* Baltimore: University Park Press.

Friedenberg, J.E., & Bradley, C.H. (1984). *The vocational ESL handbook.* Rowley, MA: Newbury House.

Garcia, S.B., & Ortiz, A.A. (1988, October). *All children can write.* Paper presented at the Council for Exceptional Children's Symposia on Multicultural and Ethnic Concerns, Denver, CO.

Glass, R.M., Christiansen, J., & Christiansen, J.L. (1982). *Teaching exceptional students in the regular classroom.* Boston: Little, Brown, & Company.

Here they come, ready or not: An Education Week special report on the ways in which America's population in motion is changing the outlook for schools and society. (1986 May 14). *Education Week, V* (35), 1-37.

Higgins, J., & Johns, T. (1984). *Computers in language learning.* Reading, MA: Addison-Wesley.

Johnson, M.A. (1988). Word processing in the English as a second language classroom. In J.L. Hoot & S.B. Silvern (Eds.), *Writing with computers in the early grades* (pp. 107-121). New York: Teachers College Press.

Johnson, D.W., Johnson, R.T., Holubec, E.J., & Roy, P. (1988). *Circles of learning: Cooperation in the classroom.* Alexandria, VA: Association for Supervision and Curriculum Development.

Krashen, S.D. (1982). Bilingual education and second language acquisition theory. In Office of Bilingual Bicultural Education, California State Department of Education (Eds.), *Schooling and language minority students: A theoretical framework* (pp. 51-79). Los Angeles, CA: Evaluation, Dissemination, and Assessment Center, California State University.

Krashen, S.D., & Terrell, T.D. (1983). *The natural approach: Language acquisition in the classroom.* Hayward, CA: Alemany Press.

McCahill, P. (1984). Microcomputer technology in the ESL classroom. *TESOL Talk, 15,* 73-81.

McKeon, D. (1987, December). Different types of ESL programs. *ERIC Digest.* Washington, DC: ERIC Clearinghouse on Languages and Linguistics.

National Coalition of Advocates for Students. (1988). *New voices: Immigrant students in U.S. public schools.* Boston: Author.

New York City agrees to Expand Its Bilingual Special-Ed Faculty. (1988, September 7). *Education Week, VIII*(1), 7.

Nuttal, E.V., Landurand, P.M., & Goldman, P. (1984). A critical look at testing and evaluation from a cross-cultural perspective. In P. Chinn (Ed.), *Education of culturally and linguistically different exceptional children* (pp. 42-62). Reston, VA: The Council for Exceptional Children.

O'Malley, J.M. (1983). *The 1980-81 Teachers Language Skills Survey. Final report.* Rosslyn, VA: InterAmerica Research Associates.

Ortiz, A.A., & Maldonado-Colon, E. (1986). Reducing inappropriate referrals of language minority students in special education. In A.C. Willig & H.F. Greenberg (Eds.), *Bilingualism and learning disabilities: Policy and practice for teachers and administrators* (pp. 37-50). New York: American Library Publishing Company.

Oxford, R.L. (1990). *Language learning strategies: What every teacher should know.* New York: Newbury House Publishers.

Oxford-Carpenter, R. (1985). *A new taxonomy of second language learning strategies.* Washington, DC: ERIC Clearinghouse on Languages and Linguistics, Center for Applied Linguistics.

Plata, M. (1986). Instructional planning for limited English proficient students. *Journal of Instructional Psychology, 13*(1), 32-39.

Reid, J.M. (1987). The learning style preferences of ESL students. *TESOL Quarterly, 21*(1), 87-111.

Savignon, S. (1983). *Communicative competence: Theory and classroom practice.* Reading, MA: Addison-Wesley.

Schniedewind, N., & Salend, S.J. (1987). Cooperative learning works. *Teaching Exceptional Children, 19*(2), 22-25.

Spolsky, B. (1988). Bridging the gap: A general theory of second language learning. *TESOL Quarterly, 22*(3), 377-396.

Spolsky, B. (1989). *Conditions for second language learning.* Oxford: Oxford University Press.

Van Ek, J.A. (1977). *The threshold level for modern language learning in schools.* London: Longman.

Van Etten, G., Arkell, C., & Van Etten, C., (1980). *The severely and profoundly handicapped: Programs, methods and materials.* St. Louis: Mosby.

Ventriglia, L. (1982). *Conversations of Miguel and Maria: How children learn a second language.* Reading, MA: Addison-Wesley.

Wilkins, D.A. (1976). *Notional syllabuses.* London: Oxford University Press.

Willig, A.C. (1986). Special education and the culturally and linguistically different child: An overview of issues and challenges. In A.C. Willig & H.F. Greenberg (Eds.), *Bilingualism and learning disabilities: Policy and practice for teachers and administrators* (pp. 191-209). New York: American Library Publishing Company.

chapter 7
Developing Literacy Skills in Two Languages

Frances Segan

INTRODUCTION

A supportive research base has accumulated over the years to document how bilingual students develop literacy in their first and second languages (Ambert, 1988; Chamot & O'Malley, 1987; de Villiers & de Villiers, 1978; Dulay, Burt, & Krashen, 1982; Hakuta, 1986; McLaughlin, 1984, 1985; Snow & Hoefnagel-Hohle, 1978; Wong Fillmore, 1985). The role of students' native language and culture has been highlighted. However, research on literacy development and the needs of language minority students in special education programs are only in the beginning stages. This chapter attempts to bridge the research and related literature on bilingual learners in general éducation settings with the recent body of information on the needs of language minority students in special education programs.

Since one of the major goals of bilingual special education programs is to help students to develop strong enough skills and confidence to return to general education settings (bilingual or monolingual English), the priority of developing literacy skills is central to language minority special education students.

OVERVIEW OF FIRST AND SECOND LANGUAGE ACQUISITION

Researchers such as Cummins (1983), Wong Fillmore and Valadez (1986), Mace-Matluck and Hoover (1986), and Collier (1987) have documented the fact that language minority students who have a strong foundation of oral and literacy skills in their native language learn a second language, such as English, more efficiently.

This section will review issues concerning first and second language acquisition and the special factors that impact on language minority students, especially those with handicapping conditions.

First Language Acquisition

Ambert (1988) described the first language acquisition process as a period in which children can "experiment" with language "with pride and delight" (p. 11). Presently, the Interactive Model views language acquisition not only in terms of children understanding and producing language, but also in terms of language being used for communication and purpose (McLaughlin, 1984). Ambert (1988) indicated that in reviewing recent research, she noted that native language development "appears to be the same across languages" (p. 22), but there are individual differences in development based on individual rates, chronological age, and use of language in diverse settings.

Second Language Acquisition

Second language acquisition and development can vary based on several factors such as individual learning style, personality, attitudes, and so on. (Hakuta, 1986; McLaughlin, 1985; Spolsky, 1988). Wong Fillmore (1985) identified three basic components for second language learning: (a) learners need to see the importance of acquiring the second language; (b) there is supportive language interaction between native speakers and second language learners; and (c) there are social opportunities for frequent practice of language learning skills.

Collier (1987) analyzed the length of time that a group of LEP students needed to become proficient in "cognitive-academic English." She also looked at the interaction between the age at which students began ESL study and the amount of time needed to develop cognitive-academic language proficiency.

Collier found that LEP students' scores increased over four to five years. Students reached national norms in three to five years, but not school district norms. Students in grades 4 and 6 who began all-English schooling without formal instruction in their native language did significantly poorer than those with such education. For older students with native language academic skills and concepts that were well developed, the process of second language acquisition occurred at a faster rate than for younger students. However, students in grades 7–12 tended to lose two to three years of cognitive academic knowledge while learning English. To prevent such loss and to prevent the high rate of school dropouts, secondary students need instruction in content area subjects in their native language while learning English. Even for younger students (ages 4 to 12), English for academic purposes may develop more quickly if they are given continued support in cognitive-academic language development in their native language. Collier concluded that the most "advantaged" second language learners need four to eight years to develop mastery in cognitive language proficiency in the second language.

Such findings have important implications for language minority students with educational deficits and/or handicapping conditions. For example, students who have not had the opportunity to attend school or whose educational experiences have been interrupted due to war might be quite capable or even intellectually gifted, but they might fail in a system that does not provide sufficient native language support for enough time as they develop cognitive-academic English language skills. The same may be true for mildly handicapped, bilingual students who can achieve the same skills as mainstream students, but who require more time to achieve mastery both in their native language and, especially, in English.

Issues for Teaching in a Pluralistic Society

In 1986, Spolsky identified four major areas that create potential language barriers to education: (a) the barrier of different languages among the population from the language(s) used in the school setting; (b) the barrier of different dialects; (c) the barrier of social class dialects that affect the attitudes and interaction between some educators and their students; and (d) the barrier of preferred style of verbalization that is influenced by cultural and social factors. Spolsky warned that these factors could lead to "an early mislabeling of pupils as uneducable" (p. 188).

Issues Related to LEP Students with Handicapping Conditions

Just as Spolsky (1986) had described sociocultural factors that might lead to children being labeled as "uneducable," so did Cummins (1984) note that lack of educational teaching related to children's linguistic and cultural experiences could lead to students eventually being placed in special education programs. Cummins pointed to the practice of "remedial pedagogy" (p. 89) that focuses on isolated instructional practice, such as phonic drills rather than thematic or interdisciplinary instruction, that may add or create learning difficulties for minority language students.

Cummins (1984) noted that students need to develop a threshold level of linguistic proficiency in their native language to avoid facing deficits when acquiring a second language. For example, students who are moved too rapidly from bilingual instruction into an English-only learning environment may have developed basic interpersonal communication skills (BICS) but may not have a sufficiently strong base to succeed in academic or cognitive academic linguistic proficiency (CALP) if concepts have not been developed well in the native language. Such theory is also supported by Chamot and O'Malley's (1987) CALLA Model and Collier's (1987) research.

Across the nation there is a group of youngsters termed "bilingual exceptional students," who have learning deficits or difficulties due to high mobility within states or between the United States and the child's native country. These students have also not had the educational exposure and time to develop strong literacy skills either in the native or second languages.

As Ortiz and Maldonado-Colon (1986) have indicated, care has to be taken to ascertain what culturally and linguistically relevant educational services have been provided to language minority students before they are placed in special education programs. Attention to prior interventions should be well documented to avoid cases in which students are placed in bilingual special education classes when they have not been given access to bilingual or ESL services in the general educational setting. If such interventions were given prior to referrals, the numbers of language minority students referred and placed in bilingual special education programs could be reduced.

Baca and Harris (1988) focused on the needs of migrant exceptional children. The high mobility, poor health care, and lack of exposure to native language development and instruction in ESL render them at an educational loss. Often migrant children with special education needs are identified late, thereby preventing early intervention and treatment. Some are inappropriately identified and placed in special education classes on the basis of language differences rather than true handicapping conditions.

The need for collaboration between bilingual and special educators is especially evident for migrant exceptional children. The importance of having an updated Individualized Educational Plan (IEP) that can be transmitted to the child's new school is crucial; it must indicate the need for native language and ESL instruction when appropriate. Instruction needs to incorporate the child's experiences from the community and cultural background.

Rueda (1987) concluded that there is a need to look at the interaction of bilingualism with students who are low achieving and who have been identified as having learning problems. He pointed to the early work of Leopold (1939–1949) to indicate that the bilingual child has alternative ways of perceiving objects and events. In reviewing the neo-Piagetian framework of DeAvila and Duncan (1981), Rueda suggested that there is the possibility that the mildly handicapped bilingual student may have some cognitive advantages over the monolingual English handicapped peer. He presented his theory based on earlier research that he had conducted in 1983. Rueda studied a small group of moderately proficient Spanish/English bilingual subjects and found that not only was bilingualism not detrimental to mildly retarded children, but that the bilingual group did better on some "metalinguistic items" (p. 191). Rueda (1987) indicated the need for larger samples and further research to study his findings.

It is in working through the strengths of bilingual special education students that literacy can be developed; to achieve this goal, creative curricular and instructional approaches must be used as an integral part of such instruction. For example, bilingual special education students may have special artistic talents, or they may be able to record oral stories, even when they do not like to read thick, textual materials. By providing rich experiences, students can discuss a mutually shared trip, record their experiences orally, then create class books or experience stories, and finally develop dialogue journals or picture dictionaries. Such experiences can lead to shared activities with mainstream students in bilingual general education programs or with English-dominant students, perhaps through tours or special projects or assemblies.

DEVELOPING READING SKILLS

Native literacy theory is based on the fact that language minority children often come to school with at least an oral knowledge of vocabulary and communicative experiences in the native language that they hear in their homes and communities. Some youngsters come to school with a weak native language base, but may have the flexibility to code switch between the first and second languages. Teachers need to recognize the potential for building on the students' native language base to develop skills in reading. Reading instruction in the students' native language enhances the transfer of literacy skills and provides cultural reinforcement adding to the students' self-esteem as they see their language used and respected in the school setting along with English.

This section will focus on selected studies that have looked at the development of native language and second language skills in reading.

A discussion of the implications for teaching reading skills to bilingual special education students will follow.

Transference of Reading Skills

Much attention has been given to the value of developing strong native language skills to help facilitate the transference of these reading skills to English.

Two recent studies that document with longitudinal data the effectiveness of teaching native literacy skills as a means of speeding the development of literacy skills in English include the Mace-Matluck and Hoover (1986) study and Collier's work in 1987.

Looking at 250 Spanish-speaking, low-income students participating in transitional bilingual education programs, the Mace-Matluck and Hoover study addressed these questions: "(a) What constitutes a favorable learning environment for Spanish-speaking students? (b) What instructional sequences are most effective in developing literacy skills and (c) What are the specific language and literacy outcomes?" (p. 170).

The students' entry skills were assessed at the beginning of the study. From kindergarten through fourth grade, the students' oral language and reading skills were assessed for growth. In addition, classroom observations were conducted; descriptions of teachers' instructional approaches as well as the instructional programs were made.

The results of the study showed that more than half of the students were on grade level in English by the end of second grade, with the target goal for all students beging grade level proficiency by the end of the fourth grade. The researchers concluded that transitional bilingual programs were indeed developing English literacy for all students.

One important finding indicated that unless there is strong native language support through home, school, and community, students will lose their native literacy skills. Thus, the danger of "subtractive" bilingualism, as described by Cummins (1984), was supported in this study.

Other major findings of the Mace-Matluck and Hoover study included: (a) oral language development centered around school-related topics helps prepare students for academic work; (b) students with less developed skills tend to receive instruction that is slower and more limited in scope and content than for more proficient readers; (c) students decode words in isolation faster in both languages, but their reading rate is slower in both languages; (d) students with strong Spanish oral language skills had higher growth rates in English reading comprehension; and (e) students with low oral skills in both languages exhibit negative effects in reading comprehension skills.

In developing suggestions for instruction, the researchers recommended that teachers receive help in preparing lessons that demonstrate that what is learned in Spanish can be applied in English and vice versa. A second concern is for students in transitional bilingual education programs to have enough time to develop strong literacy skills in Spanish in order to transfer these skills to cognitive academic learning tasks in English. To help bilingual students to succeed in the English-dominant classroom, teachers need to prepare them in the use of academic-textual materials, so they will have key skills to analyze such materials in both Spanish and English.

Wallace (1986) looked at multicultural reading in sociological terms. One problem that the writer highlighted is the frequency with which texts, newspapers, and magazines fail to reflect minority culture and life styles. Teachers working with language minority students in ESL should develop multicultural stories and reading experiences based on their students' life experiences.

Steffensen (1987) also pointed to the lack of cultural context in basal readers, which emphasize decoding skills rather than holistic reading approaches, which might provide opportunity to supplement students' cultural experiences. Steffensen advocated "language experience" and "experience-text-relationship" approaches, in which oral discussion occurs before and after reading to facilitate comprehension and to relate textual materials to the students' previous learning experiences.

Implications for Bilingual Special Education Students

The Mace-Matluck and Hoover (1986) study provides important implications for teachers of bilingual special education students. The study found that too much attention was given to isolated decoding and vocabulary skills. In addition, ability grouping in reading limited these students in the range of skills developed. The authors recommended better classroom management techniques focused on active instruction as a way to minimize major behavior disorders. With highly motivating learning experiences, students can become more involved in the lessons and use the strengths that they have.

Another implication comes from Simich-Dudgeon (1986) who presented a multidisciplinary model to educate language minority students with handicapping conditions. This model stressed the need for collaboration between bilingual and ESL and special education teachers and consultants. Attention focused on the extent of bilingual or ESL services the student had received in general and special education settings.

Cheng (1987) investigated "language impaired" preschoolers and recommended genuine communication in natural learning situations to enable these children to create pictures and stories. Such resources as fables, nursery rhymes, and oral games that are culturally appropriate can lead to positive reading and writing skill development. Cheng noted that if the language and culture that the children bring to the school are rejected, then they experience "feelings of tremendous dislocation and incongruence and a lack of linguistic competence" (p. 68) when this base is not valued.

Willig (1986) found that teachers fear dual-language instruction for exceptional children because they believe that it would lead to cognitive confusion. She referred to the research of the Handicapped Minority Institute at the University of Texas at Austin. The author concluded that careful assessment of bilingual exceptional students is crucial, and that individualized instruction for such children in each language should really be different from what is offered in the general education classroom setting. Willig favors "reciprocal interactive models" that permit bilingual children to learn based on their unique cultural and linguistic experiences. Willig refers to Cummins (1984) who contrasts the direct instruction model, which provides extrinsic motivation, with the reciprocal interactive model, which allows the student to develop intrinsic motivation to learn. For the interactive model to function well for second language learners, the content must have interest and immediate usefulness for the student. Flores, Rueda, and Porter (1986) utilized the reciprocal interactive model in the writing process. This approach to writing will be developed in the next section of this chapter.

DEVELOPING WRITING SKILLS

Enabling bilingual students to become competent and proficient writers in both English and their native language is related to the view of language skills as an interrelated, holistic entity. Writing experiences must be based on the students' in-school and out-of-school learning activities.

Farr and Daniels (1986) listed 15 major issues to be considered in developing positive writing experiences, especially for "nonmainstream" students (pp. 45-46). The issues of particular concern to teachers of LEP students are listed as follows:

1. Teachers need to value the linguistic skills students bring to the school, and they should use these skills to create positive writing experiences for the students.

2. Students need frequent practice in writing that is meaningful and "personally significant" for the writers.
3. Students need practice in writing for different audiences and situations.
4. Reading experiences should correlate with the writing experiences through literature or the writings of peers.
5. Students need to be exposed to models of writing and the writing process.
6. Cooperative and collaborative writing experiences with peers are recommended.
7. Individualized writing conferences with teachers can be helpful.
8. Emphasis should be on communication and sentence combining rather than focusing on grammar.
9. Attention to writing skills and grammar should be developed through the students' writings rather than through separate activity sheets.
10. Writing skills need to be used through all subject areas in the curriculum.

In reviewing these research recommendations, some points need to be highlighted. As Cummins (1984) indicated, minority language students can develop writings based on their own experiences. In this way, there is a reduction of a "cultural mismatch" between the students' life experiences and basic materials that may have unfamiliar cultural references presented in the school. In addition, students' self-esteem is enhanced because the teacher values their ideas expressed in writing, whether in the native language or in English.

Another point is the need for students to have regular, meaningful writing experiences. The level of writing can vary from drawing a picture, writing a two- to three-word sentence, to journal writing and compositions. Often, limited-English-proficient students, especially in special education programs, are working on oral language and vocabulary development; sometimes they are low-level readers. But all can be encouraged to draw, to develop class books or individual picture books or dialogue journals that will be personal, and that will bring together the four language skills.

After reviewing research on writing in bilingual education and ESL programs, Rodriguez (1988, pp. 97–98) reinforced the importance of a number of issues: (a) LEP students develop writing skills through interaction with peers and teachers as well as through content, purpose, and structure of the writing task; (b) the LEP child needs to feel that his/her writings are valued by the teacher; (c) cooperative learning environments support the learning styles of LEP students; (d) human resources, such as parents, peers, teachers, and community personnel, can serve as role models; and (e) LEP children need time to become proficient writers in English.

Practical Writing Experiences

Russo (1987) highlighted several motivating and interactive writing activities that teachers can utilize to stimulate interest in writing: (a) class writing, consisting of language experience stories; (b) small-group writing, consisting of class/group developed books; (c) community writing that encourages students to work with a peer to prepare to interview someone in the community. These activities involve preparing questions beforehand, note-taking during the interviews, and then making a follow-up story. Other activities can include individual writing through dialogue journals, letters to pen pals in other countries, or letters to friends in mainstream classes within the same school.

Raimes (1983) presented a variety of techniques to develop writing skills for ESL learners. The author suggested the communicative and process approaches to writing. The use of pictures can result in the production of whole-class posters to stimulate writing; students can bring pictures or drawings of personal interest to them to encourage sharing with peers. Students can design maps and write about their neighborhoods.

Other activities to stimulate writing experiences include: brainstorming activities prior to writing assignments to help students create needed vocabulary, comments, and questions. Similarly, role-playing activities and writing short dialogues based on the students' experiences can also incorporate all four language skills.

Implications for Developing Writing Skills in Bilingual Special Education Students

In planning for and selecting appropriate writing activities for bilingual special education students, teachers must identify those instructional practices which strengthen students' skills and life experiences as compared with those instructional activities which may actually prevent the students from expanding their writing skills.

In the challenge to provide individualized instruction, the practice of using rexographed sheets, copying, and doing seat work exercises actually limits students' creativity and motivation to write. Willig (1986) advocates culturally relevant and purposeful reading and writing experiences for students.

Flores et al. (1986) noted that special education students are often traditionally taught from a part to a whole in a hierarchical and sequential task approach. The authors conducted a study of mildly handicapped special education students (some bilingual; some trilingual) who were exposed to "holistically based" writing experiences. The program made use of "interactive" (dialogue) journals; emphasis was placed on communication rather than grammar. Students were encouraged in this way "to take risks" and not to fear making errors; they made drawings and enjoyed collaborative experiences with teachers and peers. These students developed more expanded writing skills through this approach than if they had continued with the traditional writing exercises that focus on discrete tasks. For example, students may be bored doing a rexographed sheet on the verb "to be," but might enjoy creating drawings and stories related to a zoo trip.

Goldman and Rueda (1988) pointed out that writing experiences have often been limited to give bilingual special education students more time for oral language development and reading skills. However, they indicated that writing experiences may actually help students to reinforce the language that they are learning through oral and reading experiences. Often the discrete skills of spelling, punctuation, and penmanship have been emphasized over thematic and expressive writing for these students.

The researchers cited two theoretical perspectives: (a) the cognitive process within the individual that affects information processing as well as the ability to meet writing tasks of process and product; and (b) the functional interactive perspective that focuses on the communicative aspects of written language and literacy. Citing Hudelson's (1984) research that indicated that bilingual general education and bilingual special education students develop stronger writing skills for having tried to express themselves in writing and by having made errors in the past, Goldman and Rueda concluded that bilingual special education students should not be prevented from initiating writing skills, even though they may have developmental delays in some aspects of language. Writing for bilingual general and bilingual special education students should be rich in content and have a high "cognitive load" so that students can generate their own writings.

The functional-interactive approach emphasizes the interpersonal context of learning and has its roots in the sociohistorical perspective of Vygotsky (1978). The teacher is central in organizing successful beginning practice and experiences to help the child move from activity with support to the level of having the confidence and skills to function on an independent level. It is the level of the child's participation that increases and develops in this process.

Functional learning environments provide opportunities for communication. Dialogue journals that provide interaction between the writer and teacher allow students to choose topics and, simultaneously, can enable the teacher to learn more about the second language learner.

Researchers have studied the use of writing journals with exceptional children. Rueda (1987), for instance, worked with a microcomputer with English speakers of Hispanic backgrounds; Goldman and Rueda (1988) looked at narrative writing of exceptional children working in pairs or on an individual basis.

Rueda observed teachers and students developing interactive journals using a specially developed software program called the "Dialog Maker." He found that teachers tended to personalize topics rather than focus on classroom-related "strategies" in the dialogue journals. The author hypothesized that such personalization may help language minority students who at first may feel alienated from the cultural context of the classroom. The journals encouraged students to want to continue to write and appeared to be a useful approach with both Hispanic and non-Hispanic students in the resource room.

Goldman described the work of two bilingual special education students working together on computer stories. Of special interest was the use of Spanish by the students for particular topics and language functions. Goldman stressed the importance for teachers to allow students to interact in languages other than English. Teachers need to be aware of the "cognitive load" of a particular task and to decide if students will be able to perform it and in which language(s).

LITERACY IN CONTENT AREA INSTRUCTION FOR BILINGUAL SPECIAL EDUCATION STUDENTS

In reviewing research and recommendations for developing literacy skills in both the native language and in English, the general trend indicates that literacy skill development should not be delayed for mildly handicapped bilingual special education students; rather, it should integrate the four language skills.

Collier and Kalk (1984, p. 216) listed various steps in curriculum development for bilingual exceptional children. Among their more important recommendations, individualized lessons for linguistic and cultural considerations, for exceptionality, and for special learning needs, were significant. Segan (1986) favored curriculum and instructional activities that are both multicultural and interdisciplinary in approach. Trips and community resources can stimulate activities that will lead to relevant reading and writing experiences.

These examples of how literacy skills in the native language and in English can be developed are presented:

Career Education: Plan to visit a bilingual bank in the local community. Before the trip, review the different jobs and services that exist in the bank. Have students work in groups to develop questions to interview bilingual workers. After the trip, students can create bulletin boards, develop language experience stories, or write about their personal reactions in dialogue journals. Interacting with successful bilingual role models can provide motivation and enhance students' self-esteem.

Science: Visit the local botanical garden and have students draw pictures of at least two plants or trees that come from their native country or (if born in the U.S.) from their parents'/grandparents' native country. Have students read and copy the names of the plants in English, Latin, Spanish, Chinese, and so on. After the trip, students can discuss and write about the kind of climate and conditions maintained in the conservatory to grow orchids, rice, bananas, cactus, and so on. Students can develop a collection of pictures of flowers and trees that grow in the United States and their native country. Students can read or write creative stories about trees and plants (e.g., Puerto Rico—Flamboyan tree).

These examples provide concrete experiences that transform oral discussions into literacy development activities.

SUMMARY

To develop literacy skills for mildly handicapped, language-minority, special education students, teachers may need to move from discrete, task-analysis approaches and arrive at an enriching, holistic form of instruction. Students need to be motivated by thematic or topical units that allow them to try to create language through discussion, art, oral recordings, reading, and writing. To hamper such expansion limits the possibilities for literacy development and prevents students from relating their life experiences to classroom learning.

Teachers in the past often feared that bilingualism would have negative effects on the exceptional child, and that these students could not participate in more expanded literacy activities until they had mastered basic skills. Current research supports the possibility that bilingualism can provide certain advantages for students, and that rich learning experiences can develop literacy skills better than isolated exercises for students with special needs.

REFERENCS

Ambert, A. (1988). Trends in bilingual special education: The double bind. In A. Ambert (Ed.), *Bilingual education and English as a second language: A research handbook 1986-1987* (pp. 226-262). New York: Garland.

Baca, L., & Harris, K.C. (1988). Teaching migrant exceptional children. *Teaching Exceptional Children, 20*(4), 32-35.

Chamot, A.U., & O'Malley, J.M. (1987). The cognitive academic language learning approach: A bridge to the mainstream. *TESOL Quarterly, 21*(2), 227-249.

Cheng, L. (1987). English communicative competence of language minority children: Assessment and treatment of language "impaired" preschoolers. In H. Trueba (Ed.), *Success or failure? Learning and the language minority student.* Cambridge, MA: Newbury House.

Collier, C., & Kalk, M. (1984). Bilingual special education curriculum development. In L. Baca & H. Cervantes (Eds.), *The bilingual special education interface.* St. Louis, MO: C.V. Mosby.

Collier, V. (1987, September). Students and second language acquisition. *NABE News,* pp. 4-5.

Cummins, J. (1983). Bilingualism and special education: Program and pedagogical issues. *Learning Disability Quarterly, 6*(4), 373-386.

Cummins, J. (1984). *Bilingualism and special education: Issues in assessment and pedagogy.* San Diego, CA: College-Hill.

DeAvila, E.A., & Duncan, S.E. (1981). Bilingualism and the metaset. In R. Duran (Ed.), *Latino language and communicative behavior.* Norwood, NJ: Ablex.

de Villiers, J.G., & de Villiers, P.A. (1978). *Language acquisition.* Cambridge, MA: Harvard University Press.

Dulay, H., Burt, M., & Krashen, S. (1982). *Language two.* New York: Oxford University Press.

Farr, M., & Daniels, H. (1986). *Language diversity and writing instruction.* New York: ERIC Clearinghouse on Urban Education, Institute for Urban and Minority Education, Teachers College, Columbia University, and Urbana, IL: National Council of Teachers of English.

Flores, B., Rueda, R., & Porter, B. (1986). Examining assumptions and instructional practices related to the acquisition of literacy within bilingual special education students. In A. Willig & H.F. Greenberg (Eds.), *Bilingualism and learning disabilities: Policy and practice for teachers and administrators* (pp. 149-165). New York: American Library.

Goldman, S.R., & Rueda, R. (1988, April). Developing writing skills in bilingual exceptional children. *Exceptional Children* (Special issue on research and instruction in written language), *54*(6), 543-551.

Hakuta, K. (1986). *Mirror of language: The debate on bilingualism.* New York: Basic Books.

Hudelson, S. (1984). *Roberto and Janice: Individual differences in second language writing*. Paper presented at the National Association of Bilingual Education, Washington, DC.

Leopold, W.F. (1939-1949). *Speech development of a bilingual child: A linguist's record* (4 vols.). Evanston, IL: Northwestern University Press.

Mace-Matluck, B.J., & Hoover, W.A. (1986). Language, literacy and instruction in bilingual settings: Issues and implications of findings from a recent longitudinal study. In A. Willig & H.F. Greenberg (Eds.), *Bilingualism and learning disabilities: Policy and practice for teachers and administrators* (pp. 169-187). New York: American Library.

McLaughlin, B. (1984). *Second language acquisition in childhood: Volume 1. Preschool children*. Hillsdale, NJ: Lawrence Erlbaum.

McLaughlin, B. (1985). *Second language acquisition in childhood: Volume 2. School-age children*. Hillsdale, NJ: Lawrence Erlbaum.

Ortiz, A.A., & Maldonado-Colon, E. (1986). Reducing inappropriate referrals of language minority students in special education. In A. Willig & H.F. Greenberg (Eds.), *Bilingualism and learning disabilities: Policy and practice for teachers and administrators*. New York: American Library.

Raimes, A. (1983). *Techniques in teaching writing*. New York: Oxford University Press.

Rodriguez, A. (1988). Research in reading and writing in bilingual education and English as a second language. In A. Ambert (Ed.), *Bilingual education and English as a second language: A research handbook 1986-1987* (pp. 61-117). New York: Garland.

Rueda, R. (1984). Cognitive development and learning in mildly handicapped bilingual children. In P. Chinn (Ed.), *Education of culturally and linguistically exceptional children*. Reston, VA: The Council for Exceptional Children.

Rueda, R. (1987). Social and communicative aspects of language proficiency in low-achieving language minority students. In H.T. Trueba (Ed.), *Success or failure? Learning and the language minority student*. Cambridge, MA: Newbury House.

Russo, G.M. (1987). Writing: An interactive experience. In W. Rivers (Ed.), *Interactive language teaching*. London, England: Cambridge University Press.

Segan, F. (1986). Curriculum and instructional planning for bilingual students in special education programs. *The Journal of NYSABE, 2*(1), 32-41.

Simich-Dudgeon, C. (1986). A multidisciplinary model to educate minority language students with handicapping conditions. In A. Willig & H.F. Greenberg (Eds.), *Bilingualism and learning disabilities: Policy and practice for teachers and administrators* (pp. 95-110). New York: American Library.

Snow, C.E., & Hoefnagel-Hohle, M. (1978). The critical period for language acquisition: Evidence from second language learning. *Child Development, 49*, 1114-1128.

Spolsky, B. (Ed.). (1986). *Language and education in multilingual settings*. San Diego, CA: College-Hill Press.

Spolsky, B. (1988). Bridging the gap: A general theory of second language learning. *TESOL Quarterly, 22*(3), 377–396.

Steffensen, M. (1987). The effect of context and culture on children's L$_2$ reading: A review. In J. Devine, P. Carrell, & D.E. Eskey (Eds.), *Research in reading in English as a second language* (pp. 41–54). Washington, DC: Teachers of English to Speakers of Other Languages.

Vygotsky, L.S. (1978). *Mind in society.* Cambridge, MA: Harvard University Press.

Wallace, C. (Ed.). (1986). *Learning to read in a multicultural society.* Great Britain: Pergamon Press.

Willig, A. (1986). Special education and the culturally and linguistically different child: An overview of issues and challenges. In A.C. Willig & H.F. Greenberg (Eds.), *Bilingualism and learning disabilities: Policy and practice for teachers and administrators.* New York: American Library.

Wong Fillmore, L. (1985). Second language learning in children: A proposed model. In National Clearinghouse for Bilingual Education (Eds.), *Issues in English language development* (pp. 33–42). Roslyn, VA: InterAmerica Research Associates, Inc.

Wong Fillmore, L., & Valadez, C. (1986). Teaching bilingual learners. In M.C. Wittrock (Ed.), *Handbook of research on teaching.* New York: Macmillan.

chapter 8

Written Communication for Exceptional Students from Culturally and Linguistically Diverse Backgrounds

Debra A. Colley

Exceptional students from culturally and linguistically diverse backgrounds come to school with many values and experiences that impact the learning environment in the classroom. The interrelationships of language and culture on cognitive and learning processes transcend skill acquisition in all curricular areas. Written communication, from a cognitive perspective, provides a vehicle to develop cognitive skills, to reinforce language development in the native language, and to assist in the transition of academic skills from the first language to the second language of the students.

This chapter discusses the development of written communication skills from a cognitive perspective. Embedded in this perspective of writing for culturally and linguistically diverse exceptional students are considerations associated with cognition, language, and cultural/learning experiences. The chapter emphasizes written communication as a cognitive process, describes a framework for the understanding of written communication skills, and provides theoretical bases within each of the components of the framework.

PRODUCT OF WRITING

Historically, research and theory in the development of writing skills have focused on the product of writing (Nodine, 1983; Smith, 1982). In the assessment and teaching of writing within this perspective, successful writing is contingent upon spelling, written grammar, organization, handwriting, and composition skills. This approach emphasizes the mechanical features of writing. The improvement of writing would be used, therefore, on rote drills, memorization of spelling and composition rules, handwriting practice, and other such activities. This approach does not consider the many variables related to culture, learning, and cognition as well as the importance of communication as the underlying purpose of writing.

To exemplify this, consider Marcos who is nine years old and in the third grade. Marcos is currently receiving special educational services in a bilingual resource room where he spends five hours each week. In his mainstreamed third-grade classroom, a writing hour takes place each week on Wednesday morning. After being what appeared to be actively engaged in writing for one hour, he very proudly brought his page-and-one-half composition to his resource room teacher. Figure 8.1 illustrates the first few lines of Marcos' written communication.

Marcos appeared to know the appropriate behavior for writing class and some mechanics. He sat quietly writing (or appearing to write) for close to one hour. His writing (at a quick glance) looked similar to the format and style of other students. He had relatively mastered the mechanics of handwriting as evidenced by his letter formation, spacing, and alignment. He knew the basic composition format with the title of the story on the first line and the first sentence of the paragraph indented. In fact, Marcos was confident in his ability to begin each sentence with a capital letter and end each sentence with a period. When asked to read his story, however, he was unable to do so.

The written composition composed by Marcos is partially the outcome of a product-oriented focus on writing. Communication and the process of expressing ideas in writing were clearly not evidenced.

PROCESS OF WRITING

Current emphases address the cognitive process that students engage in during writing (Lerner, 1985). The cognitive process involves thinking, selecting, and organizing tasks throughout the writing act. This ability to write down ideas requires numerous underlying prerequisite skills. In order for students to be actively involved in this process, facility in language, cognitive abilities, and the use of learning and cultural experiences are interrelated with writing. The process of written communication, therefore, presents many challenges to exceptional students—challenges that may be associated with existing disabilities.

For exceptional students from culturally and linguistically diverse (CLD) backgrounds, writing can provide an opportunity to integrate linguistic and cognitive tasks and to effectively utilize the background and cultural experiences that such students bring to the classroom. In

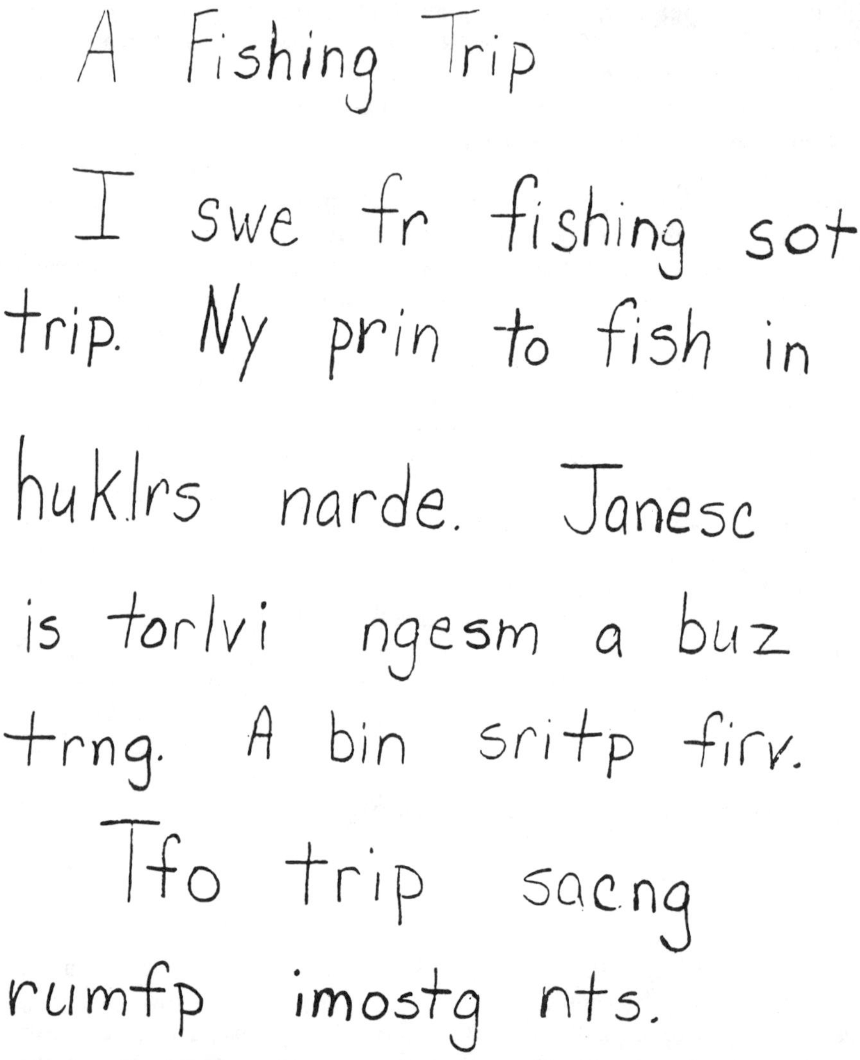

A Fishing Trip

I swe fr fishing sot
trip. Ny prin to fish in
huklrs narde. Janesc
is torlvi ngesm a buz
trng. A bin sritp firv.
Tfo trip sacng
rumfp imostg nts.

Figure 8.1 Sample of the written composition of a third-grade, learning-disabled student that depicts the outcome of a product-oriented focus in writing.

order to accomplish this, writing is viewed as a holistic, pragmatic process. Thus, written communication can provide a cornerstone to academic development through bilingual instructional services in special education or mainstreamed programs.

From a holistic perspective, reading, writing, listening, and speaking develop together as students experience language (Rhodes & Dudley-

Marling, 1988). As the repertoire of linguistic experience expands, all language expressions benefit and continue to interact. Written and oral language, therefore, develop in concert with each other. In other words, principles that govern the development of oral language apply to written language as well.

Written communication, likewise, is viewed as a process in which language is used and understood in a context that contributes to meaning (Halliday, 1978). The purpose of writing becomes primarily communication and students use active strategies to convey meaning from printed words.

To meet this purpose, the writing process capitalizes on writers' knowledge of the world as well as knowledge of language when they read and write. The combination of sound-symbol and word-ordering rules, the structure of stories, and the meanings of words from experiences and contexts from the student's repertoire can all contribute to the expression of meaning through writing (Rhodes & Dudley-Marling, 1988).

This use of written language to express meaning in different contexts also falls within the realm of pragmatic research. From a pragmatic framework, language represents an ideational and interpersonal tool for communicating in which language integrates structural and conversational rules, using linguistic contexts and the interactional skills and rules that are involved in communication (Craig, 1983; Scholl, 1981). In this way, language is used for communicative purposes; each utterance has an intention that is related to a specific function; and meaning is conveyed indirectly through the use of contextual cues and referents (Sridhar, 1981).

A COGNITIVE FRAMEWORK

Written communication for CLD exceptional students is presented in this chapter as a holistic, pragmatic process. As such, written communication becomes a communicative act by which students convey meaning and intentions in diverse contexts through writing. Exceptional students, however, may exhibit disabilities in relation to their ability to write (Lerner, 1985). Likewise, for students from culturally and linguistically diverse backgrounds, the process of writing cannot be understood without analyzing the interrelationships between language, culture, and cognition.

Figure 8.2 portrays a cognitive framework for the development of written communication skills among exceptional students from CLD backgrounds. The framework depicts three major components that im-

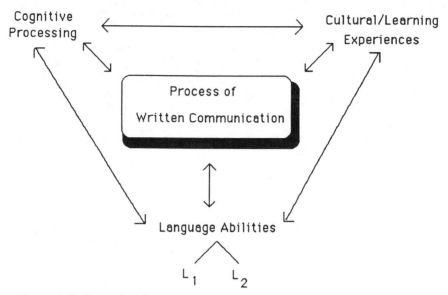

Figure 8.2 Cognitive framework for the development of written communication skills among exceptional students from culturally and linguistically diverse background.

pact upon the written communication process: (a) cognitive processing, (b) cultural/learning experiences, and (c) language abilities in the native and second language of the students. In addition, interrelationships between each of the components are depicted. The total emergence of writing skills among CLD exceptional students comes into focus as the interrelations of all components are analyzed, applied, and incorporated into the development of individualized educational programs.

The following sections of this chapter will describe each of the components in the cognitive framework. As each is described, it is important to keep in mind that exceptional students may exhibit disabilities in each area and that individualized programming will be contingent upon the interrelationships between the components.

Cognitive Processing

As depicted in Figure 8.2, cognitive processing is a primary component in written communication. Within a holistic, pragmatic orientation, the process of communicating through writing is based on a student's ability to select, organize, and process tasks. Such abilities penetrate information-processing aspects of communication, comprehension of oral and written language, and the ability to systematically monitor cognitive/ academic activities.

Cognitive abilities of children and youth have been explained through research on cognitive functioning and information processing. For example, information-processing research views cognitive development as "intricately interrelated and sequenced cognitive operations or processes that construct or create, receive, transform (recode, reduce, elaborate), store, retrieve, and otherwise manipulate units of information or knowledge" (Flavell, 1977, p. 5). Information is not processed in a passive manner, but must be acted upon in order to be processed.

In an active and modifiable cognitive process, according to Feuerstein's (1979) theory, the student is seen as an open system, amenable to considerable modification under appropriate social, cultural, and educational policy. The development of cognitive structures is a function of the organism interacting with the environment through direct exposure to sources of stimuli and mediated learning experience.

Mediated learning experience refers to the way in which a parent, sibling, or other caregiver selects, organizes, and transforms stimuli emitted by the environment (Feuerstein, 1979). Through the process of mediation and direct exposure to stimuli, an individual's cognitive structure is affected. It is this exposure to stimuli and one's capacity to modify experiences that will serve as the foundation for students' written communication skills.

As individual students use their foundation of experience and develop active strategies to interact through writing, metacognitive skills emerge. Research in the area of metacognition has investigated one's awareness of systematic thinking strategies needed for learning. Such research demonstrates that the awareness and monitoring of cognitive activities plays an important role in oral communication skills, oral comprehension, reading comprehension, language acquisition, attention, memory, and problem solving (Flavell, 1981a). Metacognition, therefore, also plays an important role in the development of written communication skills.

Cognitive monitoring occurs as a result of interactions among: (a) metacognitive knowledge (knowledge and beliefs that one has acquired and stored); (b) metacognitive experiences (conscious experiences that are related to any aspect of the social, affective, or cognitive task); (c) cognitive goals (the objectives being pursued); and (d) cognitive actions (knowledge of different types and the appropriateness of cognitive strategies) (Flavell, 1981b; Mann & Sabatino, 1985). Through the interrelationship of these four areas, strategies needed to reach a particular goal are selected. The use of the strategies leads to a new experience and knowledge as to how things are going. The interaction between new experiences and previous knowledge continues as each new metacognitive experience is interpreted according to previous metacognitive knowledge. This enables the individual to evaluate whether or not new experiences are internally consistent with previous knowledge and if they are sufficient to meet the requirements of the goal (Flavell, 1981b).

The process of cognitive monitoring cannot take place, however, unless the student understands the information being presented. Thus, they are required to extract and recall important facts and knowledge. Comprehension is required for both oral and written information. Written communication requires varying degrees of understanding, and therefore involves cognitive processing in terms of inferential abilities and skills that allow the student to transform, elaborate, and extend information to writing (Markman, 1981).

In addition to these cognitive processes, other factors that affect language comprehension through writing must be discussed. Contextual factors and background knowledge are important in written communication and language comprehension. Lund and Duchan (1983) have identified four contextual areas that affect language comprehension: (a) the situational context (features of the present situation in which comprehension takes place), (b) the intentional context (the intention that is being conveyed), (c) the listener context (the background knowledge to which the listener relates and the role relationship between the listener and speaker, and (d) the linguistic context (linguistic information embedded in sentences and shared by the speaker and listener).

Understanding written language, therefore, will not only come from the information in sentences, but will also be supplemented and organized from the background knowledge supplied by the writer (Lund & Duchan, 1983).

The relevance of past knowledge in the communication process has also been researched in terms of schema theory. This theory suggests that on the basis of past experiences, people construct schemas of related information that can influence the way they understand, interpret, and integrate new experiences (Anderson, 1977). Schemas have been defined as clusters of knowledge developed from past experiences that represent an aspect of a concept that is encountered by the individual (Thorndyke & Hayes-Roth, 1979). Incoming information is integrated with old information which has been stored in schemas. When the information is recalled, elements of the existing knowledge and the new knowledge influence one's understanding and interpretation. Current research suggests that differences in comprehension are related to the individual's construction of schemas based on past experiences and the use of these schemas in the interpretation and storage of comprehension material (Anderson, 1977; Bransford & Johnson, 1972; Thorndyke & Hayes-Roth, 1979).

Since written communication involves past knowledge and experience, language abilities, underlying cognitive processes, and comprehension, some students may experience difficulty judging their own writing. The ability to monitor what is understood underscores the academic tasks that take place in the classroom. Through the ability to monitor, students know when to ask questions, reread information, and when they need extra help. This type of comprehension requires a certain amount of information processing. A discrepancy between the amount of information processing that is needed and the actual amount that is used will lead children into thinking that something is understood when in reality it is not (Markman, 1977). The greater this discrepancy, the greater the possibility of poorly monitoring comprehension.

In order for individuals to monitor their comprehension, degrees of information processing are required. According to Markman (1979), some processing is at a relatively superficial level and involves embedded representations within single sentences. Higher degrees of monitoring, however, require relating, comparing, integrating, and encoding information over time.

In three separate studies, Markman (1979) found that in order for children to monitor their comprehension, they have to encode and store the information, draw the relevant inferences, retrieve and maintain the propositions in memory, and compare them. This was not found to be spontaneously carried out by children in third through sixth grade.

Recent research indicates that comprehension monitoring in children may undergo developmental changes and that younger children are generally quite poor in this monitoring task. Developmental differences would be expected when comprehension monitoring requires: (a) information that young children cannot obtain, and (b) the use of judgments that are difficult for children at young ages. Information retrieval and judgments require inferential skills and processing abilities that are beyond the cognitive skills of young children (Markman, 1981). In addition, comprehension monitoring requires separating facts into higher order structures. Cognitive abilities, from concrete to abstract processing, are operating throughout comprehension monitoring tasks.

Exceptional students, however, may exhibit disorders in the cognitive processing skills that are needed for processing, understanding, and monitoring written communication. Difficulties in cognitive processes that allow a student to transfer, reduce, elaborate, store, recover, and use cognitive input have been well documented among exceptional students (Lerner, 1985; Payne & Patton, 1981).

Disabilities in basic psychological processes and underlying mental abilities needed to process and use information are exhibited by many exceptional students. By the very definition of disorders that affect mental and learning processes, we can expect differences in cognitive development among students with handicapping conditions. Differences may be classified according to cognitive theory and would, therefore, be associated with developmental or maturational neurological, perceptual or motor, informational processing, and/or social learning theory. The cognitive processing abilities of CLD exceptional students, therefore, must be understood and carefully analyzed as they emerge from the written communication process. Since the cognitive perspective of writing considers the impact of cognition, language, and culture on writing, the relationships between these variables must be further explored.

Language Abilities

The second component, depicted in Figure 8.2, that must be understood in the process of written communication is language abilities. As defined in this chapter, written communication skills develop as an extension of language. The relationships between cognitive processing and language abilities of linguistically diverse students, therefore, are embedded in this process. The nature and sequence of language development as it applies to both first and second language acquisition impacts on cognitive/academic skill acquisition and, therefore, has a major role in the development of written communication skills.

First and second language proficiency. In discussing first and second language acquisition and skills for written communication, language proficiency surfaces as a major variable. Language proficiency refers to "the degree in which the student exhibits control over the use of language, including the measurement of expressive and receptive language skills in the areas of phonology, syntax, vocabulary, and semantics and including the area of pragmatics or language use within various domains or social circumstances" (Baca & Cervantes, 1984, p. 127). Native and second language proficiency must be closely interrelated with written communication in order for successful acquisition to take place.

Literature suggests that the level of language proficiency attained by bilingual children in their two respective languages is an important intervening variable in determining the effects of bilingualism on cognitive and academic development. The threshold hypothesis of Cummins (1982, 1984) begins to explain the effect of language proficiency on cognitive and academic development. This hypothesis identifies lower threshold bilingual proficiency as a low level of language abilities in both the native and second language. This limited bilingualism may lead to negative cognitive effects as evidenced by classroom performance and cognitive abilities. Partial bilingualism is experienced by individuals who evidence native-like fluency in one language (either the first or second). This level of bilingualism does not appear to positively or negatively affect cognitive skills. A higher threshold of bilingual proficiency is evidenced among individuals who have attained native-like proficiency in both the native and second language. This attainment of a higher level of proficiency in both languages is necessary to experience accelerated cognitive growth and leads to positive cognitive effects.

Other researchers have stated similar conclusions. Duncan and DeAvila (1979) found that the bilingual students who had developed high levels of native and second-language proficiency performed better than both monolinguals and partial bilingual students. In fact, similar findings showing a correlation between a high threshold of bilingualism in both the native and second language and increased cognitive performance have been found among bilingual learning disabled students (Colley, 1987).

In this study, learning disabled students (9 to 12 years of age) who exhibited native-like proficiency in both Spanish and English scored significantly higher than Spanish-dominant, English-dominant, and bilingual students with low language abilities in both languages on numerous tasks indicative of cognitive/academic performance. The performance measurement included the students' ability to perform comprehension monitoring tasks, to process and solve problems sequentially, and to process information both simultaneously and sequentially.

As applied to written communication, this research indicates the importance of native language development. It is only after the skills are acquired in the first or native language of the student that they can be transferred to the second language (Cummins, 1984; Thonis, 1983). As listening, speaking, reading, and writing skills contribute to the development of the other skills in the native language, a pool of linguistic knowledge is developed. This pool contains what is needed to successfully communicate in writing in the native/first language of the student. In order for written communication to develop naturally from language skills, the language used for written communication must be the native or more proficient language of the student.

Once written communication skills are fully developed in the native language, the transition of writing skills to the second language must be considered. The development of competence in the second language is partially a function of the competence that has been developed in the first language (Cummins, 1984). Since skills that are necessary in the manipulation of language in a decontextualized academic situation (reduced context and more demanding content) are interdependent to first and second language, the transfer of writing skills will occur. This cannot occur, however, until competence has been developed in the native language.

The theories which address language skills used for interpersonal communication (in which context is provided and content of language is not demanding), deeper structures of language used for academic purposes, and the referential or contextual base needed for language acquisition and development also apply to written communication. Communication in the first and second language takes place in a variety of settings and contexts. The effect of the context, however, is critical in the process of sharing intents between the listener and speaker (Wiig & Semel, 1984). The individual must coordinate knowledge about the world with a set of linguistic and cultural rules in order to carry out the communicative task.

The context in which communication will take place and how that context affects language production is intrinsic to communication in the first and second language. The ability to functionally use language to communicate goals and intentions in a variety of situations and context becomes the major goal in the development of written communication skills.

Language disabilities. Written communication skills, developed as a function of language and cognition, are greatly influenced by language disabilities. Language disabilities among exceptional populations have been well documented (Carrow-Woolfolk & Lynch, 1982; Cummins, 1984; Lerner, 1985; Lund & Duchan, 1983; Polloway & Smith, 1982; Wiig & Semel, 1984). As a result, language abilities (as depicted in the jframework presented in Figure 8.2) cannot be isolated from the possible disabilities that are exhibited by exceptional individuals.

Language problems may take the form of oral or written language. Research has investigated disorders in the areas of inner language, preverbal ability that allows the individual to internalize and organize experiences; receptive language, the process of understanding verbal symbols; and expressive language, the process of producing spoken language (Johnson & Myklebust, 1976; Lerner, 1985; Meyen, 1982; Scholl, 1981).

The interplay between receptive language, cognition and integration, and language production has been discussed by Polloway and Smith (1982). In each of these three areas, difficulties can occur that would affect the language processing abilities of the individual. For instance, difficulties in reception skills may occur in acuity, attending to input received from the speaker, phonological or syntactical discrimination, formation of semantic relationships, or in the automatic processing of the linguistic input. Once the input is received, coding and integration must take place. At this cognition and integration stage, cognitive abilities and disabilities affect the processing of the linguistic information. At the language production stage, the intention of the communication; semantic, syntactical, and phonological production; and automatic processing are keys to the expression of intentions in a variety of contexts.

Language disabilities may be experienced by CLD students in their native language and may appear to surface in a second language due to (a) limited exposure and proficiency in that language, or (b) similar disabilities in the first language. This basic premise, which has resulted in much study of language differences versus language disorders, must be fully understood for the development of written communication skills among exceptional students from CLD backgrounds.

A disorder is present when language behavior, such as speaking, is affected to such an extent that it interferes with one's ability to convey messages clearly and effectively during interactions with members of the same language community (Mattes & Omark, 1984). During various stages of the second language acquisition process, students will make errors due to limited proficiency in the new language. These errors are often typical of native speakers as they acquire their own language and are, therefore, natural occurrences resulting from the acquisition process. These are not disorders but a result of limited proficiency in a second language.

Language disorders may exist. Disorders, however, will be evident in the native language of the student and may surface as a second language is acquired. In order to differentiate between a language disorder and limited abilities in a second language, disorders of content, use, and form as well as the ability to express intentions and convey meaning between the speaker and listener in a variety of contexts must also be evidenced and assessed in the native language. Juarez (1983) has reasoned that, due to the common processes underlying surface manifestations of both languages, a bilingual child will not have a language disorder in one language and not in the other.

To study language disabilities among CLD students, Taylor (1986) has developed a culturally based framework. The premise of this framework is that the study of communication abilities and disabilities must be encompassed within the culture of the student. Four processes and outcomes are described within this framework: developmental issues, precursors of pathology, assessment, and treatment. Developmental processes provide the foundation for the framework and yield various outcomes. These outcomes include adult-child interactions within the sociocultural context; cognitive, language, and communication acquisition within the native culture; and adult language competence. Precursors of pathology (pathological behaviors which are defined within the cultural group and causative behaviors such as nutritional, social, biological factors) affect the development of cognition, linguistic structures, and communication.

Language disability, aspects of communication in the first and second language, the importance of communicative contexts, and the relationship between language proficiency and cognitive development have been integrated and researched by Carrow-Woolfolk and Lynch (1982). Their integrative model of language stresses the system by which children learn, the knowledge of the linguistic code, and the social forces that regulate language performance.

To accomplish this, four dimensions of language are integrated and interrelated by Carrow-Woolfolk and Lynch (1982). These dimensions are: (a) linguistic knowledge (phonology, morphology, syntax, semantics, and pragmatics); (b) cognition (sensory, perceptual, memory, conceptual, representational, and symbolic abilities); (c) language performance (comprehension and production); and (d) the communication environment (internal values, motivations, and needs of the speaker as well as the external environmental factors). The four dimensions are interrelated in that each affects and interacts with the others. Language disabilities, therefore, that are evidenced in any of the four dimensions will affect the entire system of language and communication. This illustrates the inability to separate knowledge and production of language, cognition, comprehension, and the context in which communication takes place for CLD exceptional students.

As the language abilities and disabilities of CLD exceptional students surface in the process of written communication, interrelationships between first and second language acquisition and cognition must be considered. Native language abilities should be viewed in terms of the normal sequence of language development, appropriate use and modification of language for various communicative situations, and specific abilities; disabilities associated with the handicapping condition itself. Second language abilities must be understood in conjunction with the development of the native language and take into consideration factors that enhance successful second language acquisition. First and second language abilities, as a component of the cognitive framework, become intertwined with the written communication process and relate to other dimensions of the framework.

Cultural/Learning Experiences

The third component of the cognitive framework, depicted in Figure 8.2, is cultural/learning experiences. The development of written communication skills must relate to both cultural experiences and learning characteristics of exceptional students from culturally and linguistically diverse backgrounds.

Cultural experiences. Culture provides the experiential base in which children begin to learn and develop ways in which they like to learn. Through a strong and positive identity with one's own culture, this experiential base develops and provides the foundation for successful learning experiences in school. Culture plays a vital role, therefore, in the learning characteristics, preferences, and cognitive development of CLD exceptional students.

Cummins (1982) describes the experiential base in a particular culture as a positive factor in learning. Through this cultural base, parents transmit a strong sense of pride and culture heritage to their children. Feuerstein (1979) has found that students with this strong cultural background of experience show the capacity to learn and adapt. For these students, the prerequisites for learning and adapting to new situations have been developed within the context of their own culture. A discrepancy may exist, however, between the experiences upon which classroom content is based, the experiences to which the student can make reference, the cultural norms of the students, and the social norms of the school. This often results in school failure, learned helplessness, and a depressed self-concept (Henderson, 1980).

The cultural values and experiences that children bring to school from home are thus important as children begin their formal education. The positive use of the experiences and values that students bring from their culture becomes an important means toward improving the learning characteristics of children and improving academic success. The content of written communication must reflect, therefore, the opportunity to incorporate and build from this experiential base.

Although groups are not homogeneous and may be more traditional or more assimilated in nature, a set of norms, established through the culture of a people, is common to those who share the same perceptions, organization of experiences, belief systems, and interaction patterns. When individuals share these things, they can predict behavior, interpret the environment in similar ways, share similar feelings, and organize the way in which they learn (Trueba, 1979). Longstreet (1978) has stated that children acquire many cultural traits through contact with family, friends, neighbors, and the immediate environment of the community before the age of 10 to 12. It is at this point that children begin to develop abilities for greater abstract thinking. By the time these students begin their formal education, they have already internalized the basic values and beliefs of their culture, learned the rules of behavior for their community, and established socialization skills and expectations (Saville-Troike, 1978).

These values, beliefs, rules, and expectations play a vital role in all aspects of the student's educational experiences, since many factors that enhance successful learning, positive attitudes, and increased motivation in the classroom are specific to the cultural background of the student. The cultural values of an ethnic group have been found to affect socialization practices in the home and community; likewise, communication roles and practices, and the learning characteristics of the student as displayed through motivation, thinking, perceiving, remembering, and problem solving in the classroom situation influence school learning (Ramirez & Castaneda, 1974).

Research on cultural values has been well documented in the areas of (a) family and community identification, (b) social values and interpersonal relationships, (c) status and role definition, (d) religious ideology, and (e) nonverbal orientation modes (Castaneda, 1976; Longstreet, 1978; Nine-Curt, 1979; Ramirez & Castaneda, 1974; Rodriguez, 1982; Saville-Troike, 1978). Although these values have been researched and described separately, they are interrelated and interdependent in classroom learning.

Cultural behavior patterns and products are affected by stages of ethnicity as well as the process of acculturation itself. The "process of change" brings culturally diverse groups through stages that influence traditional values and cultural identification. In order to understand cultural values and diversity, therefore, a continuum ranging from traditional community values to mainstreamed, assimilated values must be considered. In this way, individuals within a particular cultural group can be described in terms of how closely they identify with their cultural group and value system with regard to the process of acculturation and change.

Learning characteristics of exceptional students. For students who exhibit handicapping conditions, learning characteristics must be explored as they impact on learning across cognitive tasks. Learning characteristics have been discussed in terms of social learning theories, formal and informal learning, the development of selective attention, short- and long-term memory, the transfer of information to new tasks and situations, rates of learning, interest and motivation, and preferred forms of feedback (Payne & Patton, 1981; Ross, 1976).

Social learning characteristics of exceptional students include locus of control, expectancy for failure, and outerdirectedness. Locus of control describes a person's perception of the relationship between action and outcomes; individuals with an internal locus of control believe that they are in control of their actions and positive outcomes are within their own control. On the other hand, individuals with an external locus of control believe that outcomes are determined by other sources, whether by friends or by luck (Baca & Cervantes, 1984; Ortiz, 1984).

Despite the positive learning outcomes that have been associated with an internal locus of control, the perception of positive and negative events as being the result of outside forces has been correlated with exceptional learners (Payne & Patton, 1981). In addition, an external locus of control may be found in culturally and linguistically diverse students since (a) cultural values may match what others would call the behaviors associated with an external locus of control; (b) many of these students exhibit a field-dependent cognitive style that is closely associated with an external locus of control; and (c) cultural and linguistic differences in the school may lead to failure which would reinforce the external orientation of the student.

Expectancy for failure and outerdirectedness have also been associated with exceptional learners. An expectancy for failure is based upon repeated failure in school. The exceptional student expects to fail, since this is what has been experienced so many times. As a result, the student puts less effort into the tasks at school and, therefore, experiences more failure. Outerdirectedness is an attempt by the student to avoid failure by imitating and/or relying on others for behavior cues or solutions. This characteristic is related to an external orientation. This overdependence on external cues or solutions takes over even when the task is within the capabilities of the student.

Classroom behaviors associated with impulsivity and learned helplessness have also been investigated among groups of exceptional students (Torgesen, 1982). An impulsive learning style leads the student into quickly responding to classroom tasks, solving problems, and even completing classroom work. The student often responds without sufficient time between the stimulus and response to consider possible alternatives. Learned helplessness has been attributed to past learning experiences that have been neither positive nor successful, and leads students to approach a learning task in a passive, dependent manner (Lerner, 1985).

The learning characteristics of exceptional students have also been researched in terms of selective attention and formal/informal learning. Although much information is acquired through incidental and informal learning, exceptional learners may experience difficulty in this area. Ross (1976) identified the components of the learning process as beginning with expectancy and continuing feedback in the following order:

expectancy → selective attention → organizing input for storage → memory and recall → transfer → performance → feedback. Exceptional students have been found to experience difficulty with each component (Lerner, 1985; Mercer & Snell, 1977; Payne & Patton, 1981).

Based on cultural experiences and learning characteristics, the cognitive style of the student must also be considered. Cognitive style preferences involve behaviors centering around: (a) relationships with other students; (b) the role the student expects from the teacher; (c) the student's relationship with the teacher; (d) preferred modes of gathering information and responding; and (e) preferences for learning through global, analytic, individualistic, or cooperative (personal/humanistic) strategies.

The cultural base of the CLD student, therefore, revolves around a set of learned norms, which relate to the mother's teaching and child-rearing practices at home. The learned norms, in turn, lead to the child's style of communicating, relating to others, learning preferences, incentive-motivational preferences, and group behavior in school. Exceptional children, who have been found to exhibit somewhat unsuccessful learning characteristics due to continued social and academic failure and the nature of the handicapping condition itself, may experience further difficulty in adapting to the culture of the classroom. As a result, these factors impact on cognitive processing and language acquisition and must be considered in the development of written communication skills of the CLD exceptional student.

SUMMARY AND CONCLUSION

The purpose of this chapter was to describe written communication as a holistic, pragmatic process, to present a cognitive framework for the development of written communication skills among CLD exceptional students, and to discuss theoretical perspectives for each of the components of the framework. As presented in this chapter, written communication among CLD exceptional students provides them with an opportunity to become actively involved in the communicative process through the enhancement of language and cognitive skills. Through a holistic, pragmatic process of communicating in writing, the needs and abilities of students from diverse backgrounds can become keys to successful performance and positive learning outcomes.

Congruent with the cognitive perspective described in this chapter, teachers must be able to identify performance indicators and procedures for instructional decision making. This implies the evaluation of student performance not only in written communication skills, but also in cognitive processing abilities, language abilities in the native and second language, and cultural/learning experiences as they relate to the writing process. Through a curriculum-based approach to evaluation, the necessary links can be made between instructional characteristics, student performance in all related areas, and the writing curriculum.

An evaluation system that identifies needs and abilities in relation to the process of written communication will yield instructional programs and strategies that can provide appropriate linguistic and cognitive development. In terms of the process of writing, this includes the assessment of the purpose in written language; planning, transcribing, reviewing, and revising the written message; the written product, including vocabulary, content, and fluency; and the strategies embedded throughout the process (Howell & Morehead, 1987). As written communication emerges as a holistic, pragmatic process, general and specific assessment must also be conducted in all areas depicted in Figure 8.2.

In conclusion, it is important to mention major considerations that are brought to light through this cognitive framework for written communication. The following six considerations are intrinsic to the instructional decision-making process as it applies to written communication:

1. The proficient language of the student must be used as the basis for the development of written communication skills through a holistic, pragmatic orientation.
2. The transfer of written communication skills into the second language must be based on sound second language acquisition principles and occur only after mastery of such skills in the native language.
3. Opportunities for written communication to be a vehicle for the enhancement of cognitive and language skills for all classroom activities and content should be addressed as writing is used across the curriculum.
4. Strategies that will aid students in their ability to monitor their written communication must correspond to the context of the writing situation and be purposely taught to students as a cognitive monitoring activity.
5. The cultural/experiential background of exceptional students must be used as the foundation for written communication in order to incorporate existing schema, reflect personal meaning, and capitalize on the purpose of the communicative act.
6. The learning characteristics of students, based on cultural values and school experiences, should be accounted for in terms of modifying instruction in the classroom and providing positive outcomes for all students.

This framework, therefore, provides a cognitive perspective from which teachers can derive assessment strategies and appropriate instructional programs. The components of cognitive processing, first and second language abilities, and cultural/learning experiences, are intrinsic to understanding the process of written communication and are vital to the development and implementation of individualized education programs.

As written communication presents a challenge to CLD exceptional students, so is the challenge in the hands of professionals who are responsible for the development and implementation of the written communication program. In moving away from a product orientation to a process approach to written communication, teachers must be prepared to change their teaching methods and capitalize on the abilities of CLD exceptional students who may exhibit disabilities in many related areas. Through the successful matching of cognitive and linguistic abilities, cultural experiences, the writing process, instructional methods/ strategies, and the objectives of the program, written communication can become a vehicle of academic success for bilingual exceptional students.

REFERENCES

Anderson, R. (1977). Schema-directed processes in language comprehension. In A. Lesgold, J. Pellegrino, S. Fokkema, & R. Glaser (Eds.), *Cognitive psychology and instruction* (pp. 62-82). New York: Plenum Press.

Baca, L., & Cervantes, H. (1984). *The bilingual special education interface*. St. Louis: Mosby.

Bransford, J., & Johnson, M. (1972). Contextual prerequisites for understanding: Some investigations of comprehension and recall. *Journal of Verbal Learning and Verbal Behavior, 11,* 717-726.

Carrow-Woolfolk, E., & Lynch, J. (1982). *An integrative approach to language disorders in children.* New York: Grune & Stratton.

Castaneda, A. (1976). Cultural democracy and the educational needs of Mexican American children. In R. Jones (Ed.), *Mainstreaming and the minority child* (pp. 181-194). Reston, VA: Council for Exceptional Children.

Colley, D.A. (1987). Relationship between oral comprehension monitoring and information processing among culturally and linguistically diverse learning disabled students. *Dissertation Abstracts International.* (University Microfilms No. 87-1067)

Craig, H. (1983). Applications of pragmatic language models for intervention. In T. Gallagher & C. Prutting (Eds.), *Pragmatic assessment and intervention issues in language* (pp. 101-127). San Diego: College-Hill.

Cummins, J. (1982). The role of primary language development in promoting educational success for language minority students. In California State Department of Education (Ed.), *Schooling and language minority students: A theoretical framework.* Los Angeles: Evaluation, Dissemination and Assessment Center.

Cummins, J. (1984). *Bilingualism and special education: Issues in assessment and pedagogy.* San Diego, CA: College-Hill.

Duncan, S., & DeAvila, E. (1979). Bilingualism and cognition: Some recent findings. *NABE Journal, 4,* 15-50.

Feuerstein, R. (1979). *The dynamic assessment of retarded performers: The learning potential assessment device.* Baltimore, MD: University Park.

Flavell, J. (1977). *Cognitive development.* Englewood Cliffs, NJ: Prentice-Hall.

Flavell, J. (1981a). Cognitive monitoring. In W.P. Dickson (Ed.), *Children's oral communication skills* (pp. 35-60). New York: Academic Press.

Flavell, J. (1981b). Monitoring social cognitive enterprises: Something else that may develop in the area of social cognition. In J. Flavell & L. Ross (Eds.), *Social cognitive development* (pp. 272-287). Cambridge: Cambridge University Press.

Halliday, M. (1978). *Learning how to mean: Explorations in the development of language.* New York: Edward Arnold.

Henderson, R. (1980). Social and emotional needs of culturally diverse children. *Exceptional Children, 46,* 598-605.

Howell, K., & Morehead, M. (1987). *Curriculum-based evaluation for special and remedial education.* Columbus, OH: Charles E. Merrill.

Johnson, D., & Myklebust, H. (1976). *Learning disabilities.* New York: Grune & Stratton.

Juarez, M. (1983). Assessment and treatment of minority-language handicapped children: The role of the monolingual speech-language pathologist. *Topics in Language Disorders, 3,* 57-66.

Lerner, J. (1985). *Learning disabilities: Theories, diagnosis and teaching strategies* (4th ed.). Boston: Houghton Mifflin.

Longstreet, W. (1978). *Aspects of ethnicity.* New York: Teachers College Press.

Lund, N.J., & Duchen, J.F. (1983). *Assessing children's language in naturalistic contexts.* Englewood Cliffs, NJ: Prentice-Hall.

Mann, L., & Sabatino, D. (1985). *Foundations of cognitive process in remedial and special education.* Rockville, MA: Aspen Systems.

Markman, E. (1977). Realizing that you don't understand: A preliminary investigation. *Child Development, 48,* 986-992.

Markman, E. (1979). Realizing that you don't understand: Elementary school children's awareness of inconsistencies. *Child Development, 50,* 643-655.

Markman, E. (1981). Comprehension monitoring. In W.P. Dickson (Ed.), *Children's oral communication skills.* New York: Academic Press.

Mattes, L., & Omark, D. (1984). *Speech and language assessment for the bilingual handicapped.* San Diego, CA: College-Hill.

Mercer, C., & Snell, M. (1977). *Learning theory researches in mental retardation: Implications for teaching.* Columbus, OH: Charles E. Merrill.

Meyen, E. (1982). *Exceptional children and youth* (2nd ed.). Denver: Love.

Nine-Curt, C.J. (1979). *Teacher-training pack for a course on cultural awareness.* New York: National Assessment and Dissemination Center.

Nodine, B. (1983). Foreword: Process not product. *Topics in Learning and Learning Disabilities, 3*(3), ix-xii.

Ortiz, A. (1984). Language and curriculum development for exceptional bilingual children. In P. Chin (Ed.), *Education of culturally and linguistically different children* (pp. 77-100). Reston, VA: Council for Exceptional Children.

Payne, J.S., & Patton, J.R. (1981). *Mental retardation.* Columbus, OH: Charles E. Merrill.

Polloway, E., & Smith, J. (1982). *Teaching language skills to exceptional learners.* Denver: Love.

Ramirez, M., & Castaneda, A. (1974). *Cultural democracy, bicognitive development, and education.* New York: Academic Press.

Rhodes, L.K., & Dudley-Marling, C. (1988). *Readers and writers with a difference: A holistic approach to teaching learning disabled and remedial students.* Portsmouth, NH: Heinemann.

Rodriguez, R. (1982). *The Mexican American child in special education.* Las Cruces, NM: Education Resources Information Center (ERIC).

Ross, A.O. (1976). *Psychological aspects of learning disabilities and reading disorders.* New York: McGraw-Hill.

Saville-Troike, M. (1978). *A guide to culture in the classroom.* Reston, VA: National Clearinghouse for Bilingual Education.

Scholl, H. (1981). Language disorders related to learning disabilities. In J. Gottlieb & S. Strichart (Eds.), *Developmental theory and research in learning disabilities* (pp. 130-168). Baltimore, MD: University Park.

Smith, F. (1982). *Writing and the writer.* New York: Holt, Rinehart, & Winston.

Sridhar, K. (1981). Pragmatics and language assessment. In J. Erickson & D. Omark (Eds.), *Communication assessment of the bilingual bicultural child* (pp. 199-220). Baltimore, MD: University Park.

Taylor, O. (Ed.). (1986). *Nature of communication disorders in culturally and linguistically diverse populations.* San Diego, CA: College-Hill.

Thonis, E. (1983). *The English-Spanish connection.* Northvale, NJ: Santillana.

Thorndyke, P., & Hayes-Roth, B. (1979). The use of schemata in the acquisition and transfer of knowledge. *Cognitive Psychology, 11,* 82-86.

Torgesen, J. (1982). The LD child as an inactive learner: Educational implications. *Topics in Learning and Learning Disabilities, 2,* 45-52.

Trueba, H.T. (1979). Implications of culture for bilingual education. In H. Trueba & C. Barnett-Mizrahi (Eds.), *Bilingual multicultural education and the professional: From theory to practice* (pp. 161-163). Rowley, MA: Newbury House.

Wiig, E.H., & Semel, E. (1984). *Language assessment and intervention for the learning disabled* (2nd ed.). Columbus, OH: Charles E. Merrill.

chapter 9

Content Area Instruction in Bilingual Special Education Classes

Ana Rossell

This chapter discusses the need to use a differential approach to teaching content area to students who present learning handicaps and whose linguistic backgrounds are diverse. The basic elements of this differential approach, as proposed in this chapter, are those factors that interact to facilitate the learning process in bilingual special education classes. In the first section, the appropriate selection of the language of instruction and the quality of linguistic interactions in each language are emphasized to promote cognitive academic language development in the classroom. Specific teaching strategies and curriculum adaptations, which must be culturally relevant and responsive to learning potentials are included to increase the effectiveness of content area instruction. Responsible staff must provide positive experiences and meaningful access to school curriculum areas and materials to foster the interest and motivation of linguistically and culturally diverse exceptional students.

The second section of the chapter focuses on the teaching of particular areas of the curriculum. The purpose is to help teachers integrate concepts and practice. Two sample lessons are incorporated in this section to guide teachers in the understanding and reflection on the creative nature of teaching bilingual special education students.

THE TEACHING OF CONTENT AREA SUBJECT MATTER

Content area instruction refers to such mandated curriculum areas as mathematics, science, social studies, music, art, technology, vocational and career education, health, and safety. The goal of teaching content areas is to provide students with knowledge of subject matter and with creative problem-solving skills. The foundation upon which these learning outcomes can be achieved is the teaching of the basic skills of speaking, reading, writing, and computing.

In order to teach content area concepts and skills effectively, teachers need to organize activities that involve thought-provoking, problem-solving tasks in a language that is comprehensible to each student. New Levine (1985) supports the concept that students learning English as a second language have difficulties learning content area subjects taught in a language that they understand and speak imperfectly. She indicates that these difficulties intensify after grades 3 and 4 when vocabulary level increases and the use of textbooks is required for most classroom instruction.

The dual responsibility of teaching language skills and content area concepts and skills simultaneously complicates the task of teachers, who must also address the special educational needs of bilingual students who are handicapped in learning. Content area instruction for second language learners in bilingual special education classes requires addressing the curriculum objectives of the school system by actively involving handicapped students in activities and lessons that are exciting and well-integrated into the reality of their everyday lives. An effective educational intervention calls for the use of curriculum adaptations and modifications tailored to the students' strengths and potential, as well as well-planned strategies that promote language concepts, second language acquisition, and cognitive development.

Language and cognitive development for bilingual students consists of utilizing the resources of two languages, the native language or language of the home, and English, their second language. Extensive research in recent years has provided evidence that bilingualism is a cognitive asset that leads to a more flexible, resourceful, and creative intellectual development (Bozinou-Doukas, 1983). It is then very important, when referring to bilingual handicapped children, to separate bilingualism from handicapping condition. According to Bozinou-Doukas, bilingualism needs to be considered in planning for instruction, instead of dismissing it as a cognitive deterrent. Several studies indicate the need for addressing both issues separately, and for delivering better instruction in both first and second languages.

The number of motoric, psychological, perceptual, verbal, social, or intellectual processes that may be impaired in a truly handicapped child determines the need to address the remediation of those symptoms by utilizing all the resources of bilingual youngsters. This must include their culturally based schemata, or previously acquired values and knowledge. Difficulties in mastering certain cognitive tasks may not necessarily be related to a disability condition but to different schemata (Carrell & Eisterhold, 1983; Finocchiaro, 1986). Process deficits caused by any handicapping condition can, in many cases, be better addressed by providing remediation in the native language.

There are various cultural and linguistic factors to consider when deciding on the language of content area instruction for handicapped children. While some students will be more skillful in one of the two languages, others may not have developed age or grade level proficiency in either language. For students with stronger skills in the native language, the teaching of content area subjects in the native language will assure students' normal academic progress according to abilities and potential, provided effective bilingual teaching conditions take place (Cummins, 1984; Thonis, 1970).

The transfer of knowledge from the native language to English is facilitated when intensive English as a second language instruction is delivered using communicative approaches in a low-anxiety environment (Krashen & Terrell, 1983). Communicative approaches promote natural acquisition of a second language as a sequential developmental process similar to first language acquisition. A communicative approach develops listening, comprehension, and oral skills in a variety of curricular topics that motivate and interest students. The topics may range from everyday social and survival skills to areas of high interest and content levels. This approach also emphasizes the development of such cognitive skills as observation, awareness, perception, conceptualization, and judgment (Bernstein & Tiegerman, 1985). Activities should include visually demonstrable subject matter such as science experiments, role playing, story telling, interactive problem solving, games, arts and crafts, music, and physical movement (Krashen, 1982).

Linguistic approaches for learning the second language are introduced later and selectively. These approaches emphasize reading, writing, test taking, and competing in classroom academic work. They are best introduced when students are ready to monitor their own progress in more complex concepts and sentences. Students acquiring a second language will self-correct their expressive language over time, as they progress through the various stages of language and cognitive development (Krashen, 1981). When the initial stages of natural and oral language acquisition have been mastered in a variety of positive experiences, the more advanced stages of language learning will successfully emerge. Syntactic structure and graphic representation of language can then be emphasized. Rewarding communicative experiences with language and concrete ideas prepare students for these advanced stages.

Students placed in a bilingual special education setting bring different levels of cognitive abilities that need to be addressed regardless of which language is used or what level of English proficiency has been achieved. If learning is indeed based on the interdependence of language, cognition, and social development, as proposed by Piaget (1952), knowledge will be acquired more easily in the native or dominant language through experiences that are rich in content and interaction, and which are relevant to the cultural background of the students. This can best be achieved when bilingual special education programs are specifically designed to address those objectives. The basic characteristics of such programs will be discussed in the next sections to follow.

CONTENT AREA INSTRUCTION IN BILINGUAL SPECIAL EDUCATION PROGRAMS

Effective bilingual special education programs aim to develop language proficiency in both English and the native language, and provide for the successful acquisition and learning of academic and basic skills. The program consists of individualized instruction delivered in small groups by qualified bilingual special education teachers. The composition of the groups is based on the similarity of language background and academic needs of the students. The program addresses specific student needs made explicit in the Individualized Education Program (IEP). The goals and objectives of the IEP are language-specific. While some goals indicate that instruction in certain content areas is delivered in the native language, or utilize an English as a Second Language (ESL) approach, other goals indicate how each student will develop the native language and English as part of the Language Arts program.

Some of the key features of an effective bilingual special education program that is conducive to successful content area development are: (a) a multicultural education framework; (b) an appropriate learning environment; (c) the adequate selection and use of the language(s) of instruction; (d) the adaptation of curriculum and teaching strategies; and (e) a supportive school administration and staff team work.

MULTICULTURAL EDUCATION FRAMEWORK

Multicultural education can be seen as the overall framework within which instruction in each specific content area takes place. An education that is multicultural in nature allows for instruction to be presented within a culturally familiar context, while exposing students to other cultures and demonstrating the recognition and value of diverse groups.

Multicultural education begins with acknowledgment of the ethnic and cultural background of students. Content instruction is intended to be relevant and meaningful to all students regardless of their differences. Textbooks, materials, and concepts serve to develop a sensitivity toward different cultures. Students are encouraged to understand facts and ideas from different perspectives, and to enlarge their knowledge base, skills, and viewpoints on selected topics. Emphasis is placed on the diverse cultural traits, attributes, costumes, and artistic expressions of people from different countries.

Teachers need to infuse concepts of multicultural education and attitudes of multicultural understanding during instruction in all subject areas. It is this which allows students to develop a positive self-concept and a positive attitude toward learning so that they can achieve their optimal personal and academic potential. They need to learn respect, understand, and enjoy the diversity of cultures that surround them. Multicultural understanding produces positive effects in self-concept development and in interaction with others. In this way, multicultural education becomes the foundation upon which all learning is built.

APPROPRIATE LEARNING ENVIRONMENT

Given that special education classes are small, the range of abilities and disabilities tends to be wide, with variations expected within each child's own developmental levels. Bilingual handicapped students are more like other children than unlike them; they have the same need for affection, security, sense of achievement, and self-respect. Teachers must keep this in mind in order to create a classroom environment which is both therapeutic and educational.

Classroom organization takes into account the arrangement of physical space and seating patterns, provides for learning centers, and for tasteful decorations using students' art or academic work. A variety of manipulatives and other materials are well organized and available at the varied grade levels of the students. Specialized equipment is provided according to individual needs; materials and presentations reflect the students' cultural and linguistic backgrounds. Selected books and materials in the content areas are relevant to the cultures in the class and are available in the native language and English. Materials must be comparable in content to those offered to monolingual students.

When a bilingual paraprofessional is assigned to the classroom, the paraprofessional assists in second language acquisition, in planning for instruction, in helping students become active members in the class, and in the communication process between parents and school. Bilingual students may need repeated formal instruction on school procedures and routines.

An effective learning environment, then, maximizes student engagement in academic activities by careful allocation of time. Adequate programming facilitates instruction in all required content area subjects and provides for continual cognitive and language development. Decisions about scheduling, language of instruction, departmentalization of subjects, or team teaching play an important role in creating excitement and social and intellectual growth during instruction.

According to Tikunoff (1983), bilingual teachers can develop maximum school functional proficiency in their limited-English-proficient students. To accomplish this, they must deliver effective instruction in the students' native language to ensure that the lessons are clearly understood. They must communicate clearly by giving accurate directions, specifying tasks, and presenting new information by contextualizing, explaining, outlining, summarizing, and reviewing. It is necessary to monitor progress by reviewing work frequently and modifying instruction to maximize success. It is important that teachers provide immediate positive or corrective feedback so that students are reinforced for correct responses and learn to minimize errors. To develop students' attention and interest, it is important to maintain task focus, pace instruction appropriately, promote involvement and oral participation, and constantly communicate expectations for correct performance. Tikunoff maintains that effective teachers consider that, until limited-English-proficient (LEP) students are able to participate competently in English, their cognitive progress is dependent upon effective bilingual instruction.

APPROPRIATE USE OF THE LANGUAGE(S) OF INSTRUCTION

A bilingual program for handicapped students seeks to assure that students do not lag behind in the acquisition of subject matter. This entails, in many cases, the use of the native language as a medium of instruction. Subject matter plays an important role in cognitive development. Children who fall behind in subject matter because they do not understand the language of instruction may also be missing the stimulation necessary for their continued intellectual development (Krashen, 1983).

The languages of content area instruction in a self-contained bilingual special education class are, of course, the native language and English. Since students are not proficient in English, English as a Second Language teaching strategies are needed to introduce concepts.

Teachers should try to keep the use of each language separate, and limit code switching or the interchangeable mixing of both languages

(Jacobson, 1981). The use of translation during instruction makes students tune out the language they do not understand, and encourages them to wait for the translation (Gaardner, 1978; Wong-Fillmore, 1980).

The most common variations in the use of languages during content area instruction fall into two categories: concurrent approaches and alternate language approaches.

Concurrent approaches involve the use of the two languages of instruction, the native language and English, during the development of a lesson. Classroom situations and lesson planning influence the amount of use of either language. A teacher may teach content area in English while using the native language to clarify concepts and to support understanding through familiar vocabulary. This is a type of code switching that may occur naturally among children in a bilingual class when they need to revert to their native language during active participatory activities. While this may be the result of the natural flow of classroom interactions, it is also the result of the recognition that the two languages are different and could be used to resolve different functional situations. Students who code switch when they do not find the appropriate words in one language are said to be "good" language learners since they use both languages as sources for expressing more complex ideas (Ortiz, 1984). Teachers can control and limit code switching in the classroom by simply rephrasing a student's response in only one language, and by not code switching arbitrarily themselves.

Ovando and Collier (1985) refer to studies that recommend that, if any code switching is used in the classroom, it should not be used in direct translation and that intersentential code switching (switching after each sentence) is best. They also recommend that intrasentential code switching (within a sentence) by students should be accepted but not used or encouraged by the teacher.

A concurrent language approach in content area consists of the effective use of the two languages during instruction. Teachers can introduce the topic in one language, usually the native language, and then develop the lesson in English, using contextualized vocabulary, simple expressions, and constant evaluation of progress in understanding. The summary of the lesson is then facilitated in the native language to ensure total comprehension by all students. The application, homework, or evaluation can be done in the student's dominant language. If time allows, some type of review should be done in both languages separately, according to particular students' language strengths and needs. For example, one exercise in English may consist of underlining main ideas, or recognizing orally true and false statements, while another exercise may consist of sequencing sentences that tell the story or event in the native language. The class can also be divided into dominant-language groups, each involved in different projects that will allow them to show cognitive progress and content area understanding in their dominant or preferred language.

Alternate language approaches require separation of the two languages as much as possible. While some subjects are taught entirely in one language, others are taught entirely in the other language. Or, one language is used in the morning and the other in the afternoon. Other variations allow for team teaching in which one teacher will use one language, and the other teacher the other language.

The adoption of any of these modalities in the use of languages requires a clear definition of the purpose and the goals of the bilingual program. In a transitional model, for example, during the special education students' first year in a bilingual class, all content area subjects are best taught in the native language. As the students become more proficient in English through developmental English as a second language lessons, certain subjects are introduced in English utilizing English as a second language strategies, or a variation of the concurrent language approach. The use of one language or the other must be explicitly indicated in the student's individualized education plan, which is updated as changes in language of instruction are noted.

It takes several years of learning English as a second language for limited English proficient students to develop language abilities at a comparable level to English-speaking students (Cummins, 1984). Meanwhile, they may not be ready to respond to classroom academic demands or to comprehend content area instruction totally in the second language. Content area instruction in English presents difficulties when skills in comprehension, analysis, and inferencing are not present yet. The development of these higher cognitive skills is dependent on language proficiency. There is the need to develop the content area curriculum in a language that provides for meaningful participation on the part of students.

The models proposed by the New York City school system (New York City Board of Education, 1987a) and by the New York State Education Department (1987) recommend the use of language according to the student's assessed proficiency in both languages. Content area and reading instruction in the native language plus intensive English as a second language instruction are required when a student speaks no English, has very limited proficiency, or has developed only basic social skills in English, not being proficient enough for the cognitive and linguistic demands of instructional tasks. When the student has acquired sufficient academic language proficiency in English, the amount of content area instruction using an English as a Second Language approach increases. The range of bilingual instruction for a particular student may vary from receiving instruction in the native language 80 percent of the time, and instruction in English as a second language 20 percent of the time, to instruction in the native language 20 percent of the time and instruction in English 80 percent of the time. Given that linguistic needs are determined by ongoing evaluation, the individualized education program (IEP) reflects the students' achieved levels of proficiency in both languages and states goals and objectives in content areas indicating the languages of instruction.

ADAPTATION OF CURRICULUM AND TEACHING STRATEGIES

Students learn best when they proceed in small steps. If they are consistently given work that is too difficult, they are likely to give up and become "motivation problems" (Brophy, 1982). Recent research indicates that students require a very high success rate in order to progress efficiently. This can be accomplished when they move along in small steps and can experience consistent success along the way. Active teaching of small groups generally produce effective learning of content because teachers can monitor students' progress and provide feedback and remedial instruction. When students are expected to learn on their own or from texts, teachers cannot be sure students understand the tasks thoroughly. Students in special education classes require a great deal of interaction with teachers who can provide feedback and opportunities for overt practice.

Students in special education must have access to the full range of programs and services available in each school (New York City Board of Education, 1987b) to assure that these students achieve their maximum potential. For these students to benefit from instruction based upon the same curriculum used in general education classes, teachers must constantly evaluate and revise lessons to select different adaptations that meet student needs. This implies that teachers must engage in two types of instructional planning. First, based upon the analysis of the general education curriculum, teachers, considering the prerequisite skills and knowledge needed to succeed, select instructional objectives at the appropriate level of difficulty of students. This task of selecting instructional objectives that match individual student needs is the first curriculum adaptation strategy that helps special education teachers design effective and efficient instruction. Second, once appropriate objectives are identified, teachers determine what teaching strategies and adaptations must be implemented to meet student needs. In this step teachers evaluate and adapt objectives, materials, instructional presentations, methods of explaining task directions, activities that motivate students and reinforce learning, and methods to assess student progress and learning attitudes.

An adaptation of objectives may consist of the need to break down an objective into two or more sequential objectives which, when taught in proper sequence, will result in mastery of the original objective. Another type of adaptation may consist of the combining of two or more objectives to eliminate detail while retaining essential information. This should enable students to grasp key concepts common to both objectives.

Materials may also require adaptations to be appropriate for special education instruction. Some of the adaptations are of particular importance to special education students who are limited in English proficiency. Some examples of adaptation of materials are the enlarging of printed material by increasing letter size; the reduction of information on a page, by underlining, framing, or separating specific items, or the reducing of the number of problems or questions. Colorful pictures and manipulatives can illustrate vocabulary and concepts or become a stimulus for a learning experience. The same can be accomplished with tape-recorded or videotaped material, and computer software at various linguistic levels. Other strategies for adapting materials to student needs include using precut or color-coded material, utilizing arrows to prompt directionality, and providing for the tracing of shapes, pictures, maps, words, or phrases.

Materials in both languages should be used, as well as labeling in the two languages. A picture file made by teacher and students is always useful to illustrate, compare, contrast, and categorize concepts in any language.

Learning centers help keep particular subject area materials functionally grouped.

Adaptation of instructional presentation includes utilizing a variety of teaching modes that provide for visual, auditory, kinesthetic, and tactile learning approaches, as well as for increased repetition and opportunities for practice. Multisensory approaches increase acquisition and recall of knowledge and language.

Students' different learning styles may call for the use of several modes of presentation simultaneously, which enhance recognition, interpretation, and memory. These modes include drama, art, music, literature, poetry, and total physical response; oral model and focusing on essential information are also crucial.

Students learning a second language need to develop methods for listing, classifying, and storing concepts, which can be accomplished by using semantic mapping, fact cards, and summaries in both languages.

To help students understand what is expected of them, directions can be simplified, illustrated, repeated by a classmate, or rewritten by the students in their own words.

Diverse strategies for adapting and reinforcing the curriculum make instruction meaningful. Properly adapted methods and criteria for evaluation ensure that specific curriculum objectives are met and that successive approximation of goals are being accomplished.

The adequacy of current available curricula also needs consideration (Ortiz & Garcia, 1988). Schools need to continually adapt, supplement, or validate programs to make them meaningful for the multicultural populations they serve. For example, bilingual education and English as a second language programs (ESL) were developed in recognition that limited-English-proficient students could not master the regular curriculum without a program of study to help them become competent in English. Native language curricula were incorporated to ensure that LEP students did not fall behind English-speaking peers on grade level subjects or skills while they learned English as a second language.

EFFECTIVE SCHOOL ADMINISTRATION AND TEAM WORK

Bilingual special education teachers need to have the support of school administrators and colleagues when they design and implement learning activities. Schoolwide support should be based on an understanding of child development and knowledge of students' cultural backgrounds. It is imperative that the goals of the program in each particular school be developed jointly by the school administrators, principals, supervisors, clinical and instructional personnel, as well as parents. The clinical, pedagogical, and administrative issues related to each bilingual special education program must be addressed by all levels of school personnel. The education and integration of the bilingual special education student is a team responsibility. School administrators should foster greater awareness of the special needs of pupils with linguistic and cultural differences. A school's commitment to these students can be achieved only through the efforts of well-informed, effectively trained, caring individuals.

CURRICULUM AREAS

Teaching content area is a strategic process in which the teacher shares the roles of planner and mediator of learning. Teachers must know the content thoroughly, understand thinking processes appropriate to learn-ing, and differentiate strategies to match student needs (Jones, Sullivan Palincsar, Sederburg Ogle, & Glyn Carr, 1987).

This section introduces teachers to specific curriculum areas selected to discuss processes and strategies that are, according to recent research on learning, relevant to diverse needs and cultural and linguistic back-grounds of students.

Language Arts

One main purpose of the language arts curriculum in the bilingual class is to develop communicative and cognitive academic language skills in English and the native language. Students in a class are at different stages of development in both languages. Teachers need to know the language status of their students in terms of proficiency in each language, use of language at home, language preference and competence, and the possible presence of a linguistic disorder or impairment. The identifi-cation of these characteristics facilitates grouping students with similar patterns of language use or proficiency. The use of grouping for language development activities is important because it permits students to work together with the teacher for a short, but meaningful time each day, in adult-directed learning activities, while also providing for opportu-nities for self-directed small-group practice activities. Teachers plan according to a particular group's interests, skills, and developmental gains by observing the motivational and affective factors that influence linguistic and cognitive acquisition.

Classroom language modeling is important. The adults in the class-room should talk to students in a comprehensible, direct, and polite manner, and in a soft voice. Reading to younger children in both languages is an excellent source of language modeling.

Opportunities to acquire and learn language should permeate the entire school curriculum. In whatever area students are working they should be encouraged to practice the various language skills. Bilingual teachers need to integrate both languages creatively in order to provide for an enriched and successful language-learning environment. Both languages, however, are taught monolingually, that is, English as a Second Language (ESL) is taught in English only, and the native language in only that language.

Native language arts. The native language serves as the link with the home and the bilingual social context in which students grow up. Students need to further develop the native language for successful interactions and negotiations in the home and the community, and for future job or career opportunities. In the bilingual class the native language is needed to advance in topics that require higher cognitive and thinking skills.

Teachers can help students build a solid cognitive base through instruction in the native language and by providing a rich native language environment that enhances the skills of listening, speaking, reading, and writing. Live language, songs, and games become meaningful for students and provide the backbone for the development of reading and writing skills.

Valdez (1981) lists these basic native language arts objectives that bilingual children need to develop: (a) listening, observing, and speaking skills; (b) basic reading skills; (c) language skills through experiences with books; (d) spelling abilities; (e) competence and creativeness in oral and written communication; (f) effective language skills for use in daily life; (g) skills in use of mass modes of communication; and (h) competent use of language and reading for vocational purposes.

Teachers and paraprofessionals need to be fluent in the language and become familiar with methods and materials specific to the teaching of the particular language. Adaptation of speed, amount of help given, and achievement expected must be carefully considered for each student.

English as a second language. For many students, the first significant contact with English occurs in school. Instruction in English as a second language must become a part of the student's IEP (Ortiz, 1984). A common misconception, according to Ortiz, is that bilingual students should be given as much time as possible to master the English language. Contrary to this opinion, increased exposure or submersion in English does not improve or hasten second language acquisition (Krashen, 1982). During specific instruction in English as a second language students are given the necessary amount of time and help to develop communicative competence in English (Backman & Savignon, 1986). However, a pull-out program in which students are removed from the self-contained special class for language instruction only is not recommended in special education. Special education teachers need to become familiar with diverse methods and techniques on second language teaching; students need to develop the language through meaningful classroom experiences. The ability to use English as a medium of thought in content area, however, takes several years (Cummins, 1982).

A content-based English language development program has been proposed by Chamot and O'Malley (1986) as an alternative to ESL classes that focus on linguistic instruction only. A content-based curriculum provides for transitional language activities geared to develop the necessary skills of listening, speaking, and writing, associated with the particular subject matter. Reading and language arts are taught as part of content area subjects such as science, mathematics, and social studies. The cognitive and metacognitive learning strategies used in this type of program are of particular interest for adaptation to special education instruction.

Reading. The development of reading skills is of paramount importance to bilingual special education students. Reading is basic to every other interest or subject. According to Thonis (1970), children use their previous language experiences during the process of learning how to read. Children learn about sounds, that they have certain meanings, and that actions result from their use. Oral language becomes, then, an integral part of the reading process. From the standpoint of language readiness, students are better prepared to learn written symbols in their native language than in English. By beginning reading instruction in the native language, literacy and progress in reading are promoted. Positive attitudes toward learning, school, and self are enhanced which, in turn, facilitate the students' successful transfer to reading English.

An effective plan for teaching limited-English-proficient (LEP) students to read in English requires that skills in oral English precede written English. LEP children are taught to understand and speak English before beginning reading instruction in English (Harris & Spivay, 1979; Thonis, 1970). Before introducing reading, ability and experiences in oral English, as well as native language ability and reading level, must be considered. Teachers need to be resourceful and familiar with different methods and approaches to teach reading, with special remedial techniques, reading skills inventories, and with the LEP students' abilities, learning modalities, and difficulties. This is essential in order to adapt the appropriate reading program, materials, and pace. Remedial reading for students with learning disabilities that involve reading should be done in the native or dominant language. How students learn to read depends on the students' background, attitudes, and cultural environment (Carrasquillo, 1984).

Reading in the content areas. For students who do not speak English as a native language, the reading requirements of individual subjects are often unrealistic. When teaching science, mathematics, or social studies, teachers are often unaware of the heavy burden imposed by print upon both native and non-native speakers of English (Thonis, 1970). This is particularly relevant to special education students whose impairments impede learning to read by conventional methods. If information is only available in the second language, LEP students in special education are certain to make little progress. If students understand and speak the native language but have not been taught how to read in it, reading subject matter in the native language is also unrealistic.

Thonis discusses some programmatic alternatives to the presentation of subjects in written English. She argues that the selection of an appropriate medium by which to convey content would depend upon the language strengths and maturity of students. If learners understand and speak English with some adequacy, but have not yet learned to read and write well, subject matter should be offered orally, well-supported by pictures, films, filmstrips, charts, demonstrations, realia, and other aids to meaning. If students are dominant in the native language, subject matter should be made available in the native language, as this will enable them to acquire and extend their mastery of concepts, ideas, and content. Still another alternative is the presentation of subject matter in both oral and written forms which have been simplified for the LEP special education student. Specific vocabulary items may be explained in words more familiar to the students; sentences may be made shorter and structures simpler.

The language-experience approach is an excellent way to initiate students into print via the pupils' own language (Jeffree & Skeffington, 1986). In the process of providing language experiences in a variety of topics, a great many reading skills are developed. Content area can become an excellent source for students to illustrate, write, and read their own books.

A suitable reading program to address the specific reading skills of students can be designed in the context of content area topics. Reading skills can be mediated through content area. Mediation is a strategy to make problem readers participate in a wider range of literacy events (Cochran-Smith, 1988). Through this process teachers read with the student, and they fill in some of the gaps that exist between the student's ability and the print they are attempting to read. With time, teachers provide less and less help since the students progress in making use of print by themselves.

Mathematics

All students are expected to receive daily instruction in mathematics at grade level. The language(s) of math instruction for LEP students in bilingual special education classes must be clearly specified in each student's Individualized Education Plan (IEP). The language of instruction is the native language when this is the strongest or dominant language. Students can think faster and with more accuracy in their primary language. Mathematical terminology in English can be introduced gradually, using an alternatve language approach in which main or selected concepts are presented in English during a summary of the lesson after the lesson has been completed in the native language. The terminology and concepts are then reinforced in meaningful contexts during English as a Second Language instruction.

Math instruction in English is implemented in an English as a second language approach by teaching the cognitive aspects of the curriculum, the mathematical skills, and the second language at the same time. As with other subjects, the language is simplified, the concepts are represented in manipulatives or audiovisual materials, and semantic features of the language are adequately explained in context.

Along with establishing the language of instruction, the teacher's challenge is to select the combination of approaches to meet every student's instructional objectives in mathematics. Thematically related topics or units of instruction that integrate mathematics with other disciplines should always be alternated with specific math skill development lessons. Such thematic approaches are more conducive to the application of already learned math facts and basic computation skills.

Many students may not have mastered math facts before working with math problems, thereby increasing the difficulty of the task. Sometimes this difficulty may be incorrectly attributed to a linguistic weakness that requires more language instruction, which can delay attacking the real troublesome area. Reinforcement of math facts in the strongest language is the best way to accelerate a bilingual students who is considerably delayed or ready to give up on math work.

Since the acquisition of mathematical concepts involves mastery of words and linguistic structures that carry complex meanings, LEP students most commonly will encounter difficulties in the following areas, according to a Lansing Board of Education (1988) publication: word/symbol recognition; the processes followed in basic computation and problem solving; and mathematical reasoning. The benefits of making specific linguistic adaptations to enable students with special needs to learn those processes have been documented in research (Ekwall & Milson, 1980). Allowing students to verbalize prior to engaging in written numerical work results in an increase of correct responses. The facilitation of language fluency helps in the development of cognitive skills involved in learning math.

The following is a list of suggestions for teaching mathematics to LEP students in special education programs (Segan & Rossell, 1986):

1. Provide materials that allow LEP students to involve their senses (touch, sight, smell, etc.); involve LEP students in many different types of manipulative acitivities.

2. Use concrete items to illustrate mathematical concepts: milk cartons, coins, beads, flannel board, and so on; use cultural games such as dominoes as well as counting devices such as the Chinese abacus. (Most of these learning tools can be made by the students; giant dominoes can be made out of cardboard or wood; and abacuses can be made from wood, nails, and bottle caps or beads.)
3. Clarify specialized math vocabulary and expressions that may cause difficulty for LEP students, for example, "power," "round off," and so on; provide practice in how to read a word problem, how to analyze its vocabulary and content, and then how to plan a sequence of actions to solve the problem; focus on "what is given" and "what is asked for"; utilize rebuses that may help LEP students in comprehending story problems.
4. Personalize word problems by adding students' names and the name of familiar stores, people, and so on from the community or their daily life experiences.
5. Emphasize the contributions of different cultural groups to the field of mathematics, such as the Mayan, the Greek, and so on.
6. Compare the use and value of coins and currency used in the United States with those used in the students' native countries; contrast standard and metric measurement systems; have students make picture books to assist them in learning measurement concepts.
7. Develop card files and language master cards with key vocabulary and symbols to help students review on their own; use counting games, songs, and so on, to develop math vocabulary and concepts through oral and written modes, and to reinforce them through rhythms and intonations.
8. Be aware that students may know how to do division in a different way from the approach used in the United States. For example:

$$25\,/\,\underline{4} \qquad\qquad \text{versus} \qquad\qquad \underline{6}$$
$$1\ \ 6 \qquad\qquad\qquad\qquad\qquad 4\ \ /\,25$$
$$\qquad\qquad\qquad\qquad\qquad\qquad\qquad -\,\underline{24}$$
$$\qquad\qquad\qquad\qquad\qquad\qquad\qquad 1$$

(The first process stresses the partitioning of the whole; the second, the number of given sets in a whole.)
9. Be aware that students in other countries may write numbers differently: that is, 10,000 as 10.000 and $1.50 as $1,50. Note the following numerical system outside of the United States:

$$1.000.000 = 1 \text{ million}$$
$$1.000.000.000 = 1 \text{ thousand million}$$
$$1.000.000.000.000 = 1 \text{ billion}$$
$$1.000.000.000.000.000 = 1 \text{ thousand billion}$$

Teachers must develop an understanding of the various difficulties handicapped LEP students may encounter as they try to learn mathematics. Repeated, precise educational diagnosis of student difficulties is essential for the proper selection of strategies. It is also important that teachers understand that all children can become good math learners.

Science and Social Studies

The teaching of science and social studies provides excellent opportunities for the development of language and for the acquisition of a second language. While science and social studies concepts are built as linguistic concepts are developed, language skills are constantly reinforced through the progressive development of intellectual and investigative skills. The introduction of second language skills in a meaningful science or social studies context facilitates the earlier acquisition of those advanced language skills which help develop cognitive skills.

Simple lessons that integrate content area and ESL are enriching experiences because they provide much practice in the application of language in real-life activities and daily conversations. Science lessons demand little initial reading but maximize observation, reasoning, manipulation of materials and equipment, and experimentation. Science activities can be structured around following verbal and visual directions and active participation. Social studies lessons prepare students for reading since they maximize listening, listening with comprehension, reasoning, discussing events and their consequences, and manipulating new words and new ideas.

Science and social studies subject matter must be presented in ways that promote oral language exchanges in both natural and formal situations. In these content areas in particular, teachers need to prepare lessons with an emphasis on activity, not on traditional lectures or book situations. Students need to get involved in doing, building, observing, making deductions, listening and analyzing news and events, and interacting with both the natural environment and the social system in which they live. Only by creating and maintaining such an interactive learning environment can these subjects be effectively presented to special students.

An adapted academic curriculum includes activities in which there are varied kinds of work for individuals, pairs, small groups, as well as the whole class. Students interact in flexible groupings where verbal interaction and cooperation are encouraged. They learn optimally through specific projects that are interesting and relevant to their lives. Examples of such activities include the study of maps, obtaining information from a nearby museum, an art show, a movie, a special TV show, preparing a trip, a dialogue, and interview, and collecting or taking pictures from people, natural phenomena, and events. Texts at grade level should be made available in English and the native language for students and parents to use as references.

Science and social studies are subjects that make students discover over and over the world that surrounds them. These discoveries help students expand their vocabulary and conceptualization while they learn to understand themselves and their place in the world. When they realize that they are part of a group, a family, a city, a nation, the world, they feel accepted, and can then participate, contribute, and lately modify their environment and social context. By acquiring a sense of curiosity and wonder about how and why things function, how changes occur and what effect actions have, children acquire a sense of control over their environment, as well as a deeper understanding and respect for it.

Occupational Education

The purpose of an occupational education curriculum or sequence is that students develop broad, transferable employment skills, as well as job-specific skills. Student leadership skills are also integrated in the objectives of the program. Sequences for high school students may include units in agriculture, business/marketing, health occupations, home economics, technical and industrial arts, and trade and industrial education. A general introduction to occupations is part of the curriculum. Students can learn about technology and home and career skills in the junior high or intermediate school in order to develop an experiential foundation in occupational education. Occupationally related math and science courses can be offered for students pursuing a high school diploma.

A meaningful occupational program for handicapped LEP students must be designed based on the relationship between a student's characteristics, cultural background, and the labor market in the area of future accessibility to the student. In the case of students who cannot adjust easily to societal demands, occupational education can increase the ability to connect productively with the social group and to develop adaptation through interpersonal exchanges and active participation. A functional ability in each language in the specific vocational area is one general goal for students in bilingual programs.

Music and Art

The music and art curricula have enormous educational value, which is of particular interest in bilingual special education classes. When music and art are made part of classroom activities, they can create the balance in which students are clearly challenged but not overwhelmed (Ovando & Collier, 1985). The educational advantages of the music and art activities are the development of different competences, which can take place during pleasant, nonthreatening experiences. The following is a summary of areas that are facilitated through the integration or direct teaching of music and art:

Sociocultural value:
    develops aesthetic appreciation
    promotes creativity and resourcefulness
    develops organization and value
    incorporates elements of diverse cultures
    helps identify talents, interests, and vocations

Cognitive-academic value:
    develops keen understanding of content
    promotes practice and reinforcement of skills
    complements and enriches curriculum
    promotes abstract thinking

Linguistic value:
    develops the four language skills
    introduces vocabulary in context
    reinforces grammatical structures
    promotes communication

Emotional and psycho-motoric value:
    motivates participation
    can be therapeutic
    relaxes or cheers students

promotes nonverbal expression

utilizes visual imagery

promotes psychomotor development through synchronized movement, gestural communication, physical response, and use of body
parts

The music and art programs generally integrate the following types of
activities:

music listening	drawing	collage
singing	painting	weaving
rhymes	sculpture	stitchery
chants	pottery	printmaking
jump rope rhymes	crafts	fingerplay
action songs	puppetry	skits/drama
theater production	photography	dance
musical instruments	jewelry making	origami
face painting	mask making	piñatas

It is important to set up an art center in each class. There should
be enough materials for everyone to use. Basic materials include: scissors,
glue, oaktag, construction paper, and paint. "Scrounge" materials include
cloth straps, buttons, yarn, tissue, styrofoam pieces, and other collec-
tions.

Songs in various languages and crafts from different cultures provide
for essential experiences in bilingual special education classes.

Artistic or musical activities can also be part of celebrations or school
events. These activities tend to be more elaborate and require rehearsals.
They can be very rewarding for students. A well-rounded educational
plan must keep a strict balance between time on academic tasks and
other cultural or artistic events.

Lesson Planning

The following sample lesson plans integrate area and language development. The first lesson is applicable in a readiness class with a small
group of learning handicapped students from bilingual backgrounds. Its
aim is to develop mathematics (counting and sequencing skills), English
as a second language (numbers and animal words), linguistic practice
(verb gerunds), and the cognitive skills of correspondence (matching
word/symbol) memorization of a poem, and prewriting skills (recon-
struction of story with pictures).

Grade level: Kindergarten
English as a second language (ESL) level: Beginning
Subjects: Math and ESL
Topic: Numbers 1, 2, 3. Number words one, two, three.
Annual goals: Develop math language
     Develop counting skills

Short term objectives:
 Introduce counting from 1 to 3
 Develop one-to-one correspondence
 Develop sequencing skills
ESL objectives:
 Develop language patterns through poetry
 Develop counting pattern
 Introduce verb gerund
Problem/Cognitive task:
 How to count from number one to number three
 How to represent the counting pattern with hands on, one-to-one
 correspondences
Content vocabulary:
 one-two-three
ESL vocabulary:
 sentence patterns—one, two, three
 counting patterns—one, two, three
 animal words—kittens, frogs, bears, ducks
 verb gerunds—wearing, sitting, walking, riding
 nouns—mittens, logs, steps, trucks
Materials:
 Poem, flannel board, flannel board characters.
 Follow-up—poem folder with sentence strips.
Motivation:
 Teacher reads the poem, while introducing the flannel characters:

I see three

I see three, one, two, three.	I see three, one, two, three.
Three little kittens all wearing mittens. I see three, one, two, three.	Three little bears walking up stairs I see three, one, two, three.

| Three little frogs | three little ducks |
| sitting on logs. | riding on trucks |

Procedure:

1. Sort the flannel characters into groups.
2. Ask if anyone can count how many kittens, bears, etc., in any language.
3. Introduce the poem while showing the flannel figures.
   Recite the poem in its entirety.
4. Recite poem phrase by phrase, while pointing to visual characters. Children repeat after each phrase.
5. Have the whole group recite the entire poem while one child points to the visuals.
6. Remove flannel figures and select volunteers, one at a time, to reconstruct the poem.
7. Count other objects available in the classroom.

Evaluation:

1. Are children reconstructing the poem? (Flannel board and characters are available in library center.)
2. Can all children recite the poem?
3. Can all children count to three?
4. Are children using the poem folder and the sentence strips?
5. Worksheet: Can children color three out of five of the images?

Example:

.Color three squares

☐   ☐   ☐   ☐   ☐

.Color three stars

☆   ☆   ☆   ☆   ☆

Followup activity:

1. Developing sequencing skills—
   Which animal is first in the poem?
   Which is next? Which is last?
2. Developing sequencing and ordering skills—
   Which animal is first?
   Which is second, third, fourth?
3. Developing readiness in reading and writing—
   Make a book of this poem.
   Each child completes a page, drawing and copying a phrase.

(The above lesson was developed by Barbara McCarthy, Early Childhood Education teacher in the New York City Public School System.)

The next sample lesson plan integrates several content area subjects and the medium of cinematography. Since the film is silent, it facilitates the development of any appropriate dialogue and interpretation presented by the students. The thematic approach used in this lesson consists of discussing geographical locations where the scene may have taken place, perhaps Alaska or any other country. The countries can be located on the world map or globe. The weather conditions may lead to a science discussion on seasons, temperature, natural phenomena, and the senses. Nutrition and health topics, as well as feelings, will easily emerge.

Grade level: Third grade.
                Bilingual special education class.
ESL level: Intermediate
Subjects: Social Studies, ESL, Nutrition
Topic: How does hunger affect us?
Objectives: Students will understand effects of hunger on our senses
                and our rationality.
                Students will describe the conditions that provoked hunger.
                Students will reconstruct the possible monologues and dialogues of the movie.
Vocabulary: storm, snow, cabin, alone,
hungry, bully, funny, chase,
shoe, sole of a shoe, eat, chicken,
table, plate, salt, knife, fork.

Procedure:
1. The class will watch a sequence in the Charlie Chaplin film, *The Gold Rush*. (The scene takes place in a log cabin in Alaska in the midst of a blizzard. Charlie Chaplin and a very large brutish prospector are stranded in the cabin for days without food. Out of desperation, Charlie Chaplin cooks the sole of his shoe, salting it, setting the table for the two of them, and delicately devouring it. The bully, however, is not satisfied with the shoe. His mind begins playing tricks on him. He looks at Charlie Chaplin and sees a tasty roast chicken instead. The results are hilarious.)
2. As the students watch this *silent film,* the teacher will translate the small amounts of English subtitles into the language of the students.
3. At the end of the film clip, the teacher will use appropriate questioning techniques to ask the children about the film, introducing the vocabulary words in English.

4. Some of the vocabulary words will be reinforced by pictures. Other words, such as *hungry, bully,* and *chase* may be acted out by the students. Students may want to reenact the entire scene.
5. The students will copy the list of new words into their notebooks and into flash cards to include in their Word Bank.

Evaluation:

Students will expand scenes of the film and their implications to weather, nutrition, or imagination.

Students will write sentences using the vocabulary to describe the scenes or to create their own story.

Following the lesson, milk and cookies will be served.

(The above lesson was developed by Peter Jaffe, crisis intervention teacher in a New York City school).

SUMMARY

This chapter presented general considerations on teaching content area to limited English proficient handicapped students. Areas of consideration were the language of instruction, when to introduce reading in content area, the need for students to develop the native language and English as a second language, and curriculum adaptations that are needed in the design of bilingual special education programs conducive to effective teaching of curriculum content areas. Classroom organization, school support, and the framework of multicultural education were discussed since these are basic to the implementation of effective teaching. Specific curriculum adaptations and teaching strategies, as well as values and goals, were presented for these specific curricular areas: language arts, mathematics, science and social studies, music and art, and vocational education. The chapter concluded with two sample lesson plans to demonstrate the use of strategies and the implementation of curriculum and language development concepts through an integrative approach.

REFERENCES

Backman, L.F., & Savignon, S.J. (1986). The evaluation of communicative language proficiency: A critique of the ACTFL oral interview. *The Modern Language Journal, 70*(4), 380–389.

Bernstein, D.K., & Tiegerman, E. (1985). *Language and communication disorders in children.* Columbus, OH: Charles E. Merrill.

Bozinou-Doukas, E. (1983). Learning disability: The case of the bilingual child. In D. Omark & J. Good Erickson (Eds.), *The bilingual exceptional child.* San Diego, CA: College-Hill Press.

Brophy, J. (1982, April). Successful teaching strategies for the inner-city child. *Phi Delta Kappan,* pp. 527–530.

Carrasquillo, A.L. (1984). The most well known methods for teaching reading in Spanish. In A.L. Carrasquillo & P. Segan (Eds.), *The teaching of reading in Spanish to the bilingual student.* Madrid: Ediciones Alcala, S.A.

Carrell, P.L. & Eisterhold, J.C. (1983). Schema theory and ESL reading pedagogy. *TESOL Quarterly, 17,* 553–573.

Chamot, A.U., & O'Malley, J.M. (1986). *A Cognitive Academic Language Learning Approach: An ESL content-based curriculum.* Rosslyn, VA: National Clearinghouse for Bilingual Education.

Cochran-Smith, M. (1988). Mediating: An important role for the reading teacher. In C.N. Hedley & J.S. Hicks (Eds.), *Reading and the special learner* (pp. 109–139). Norwood, NJ: Ablex Publishing.

Cummins, J. (1982). Tests, achievment, and bilingual education. In *FOCUS* (no. 9). Rosslyn, VA: National Clearinghouse for Bilingual Education.

Cummins, J. (1984). *Bilingualism and special education: Issues in assessment and pedagogy.* San Diego, CA: College-Hill Press.

Ekwall, E.C., & Milson, J.L. (1980). When students can't read textbooks and lab manuals. *School Science and Mathematics, 80*(2), 93–96.

Finocchiaro, M. (1986). *English as a second/foreign language. From theory to practice.* New York: Regents Publishing Company, Inc.

Friedenberg, J.E., & Bradley, C.H. (1988). *A handbook for vocational ESL.* Bloomington, IL: Meridian Education Corporation.

Gaardner, A.B. (1978). Bilingual education: Central questions and concerns. In H. LaFontaine, B. Persky, & L.H. Golubchich (Eds.), *Bilingual education* (pp. 33–38). Wayne, NJ: Avery Publishing.

Harris, A.J., & Sipay, E.R. (1979). *How to teach reading— A competency based program.* New York: Longman.

Jacobson, R. (1981). The implementation of a bilingual instruction model: The new concurrent approach. In R.V. Padilla (Ed.), *Ethnoperspectives in bilingual education research: Vol. 3 . Bilingual education technology* (pp. 14–29). Ypsilanti, MI: Eastern Michigan University.

Jeffree, D., & Skeffington, M. (1986). *Reading is for everyone. A guide for parents and teachers of exceptional children.* Englewood Cliffs, NJ: Prentice-Hall.

Jones, B.F., Sullivan Palincsar, P.A., Sederburg Ogle, D., & Glyn Carr, E. (Eds.). (1987). *Strategic teaching and learning: Cognitive instruction in the content areas.* Elmhurst, IL: North Central Regional Educational Laboratory.

Krashen, S.D. (1981). Bilingual education and second language acquisition theory. In California State Department of Education (Ed.), *Schooling and language minority students: A theoretical framework* (pp. 51–79). Sacramento, CA: Editor.

Krashen, S.D. (1982). *Principles and practice in second language acquisition.* New York: Pergamon Press.

Krashen, S.D., & Terrell, T.D. (1983). *The natural approach. Natural acquisition in the classroom.* Hayward, CA: Alemany Press.

Lambie, R.A., & Hutchens, P.W. (1980, Spring). Adapting elementary school mathematics instruction. *Teaching Exceptional Children,* pp. 185–189.

Lansing Board of Education. (1988). *Math in a limited English world* (Manual for middle school teachers). Lansing, MI: Lansing Michigan School District, Bilingual Instructional Center.

New Levine, L. (1985). Content area instruction for the elementary school LEP student. In *TESOL '84: A brave new world for TESOL* (pp. 233–240). Washington, DC: Georgetown University.

New York City Board of Education. (1987a). *Adapting curriculum for students in special education: A teacher's handbook.* New York: Division of Special Education, Office of Curriculum and Professional Development.

New York City Board of Education. (1987b). *Bilingual special education program models.* New York: Division of Special Education, Office of Bilingual Services.

New York State Education Department. (1987). *Guidelines for services to students with limited English proficiency and special education needs in New York State.* Albany, NY: Author.

Ortiz, A.A. (1984). Choosing the language of instruction for exceptional bilingual children. *Teaching Exceptional Childdren, 16,* 208–212.

Ortiz, A.A. & Garcia, S.B. (1988). A prereferral process for preventing inappropriate referrals of Hispanic students to special education. In A.A. Ortiz & B.A. Ramirez (Eds.), *Schools and the culturally diverse exceptional student: Promising practices and future directions.* Reston, VA: The Council for Exceptional Children.

Ovando, C.M., & Collier, V.P. (1985). *Bilingual and ESL classrooms: Teaching in multicultural contexts.* New York: McGraw-Hill Book Company.

Piaget, J. (1952). *The origin of intelligence in children* (2nd ed.). New York: International University Press.

Segan, F., & Rossell, A. (1986). *Suggestions for teaching mathematics to LEP students in special education.* Unpublished manuscript, Office of Program Development, Division of Special Education, New York City Board of Education.

Thonis, E.W. (1970). *Teaching reading to non-English speakers.* New York: Macmillan.

Tikunoff, W.J. (1983). *An emerging description of successful bilingual instruction: Executive summary of Part I of the SBIT descriptive study.* San Francisco: Far West Laboratory for Educational Research and Development

Valdez, G. (1981). Pedagogical implications of teaching Spanish to the Spanish-speaking in the United States. In G. Valez, A.G. Lozano, & R. Garcia-Moya (Eds.), *Teaching Spanish to the Hispanic bilingual: Issues, aims, and methods* (pp. 3–20). New York: Teachers College Press.

Wong-Fillmore, L. (1980). *Language learning bilingual instruction.* Unpublished manuscript, University of California, Berkeley.

chapter 10

The Cognitive Academic Language Learning Approach: A Bridge to the Mainstream*

Anna Uhl Chamot
J. Michael O'Malley

The major objective of ESL Programs at the elementary and secondary levels in the United States is to prepare students to function successfully in classrooms where English is the medium of instruction for all subject areas. The approaches used to achieve this objective vary considerably, despite their common intent. A recent national survey (Chamot & Stewner-Manzanares, 1985) of the state of the art in ESL in public schools, for example, found that of 13 different instructional approaches currently in use, the most widely cited by a sample of school districts, Bilingual Education Multifunctional Support Centers, and teacher trainers in representative universities were the audiolingual method, the Natural Approach, Total Physical Response, communicative approaches, and eclectic or combination approaches. None of these approaches, whatever their other merits or deficiencies, focuses specifically on developing the English language skills used in content-area subjects, such as science, mathematics, and social studies.

Students in ESL programs develop many important skills in English and may become quite proficient in day-to-day survival in English. At the conclusion of one or more years of ESL instruction, minority-language students may perform satisfactorily on language proficiency assessment measures and be judged by their teachers as proficient in English communicative skills. They are then mainstreamed into the all-English curriculum, where typically they encounter severe difficulties with the academic program. This problem has been attributed to the increased language demands made by the academic curriculum, particularly as students move beyond the primary grade level. Various re-

---

* This article is reprinted from *TESOL Quarterly, 21,* 227–249. Copyright 1987. Reprinted by permission.

searchers have found that the development of these academic language skills lags behind the development of social communicative language skills, often by as much as 5 to 7 years (Cummins, 1983, 1984; Saville-Troike, 1984).

Before entering the mainstream curriculum, minority-language students should be able to use English as a tool for learning subject matter. This ability becomes particularly acute from the middle elementary grades onward because in these upper grades the language of subjects such as social studies, science, and mathematics becomes more academic and less closely related to the language of everyday communication than is the case at the primary grade level. By the middle elementary grades, students are expected to have mastered basic skills in reading, writing, and computation and to understand and use increasingly abstract language. At this level, and increasingly at higher grade levels, the curriculum requires that students listen and read to acquire new information, speak and write to express their understanding of new concepts, use mathematics skills to solve problems, and apply effective strategies for learning to all areas of the curriculum. For the minority-language student, these requirements of the upper elementary and secondary school entail additional language demands. Language proficiency, which may have previously focused on communicative competence, must now focus on academic competence.

A DESCRIPTION OF THE COGNITIVE ACADEMIC LANGUAGE LEARNING APPROACH

This article describes the Cognitive Academic Language Learning Approach (CALLA), an instructional method for limited-English-proficient (LEP) students who are being prepared to participate in mainstream content instruction. CALLA (pronounced /kalá/) combines English language development with content-based ESL and with instruction in special learner strategies that will help students understand and remember important concepts. Richards (1984) has pointed out that second language methods can be based on a syllabus (or curriculum) or on a theory of learning processes and instructional procedures and that many current methodological approaches reflect one assumption but not the other. CALLA makes these two approaches to language teaching methods interdependent by integrating language learning and teaching theory and the specification of content to be taught.

Richards (1984) has also indicated the importance of addressing the needs of second language learners in program planning. CALLA is designed to meet the educational needs of three types of LEP students:

(a) students who have developed social communicative skills through ESL or exposure to an English-speaking environment but who have not developed academic language skills appropriate to their grade level; (b) students exiting from bilingual programs who need assistance in transferring concepts and skills learned in their native language to English; and (c) bilingual, English-dominant students who are even less academically proficient in their native language than in English and need to develop academic English language skills.

The bridge that CALLA provides between special language programs and mainstream education is illustrated in Figure 10.1. LEP students in ESL and bilingual programs develop initial skills in understanding, speaking, reading, and writing in English, and they practice the essentials of communication for mainly social purposes. CALLA is intended for students at the intermediate and advanced levels of English proficiency who need additional experiences in English language development specifically related to three academic areas: science, mathematics, and social studies. The intent is to introduce vocabulary, structures, and functions in English by using concepts drawn from content areas. CALLA is not intended to substitute for mainstream content-area instruction or to teach the basic content expertise required in school district curricula, as is the intention of immersion and "sheltered English" programs.

The three content areas addressed by CALLA can be phased into the intermediate-level ESL class one at a time. We recommend beginning with science, since by using a discovery approach to science, teachers can capitalize on experiential learning opportunities which provide both contextual support and language development. The next subject to be introduced is mathematics, which has less contextual support and a more restricted language register than science. Social studies is the third subject introduced in the CALLA Model, since of the three, it is the most language- and culture-dependent; in addition, it includes many topics which are not easily amenable to experiential learning activities. A fourth subject area, English language arts, is a planned addition to the model. Because language is the focus of study as well as the medium through which lessons in literature and composition are taught, this subject is the most language-dependent of all, and it is also probably at least as culture-dependent as social studies.

The CALLA Model has three components: (a) a curriculum correlated with mainstream content areas, (b) English language development integrated with content subjects, and (c) instruction in the use of learning strategies. Each of these components is examined separately, following a discussion of the theoretical framework underlying CALLA. The final section of this chapter provides guidelines for integrating these components into a single instructional approach.

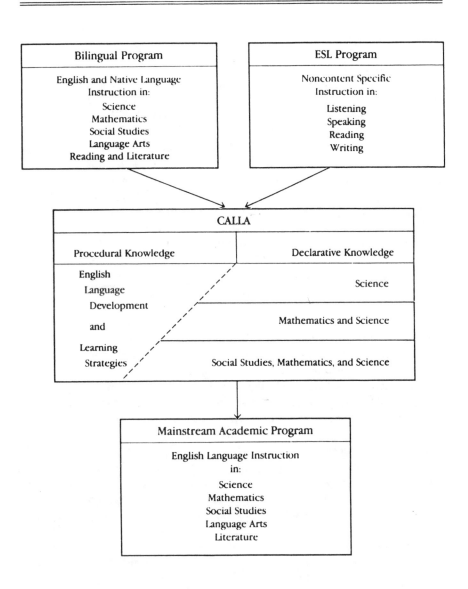

Figure 10.1. The CALA Model: A Bridge to the Mainstream.

THEORETICAL BACKGROUND

A brief examination of the theoretical base for CALLA illustrates the relationship between this instructional approach and current developments in cognitive psychology. Recent efforts to describe both second language acquisition and learning strategies within the cognitive theory proposed by Anderson (1981, 1983, 1985) provide the necessary theoretical foundation (O'Malley, Chamot, & Walker, 1987).

In Anderson's view, information is stored in memory in two forms: *declarative knowledge,* or what we know about a given topic, and *procedural knowledge,* or what we know how to do. Examples of declarative knowledge include word definitions, facts, and rules, including our memory for images and sequences of events. This type of knowledge is represented in long-term memory in terms of meaning-based concepts rather than precisely replicated events or specific language. The concepts on which meaning is based are represented in memory as nodes that are associated with other nodes through connecting associations or links. These interconnected nodes may be organized into propositions, which show the relationships of arguments in sentences; into hierarchies, which show classification relationships with similar concepts in memory; or into larger units of memory called schemata, which reveal a configuration of interrelated features that define a concept. In any of these representations, the strength of associations in the link between nodes is largely due to prior learning experiences.

Procedural knowledge underlies our ability to understand and generate language. According to Anderson's theory, procedural knowledge is represented in memory by production systems, which are the basis for explaining how complex cognitive skills such as language are learned and used. Production systems are rule-based conditional actions (*if-then* relationships) which are initially represented like declarative knowledge but which may become automatic through repeated practice. Production systems have been used to describe procedural knowledge in reading, mathematical problem solving, and chess, as well as language comprehension and production. Production systems have been used by Anderson (1983) to represent linguistic rules and by O'Malley et al. (1987) to represent sociolinguistic, discourse, and strategic competence.

Whereas declarative knowledge of factual information may be acquired quickly, procedural knowledge such as language skill is acquired gradually and only with extensive opportunities for practice. Anderson indicates that language is a complex cognitive process which requires explicit or implicit knowledge about language as a system and extensive practice in order to reach an autonomous stage. This theoretical distinction is a familiar one to second language teachers, who tend to alternate between teaching language as declarative knowledge (grammar, rules, pronunciation, vocabulary) and language as procedural knowledge (communicative competence, functional proficiency, fluency).

What is most important about Anderson's theory is that an interplay between declarative and procedural knowledge leads to the refinement of language ability. Anderson discusses ways in which new information is processed in working memory and accessed to long-term memory, from which it can be retrieved at a later date. He identifies three empirically derived stages that describe the process by which a complex cognitive skill such as language is acquired: (a) a cognitive stage, in which learning is deliberate, rule based, and often error laden; (b) an associative stage, in which actions are executed more rapidly and errors begin to diminish; and (c) an autonomous stage, in which actions are performed more fluently and the original rule governing the performance may no longer be retained. Thus, as the same procedure is used repeatedly, access to the rules that originally produced the procedure may be lost.

Although he does not mention learning strategies, Anderson's description of these cognitive processes is congruent with the types of learning strategies which have been identified in research with LEP students (Cohen & Aphek, 1981; Naiman, Frohlich, Stern, & Todesco, 1978; O'Malley, Chamot, Stewner-Manzanares, Kupper, & Russo, 1985; O'Malley, Chamot, Stewner-Manzanares, Russo, & Kupper, 1985). A number of the mental processes Anderson discusses serve to explain how strategies are represented, how they are learned, and how they influence second language acquisition. O'Malley et al. (1987) have suggested that learning strategies are declarative knowledge which may become procedural knowledge through practice. Learning strategies are conscious and deliberate when they are in the cognitive and associative stages of learning but may no longer be considered strategic in the autonomous stage, since the strategies are applied automatically and often without awareness (Rabinowitz & Chi, 1987). As with other complex cognitive skills, the strategies are acquired only with extensive opportunities for application.

Viewing second or foreign language acquisition as a cognitive skill offers several advantages for research on language learning strategies. Anderson's model provides a comprehensive and well-specified theoretical framework for second language learning and can be adapted to provide a detailed process view of how students acquire and retain a new language. This model can also help to identify and describe the existence and use of specific learning strategies for different types of learners at various stages in second language development. Finally, a cognitive-skill model of second language acquisition can provide guidance in the selection and application of learning strategies in the instruction of second and foreign language students.

We have applied Anderson's theoretical principles to the CALLA model in the following preliminary way:

1. The content component of the CALLA model represents declarative knowledge. This includes the concepts, facts, and skills underlying science, mathematics, and social studies at the student's grade level. An extension of these content areas to include English language arts would add grammatical knowledge, rhetorical knowledge, and knowledge about literary themes, plots, and story grammars to this store of declarative knowledge.

2. The language development component of CALLA aims to teach the procedural knowledge that students need to use language as a tool for learning. In this component, students are given sufficient practice in using language in academic contexts so that language comprehension and production become automatic and students develop the ability to communicate about academic subjects.

3. The learning strategies instruction component of the CALLA model builds on Anderson's theory and suggests ways in which teachers can foster autonomy in their students. Many of the learning strategies identified in previous research (O'Malley, Chamot, & Kupper, 1986; O'Malley, Chamot, Stewner-Manzaneres, Kupper, & Russo, 1985; O'Malley, Chamot, Stewner-Manzanares, Russo, & Kupper, 1985; Rubin, 1981; Wenden, 1985) can be used as powerful learning tools.

COMPONENTS OF THE MODEL

The Content-Based Curriculum

The importance of integrating language learning with content learning has been stated by Mohan (1986):

> Regarding language as a medium of learning naturally leads to a cross-curriculum perspective. We have seen that reading specialists contrast learning to read with reading to learn. Writing specialists contrast learning to write with writing to learn. Similarly, language education specialists should distinguish between language learning and using language to learn. Helping students use language to learn requires us to look beyond the

language domain to all subject areas and to look beyond language learning to education in general. Outside the isolated language classroom students learn language and content at the same time. Therefore we need a broad perspective which integrates language and content learning. (p. 18)

The purpose of CALLA is to provide a broad framework for using language to learn through the integration of language and content.

Content-based English language development is not only important for developing academic language skills, but it is also inherently more interesting to many students than ESL classes which focus on language only. Content areas such as science, mathematics, and social studies present numerous topics related to a variety of personal interests. LEP students can be motivated not only by the topics presented but also by knowing that they are developing the concepts and skills associated with these subjects—in other words, that they are actually doing "real" schoolwork instead of merely learning a second language for applications that have yet to be revealed.

LEP students making the transition from a special language program such as bilingual education or ESL need systematic and extensive instruction and practice in the types of activities they will encounter in the mainstream class. An occasional, randomly selected ESL lesson on a topic in social studies or science will not adequately prepare students. This is especially true in the middle and upper grade levels, where the curriculum in the content areas becomes progressively more demanding, both in terms of information load and language demands. To be most effective, a content-based ESL curriculum should encompass the sequence and major-scope areas of the mainstream curriculum. The topics incorporated should be authentic and important topics for the grade level of the student.

In a beginning-level ESL class, for example, middle and upper grade (as well as primary grade) students learn to count and do simple arithmetic computation in English. But this is not an appropriate content-based, English language development curriculum for older students because it is not sufficiently challenging. A curriculum that merely reviews concepts and skills already developed in the first language can rapidly become a series of exercises in translation of vocabulary and skills from L1 to L2 and may not stimulate students to begin to use the second language as a tool for learning. Instead, students who already have a background in a content area and who have already developed English proficiency through ESL instruction need a content-based curriculum in which they use English to solve problems and develop additional concepts that are appropriate for their grade and achievement level.

For these reasons, it is important that the content component be based on the mainstream curriculum for the grade level of the students who will participate in the program. This does not mean that it should be identical to the mainstream program (which would make it a submersion model) or that it should replace the mainstream program (as in immersion and "sheltered English" programs). Rather, a CALLA curriculum includes a sample of high-priority content topics that develop academic language skills appropriate to the subject area at the student's grade level. Of course, adjustments will need to be made in the case of students whose previous schooling has been interrupted and who are therefore not at grade level in their native language. As with any instructional program, teachers should discover what students already know about a subject and then build on this previous knowledge by providing them with experiences that develop new concepts and expand previous ones.

To select content topics for CALLA lessons, ESL teachers can coordinate with classroom teachers and consult subject-area textbooks for the grade level concerned. Classroom teachers can identify the most important concepts and skills taught in the content areas they teach. Science, mathematics, and social studies textbooks can be used as a source of specific information to be presented. Having used these resources to identify lesson topics, the ESL teacher can build language development activities onto the content information selected.

To sum up, the CALLA content-based curriculum is based on authentic subject matter from the mainstream curriculum which has been selected as central to the concepts and skills that are developed at particular grade levels.

English Language Development

The purpose of English language development, the second component of the CALLA model, is to provide students with practice in using English as a tool for learning academic subject matter. Reading and language arts can be taught as part of content-area subjects such as social studies, mathematics, and science. The language demands of the different content subjects, which include the language of curriculum materials and of classroom participation, need to be analyzed so that students can be taught the actual language functions, structures, and subject-specific vocabulary that they will need when they enter the mainstream content class. These language demands, which are different from those of the beginning-level ESL class or the type of language used for social interaction, need to be specifically taught and practiced in the context of actual subject-matter learning.

Cummins (1982, 1983) indicates that two dimensions can be used to describe the language demands encountered by LEP students. The first dimension concerns contextual cues that assist comprehension, and the second concerns the complexity of the task. Language that is most comprehensible is contextualized and rich in nonverbal cues such as concrete objects, gestures, facial expressions, and visual aids. Language that is least comprehensible is language in which context cues have been reduced to such a degree that comprehension depends entirely on the listener's or reader's ability to extract meaning from text without assistance from a nonverbal context.

The second dimension, task complexity, suggests that comprehension is affected by the cognitive demands of the task. Examples of less demanding language tasks are vocabulary, grammar drills, and following directions. More cognitively demanding tasks call on the use of language for higher-level reasoning and for integrative language skills (e.g., reading and listening comprehension, speaking or writing about academic topics). By combining these two dimensions, tasks involving language use can be classified into one of four categories: easy and contextualized, difficult but contextualized, context-reduced but easy, and context-reduced and difficult.

Although context-reduced language is commonly associated with written language, oral language can also vary along the context-embedded to context-reduced continuum. Davidson, Kline, and Snow (1986) define contextualized oral language as conversational, interactive, and supported by shared knowledge and experiences. Decontextualized oral language, on the other hand, is characterized as language that is not interactive and concerns a topic on which no shared knowledge exists. This seems a fair description of much of the content and presentation style in typical subject-area instruction.

Figure 10.2 is based on Cummins' (1982) model of two intersecting continua of second language tasks. Allen (1985) has pointed out that ESL classes generally stress activities in Quadrant I and that students are then mainstreamed directly into Quadrant IV activities. The sample activities listed in each quadrant can provide teachers with information about activities appropriate to the English proficiency level and age or grade placement of LEP students. The activities listed in Quadrant I might be used in beginning-level ESL classes. LEP students' first experiences with decontextualized language could be planned around the activities listed in Quadrant II. Some of these activities relate to personal or social communication, and others relate to school activities involving mainly rote learning. Academic content is included in the activities listed in Quadrant III, but context needs to be built into the activities to assist comprehension. Activities in this quadrant require hands-on experiences and concrete referents. Finally, the activities listed in Quadrant IV represent those of the mainstream classroom at the upper elementary and secondary levels. These are the kinds of activities that LEP students have most difficulty with because they are cognitively demanding and because the language associated with them is reduced in context. Although ESL students probably need to begin with Quadrant I activities and must eventually be able to perform Quadrant IV activities, some teachers may prefer that activities in Quadrants II and III take place concurrently rather than sequentially.

An important objective of the English language development component of the CALLA model is to provide students with extensive transitional language activities in Quadrant III and gradually initiate some practice with the context-reduced and cognitively demanding activities of Quadrant IV. Although some language activities may be integrated with mainstream content-area instruction in the typical school curriculum, these may consist primarily of reading for information. LEP students need to develop not only content-area reading skills, but also the listening, speaking, and writing skills associated with each subject. The number and variety of language activities in a content-based curriculum for LEP students should provide many opportunities for the development of academic language proficiency.

The following aspects of language should be included in the language development component of the CALLA model (Chamot, 1985): development of the specialized vocabulary and technical terms of each content area; practice with the language functions used in academic communication, such as explaining, informing, describing, classifying, and evaluating; development of the ability to comprehend and use the language structures and discourse features found in different subject areas; and practice in using the language skills needed in the content classroom, such as listening to explanations, reading for information, participating in academic discussions, and writing reports. By integrating these types of language activities with grade-appropriate content, a curriculum based on the CALLA model can provide LEP students with the conceptual knowledge and language skills they will need to participate successfully in the mainstream classroom.

Learning Strategy Instruction

The CALLA model uses learning strategy instruction as an approach to teaching the content-based language development curriculum de-

Nonacademic or cognitively undemanding activities	Academic and cognitively demanding activities
I	**III**
Developing survival vocabulary	Developing academic vocabulary
Following demonstrated directions	Understanding academic presentations accompanied by visuals, demonstrations of a process, etc.
	Participating in hands-on science activities
Playing simple games	Making models, maps, charts, and graphs in social studies
Participating in art, music, physical education, and some vocational education classes	Solving math computation problems
	Solving math word problems assisted by manipulatives and/or illustrations
Engaging in face-to-face interactions	Participating in academic discussions
Practicing oral language exercises and communicative language functions	Making brief oral presentations
	Using higher level comprehension skills in listening to oral texts
	Understanding written texts through discussion, illustrations, and visuals
	Writing simple science and social studies reports with format provided
Answering lower level questions	Answering higher level questions
II	**IV**
Engaging in predictable telephone conversations	Understanding academic presentations without visuals or demonstrations
	Making formal oral presentations
Developing initial reading skills: decoding and literal comprehension	Using higher level reading comprehension skills: inferential and critical reading
Reading and writing for personal purposes: notes, lists, recipes, etc.	Reading for information in content subjects
Reading and writing for operational purposes: directions, forms, licenses, etc.	Writing compositions, essays, and research reports in content subjects
	Solving math word problems without illustrations
Writing answers to lower level questions	Writing answers to higher level questions
	Taking standardized achievement tests

Context-embedded (left vertical axis, upper)
Context-reduced (left vertical axis, lower)

Figure 10.2. Classification of Language and Content Activities Within Cummins's (1982) Framework.

scribed in the preceding sections. Learning strategy instruction is a cognitive approach to teaching that helps students learn conscious processes and techniques that facilitate the comprehension, acquisition, and retention of new skills and concepts. The use of learning strategy instruction in second language learning is based on four main propositions (see Chipman, Sigel, & Glaser, 1985; Derry & Murphy, 1986; Weinstein & Mayer, 1986):

1. Mentally active learners are better learners. Students who organize new information and consciously relate it to existing knowledge should have more cognitive linkages to assist comprehension and recall than do students who approach each new task as something to be memorized by rote learning.
2. Strategies can be taught. Students who are taught to use strategies and provided with sufficient practice in using them will learn more effectively than students who have had no experience with learning strategies.
3. Learning strategies transfer to new tasks. Once students have become accustomed to using learning strategies, they will use them on new tasks that are similar to the learning activities on which they were initially trained.
4. Academic language learning is more effective with learning strategies. Academic language learning among students of English as a second language is governed by some of the same principles that govern reading and problem solving among native English speakers.

While research evidence supports the first two propositions, the transfer of strategies to new learning requires extensive instructional support. We have attempted to make learning strategy instruction a pervasive part of the CALLA program in response to this need, not only to encourage use of strategies while the students are in CALLA, but also to encourage strategy use when the students exit to the mainstream curriculum.

The fourth proposition is based in part on our own observation that strategies for language learning are similar to strategies for learning content (O'Malley, Chamot, Stewner-Manzanares, Kupper, & Russo, 1985) and in part on our positive experiences with the effects of learning strategy instruction on integrative language tasks among ESL students (O'Malley, Chamot, Stewner-Manzanares, Russo, & Kupper, 1985). While strategies for learning language and content are very similar, LEP students may have difficulty in discovering the application of strategies to content because their attention is focused on figuring out and comprehending the English language. In CALLA, the blending of language and content results in unified learning tasks to which students can apply learning strategies that facilitate the comprehension and retention of both declarative and procedural knowledge.

Strategy instruction, we believe, is necessary to provide LEP students with extra support in learning language and content, especially when they are in the process of making the transition from the simplified language of the beginning-level ESL class to the more authentic language of the intermediate and advanced level. This is not a new notion. Honeyfield (1977), in arguing against simplification of text after the beginning ESL level, suggests an alternative approach in which we would help intermediate and advanced students to "cope earlier with unsimplified materials by giving training in such skills as *inferring unknown meanings from context, giving selective attention to material in accordance with realistic reading purposes, recognizing communicative structure* [italics added], and others" (p. 440). The italicized skill descriptions are precisely what we understand as conscious learning strategies, as defined in the cognitive psychology literature.

Studies in learning strategy applications indicate that students taught to use new strategies can become more effective learners (O'Malley, 1985). In a recent experimental study, second language learners were taught to use learning strategies for vocabulary, listening comprehension, and formal speaking tasks using academic content (O'Malley, Chamot, Stewner-Manzanares, Russo, & Kupper, 1985). The results showed that learning strategy instruction was most effective for the more integrative language tasks which involved the use of academic language skills to understand or produce extended text.

Our original list of learning strategies (see O'Malley, Chamot, Stewner-Manzanares, Russo, & Kupper, 1985) was derived from research on learning strategies in first language reading and problem solving, research in second language learning, and our own initial research. This initial learning strategies list has undergone adaptations based on later research (O'Malley et al., 1986) and on our experiences in training teachers on the CALLA model. The three major categories of learning strategies, however, have continued to be useful in differentiating groups of strategies and in showing teachers how to integrate strategy instruction into their daily lessons. These major categories are as follows:

1. Metacognitive strategies: These involve executive processes in planning for learning, monitoring one's comprehension and production, and evaluating how well one has achieved a learning objective.
2. Cognitive strategies: The learner interacts with the material to be learned by manipulating it mentally (as in making mental images or relating new information to previously acquired concepts or skills)

or physically (as in grouping items to be learned in meaningful categories or taking notes on or making summaries of important information to be remembered).

3. Social-affective strategies: The learner either interacts with another person in order to assist learning, as in cooperation or asking questions for clarification, or uses some kind of affective control to assist learning.

We have selected a smaller number of strategies from the original list of those reported by ESL students (see O'Malley, Chamot, Stewner-Manzanares, Russo, & Kupper, 1985) for teachers to use as the principal instructional approach for CALLA. These, we believe, are strategies which are easy to teach, useful for both discrete and integrative language tasks, and applicable to both content and language learning.

Learning strategies for CALLA are listed and defined in Appendix 1. Some of these strategies may be known to teachers by the term *study skills.* Study skills describe overt behavior, such as taking notes, writing summaries, or using reference materials. Learning strategies, on the other hand, generally refer to mental processes which are not observable. Although this distinction between learning strategies and study skills is important theoretically, we do not believe that it is always necessary to differentiate them in practice.

Some learning strategies are particularly powerful because they can be used for many different types of learning activities. For example, metacognitive strategies which can be applied to any type of learning are selective attention, self-monitoring, and self-evaluation. Students can use selective attention to assist comprehension by attending to the linguistic markers that signal the type of information that will follow. Some examples of phrases which serve as linguistic markers are discussed in Chamot and O'Malley (1986b):

> "Today we're going to talk about . . ." indicates the main topic of the presentation. Markers such as "The most important thing to remember about . . ." indicate that a main idea is about to be presented. When students hear markers such as "For instance . . ." or "An example of . . .," they know that they can expect an example or a detail. And when students hear a marker such as "Finally, . . ." or "In conclusion, . . .," they can expect a concluding summary of the main points. (p. 11)

Self-monitoring is a metacognitive strategy which has been linked to productive language, in which students correct themselves during speaking or writing. We have discovered that effective ESL listeners also use self-monitoring to check on how well they are comprehending an oral text (O'Malley et al., 1986). The consequence of self-monitoring is that students spend more time being actively involved in the comprehension and learning task. Self-evaluation assists learning by helping students decide how well they have accomplished a learning task and whether they need to relearn or review any aspects of it.

A number of cognitive learning strategies can be used by ESL students to assist learning. Elaboration is one of the most powerful strategies and can be applied to all four language skills and to all types of content. When students elaborate, they recall prior knowledge, consciously interrelate parts of what they are learning, and integrate new information to their existing knowledge structure, or schemata. The following example (Chamot & O'Malley, 1986a) illustrates elaboration:

> The learner thinks, "Let's see. I have to read some information about the early history of California. What do I already know about California history? Well, the Spanish were there first, and then it belonged by Mexico, then there was a war between Mexico and the U.S., and now it's an important state . . ." The student goes on to read the assigned text, confirms previous knowledge, and also learns some new facts. During or after reading, the student may think, "Well, I didn't know that there were Russians in California too. Let's see, how does this fit in with what I already know about the Spanish in California?" The student uses elaboration in relating new information to previous knowledge and by incorporating it into an existing conceptual framework. (p. 18)

School tasks often require students to learn new information on topics on which they do not possess existing knowledge, so that elaboration may not be possible. It is important for students in this case to organize the new information effectively so that the information can be retrieved and future efforts to use elaboration will be fruitful. Grouping is a strategy which students without prior knowledge on a topic can use to organize or classify new information. In this way, a network, or schema, is established that will make the new knowledge accessible in the future. Grouping is particularly important in science and social studies content areas, where students need to understand classification systems and cause-and-effect relationships. To facilitate comprehension of groups or sets, students may use the strategy of imagery as a way of making mental or actual diagrams of the structure of new information. Grouping and imagery may be particularly effective in conveying knowledge structures to students whose prior education has been interrupted.

The social-affective learning strategies listed in the Appendix can be helpful for many types of learning activities. Cooperation is a strategy which has been shown to have positive effects on both attitude and learning. It is particularly useful for LEP students because by working cooperatively on a task, they practice using language skills directly related to an academic task. Questioning for clarification is also important because students need to learn how to ask questions when they do not understand. Some LEP students may not know how or when to ask appropriate questions, or even that U.S. teachers expect students to ask questions. Self-talk is an affective strategy in which students allay their anxiety by reassuring themselves about their own abilities. It has been used as a way of helping students overcome test anxiety and could be used in any situation in which students feel anxious about a learning task.

We believe that teachers can help their LEP students become more effective learners in general by showing them how to apply a variety of learning strategies to different activities that they may encounter in learning English as well as other subjects in the curriculum. Suggestions for learning strategy instruction include showing students how to apply the strategies, suggesting a variety of different strategies for the language and content tasks of the curriculum, and providing many examples of learning strategies throughout the curriculum so that students will be able to generalize them to new learning activities in other classes and even outside the classroom (Chamot & O'Malley, 1986a). Effective transfer of strategies to other classes also requires that students be made aware of the strategies they are using and be able to verbalize the conditions under which strategies can be used.

A DESCRIPTION OF A CALLA LESSON PLAN MODEL

To integrate the three components of CALLA, we have developed a lesson plan model that incorporates content-area topics, language development activities, and learning strategy instruction. In this plan, learning strategy instruction is embedded into daily lessons so that it becomes an integral part of the regular class routine, rather than a supplementary activity. In this way, students have opportunities to practice the strategies on actual lessons, and use of the strategies becomes part of the class requirements. At first, the teacher shows the students how to use the strategies and provides reminders and cues so that they will be used. Later, teachers should diminish the reminders to allow students to use strategies independently.

CALLA lessons identify both language and content objectives, so that teachers can specify both procedural and declarative tasks for their

ESL students. The lessons are divided into five phases: Preparation, Presentation, Practice, Evaluation, and Follow-Up Expansion. In the Preparation phase, teachers provide advance organizers about the lesson, and students identify what they already know about a topic, using elaboration as a strategy. In the Presentation phase, teachers provide new information to students, using techniques which make their input comprehensible. Teachers can use advance organizers and encourage the use of selective attention, self-monitoring, inferencing, summarizing, and transfer. In the Practice phase, students engage in activities in which they apply learning strategies, often in cooperative small-group sessions. During this phase, the teacher should encourage the use of strategies such as grouping, imagery, organizational planning, deduction, inferencing, and questioning for clarification. In the Evaluation phase, students reflect on their individual learning and plan to remedy any deficiencies they may have identified. Finally, in the Follow-Up Expansion phase, students are provided with opportunities to relate and apply the new information to their own lives, call on the expertise of their parents and other family members, and compare what they have learned in school with their own cultural experiences.

CONCLUSION

The Cognitive Academic Language Learning Approach, an instructional method for limited-English-proficient students at the intermediate and advanced levels of English proficiency, is intended to be a bridge between bilingual or ESL instruction and academic mainstream classes. It focuses on English language development through cognitively based content-area instruction in science, mathematics, and social studies. CALLA teaches students the academic language skills and learning strategies they need to succeed in content areas and can also help the English-dominant but still limited English proficient bilingual student acquire these types of language skills. The approach addresses the need for English language development in the four language skill areas of listening, reading, speaking, and writing. CALLA is designed to supply added support for English language development among LEP students and is not a replacement for experience in mainstream classes.

REFERENCES

Allen, V. (1985, December). *Language experience techniques for teaching subject content to elementary level limited English proficient students.* Paper presented at the Second Annual LAU Center Conference, Columbus, OH.

Anderson, J.R. (Ed.). (1981). *Cognitive skills and their acquisition.* Hillsdale, NJ: Lawrence Erlbaum.

Anderson, J.R. (1983). *The architecture of cognition.* Cambridge, MA: Harvard University Press.

Anderson, J.R. (1985). *Cognitive psychology and its implications* (2nd ed.). New York: W.H. Freeman.

Chamot, A.U. (1985). English language development through a content-based approach. In *Issues in English language development* (pp. 49–55). Washington, DC: National Clearinghouse for Bilingual Education.

Chamot, A.U., & O'Malley, J.M. (1986a). *A cognitive academic language learning approach: An ESL content-based curriculum.* Washington, DC: National Clearinghouse for Bilingual Education.

Chamot, A.U., & O'Malley, J.M. (1986b). Language learning strategies for children. *The Language Teacher, 10*(1), 9–12.

Chamot, A.U., & Stewner-Manzanares, G. (1985). *A summary of current literature on English as a second language.* McLean, VA: InterAmerica Research Associates.

Chipman, S., Sigel, J., & Glaser, R. (Eds.). (1985). *Thinking and learning skills: Relating learning to basic research* (Vols. 1–2). Hillsdale, NJ: Lawrence Erlbaum.

Cohen, A.D., & Aphek, E. (1981). Easifying second language learning. *Studies in Second Language Acquisition, 3,* 221–236.

Cummins, J. (1982, February). Tests, achievement, and bilingual students. In *Focus* (No. 9). Washington, DC: National Clearinghouse for Bilingual Education.

Cummins, J. (1983). Conceptual and linguistic foundations of language assessment. In S.S. Seidner (Ed.), *Issues of language assessment: Vol. 2. Language assessment and curriculum planning* (pp. 7–16). Washington, DC: National Clearinghouse for Bilingual Education.

Cummins, J. (1984). *Bilingualism and special education: Issues in assessment and pedagogy.* Clevedon, England: Multilingual Matters.

Davidson, R.G., Kline, S.B., & Snow, C.E. (1986). Definitions and definite noun phrases: Indicators of children's decontextualized language skills. *Journal of Research in Childhood Education, 1,* 37–48.

Derry, S.J., & Murphy, D.A. (1986). Designing systems that train learning ability: From theory to practice. *Review of Educational Research, 56,* 1–39.

Honeyfield, J. (1977). Simplification. *TESOL Quarterly, 4,* 431–440.

Mohan, B.A. (1986). *Language and content.* Reading, MA: Addison-Wesley.

Naiman, N., Frohlich, M., Stern, H.H., & Todesco, A. (1978). *The good language learner.* Toronto: Ontario Institute for Studies in Education.

O'Malley, J.M. (1985). Learning strategy applications to content instruction in second language development. In *Issues in English language development* (pp. 69–73). Washington, DC: National Clearinghouse for Bilingual Education.

O'Malley, J.M., Chamot, A.U., & Kupper, L. (1986). *The role of learning strategies and cognition in second language acquisition: A study of strategies for listening comprehension used by students of English as a second language.* McLean, VA: InterAmerica Research Associates.

O'Malley, J.M., Chamot, A.U., Stewner-Manzanares, G., Kupper, L., & Russo, R.P. (1985). Learning strategies used by beginning and intermediate ESL students. *Language Learning, 35,* 21-46.

O'Malley, J.M., Chamot, A.U., Stewner-Manzanares, G., Russo, R.P., & Kupper, L. (1985). Learning strategy applications with students of English as a second language. *TESOL Quarterly, 19,* 557-584.

O'Malley, J.M., Chamot, A.U., & Walker, C. (1987). The role of cognition in second language acquisition. *Studies in Second Language Acquisition, 9,* 287-306.

Rabinowitz, M., & Chi, M.T. (1987). An interactive model of strategic processing. In S.J. Ceci (Ed.), *Handbook of cognitive, social, and neuropsychological aspects of learning disabilities* (Vol. 2, pp. 83-102). Hillsdale, NJ: Lawrence Erlbaum.

Richards, J.C. (1984). The secret life of methods. *TESOL Quarterly, 18,* 7-23.

Rubin, J. (1981). Study of cognitive processes in second language learning. *Applied Linguistics, 11,* 117-131.

Saville-Troike, M. (1984). What *really* matters in second language learning for academic achievement? *TESOL Quarterly, 18,* 199-219.

Weinstein, C.E., & Mayer, R.E. (1986). The teaching of learning strategies. In M.C. Wittrock (Ed.), *Handbook of research on teaching* (3rd ed., pp. 315-327). New York: Macmillan.

Wenden, A. (1985). Learner strategies. *TESOL Newsletter, 19*(5), 1-7.

Appendix 1. Learning Strategy Definitions

Learning strategy	Definition
Metacognitive strategies	
1. Advance organization	Previewing the main ideas and concepts of the material to be learned, often by skimming the text for the organizing principle
2. Organizational planning	Planning the parts, sequence, main ideas, or language functions to be expressed orally or in writing.
3. Selective attention	Deciding in advance to attend to specific aspects of input, often by scanning for key words, concepts, and/or linguistic markers
4. Self-monitoring	Checking one's comprehension during listening or reading or checking the accuracy and/or appropriateness of one's oral or written production while it is taking place
5. Self-evaluation	Judging how well one has accomplished a learning activity after it has been completed

Learning strategy	Definition
Cognitive strategies	
1. Resourcing	Using target language reference materials such as dictionaries, encyclopedias, or textbooks
2. Grouping	Classifying words, terminology, or concepts according to their attributes
3. Note taking	Writing down key words and concepts in abbreviated verbal, graphic, or numerical form during a listening or reading activity.
4. Summarizing	Making a mental, oral, or written summary of information gained through listening or reading.
5. Deduction/induction	Applying rules to understand or produce the second language or making up rules based on language analysis.
6. Imagery	Using visual images (either mental or actual) to understand and remember new information
7. Auditory representation	Playing back in one's mind the sound of a word, phrase, or longer language sequence
8. Elaboration	Relating new information to prior knowledge, relating different parts of new information to each other, or making meaningful personal association with the new information.
9. Transfer	Using previous linguistic knowledge or prior skills to assist comprehension or production
10. Inferencing	Using information in an oral or written text to guess meanings, predict outcomes, or complete missing parts

Learning strategy	Definition
	Social-affective strategies
1. Questions for clarification	Eliciting from a teacher or peer additional explanation, rephrasing, examples, or verificaton
2. Cooperation	Working together with peers to solve a problem, pool information, check a learning task, model a language activity, or get feedback on oral or written performance
3. Self-talk	Reducing anxiety by using mental techniques that make one feel competent to do the learning task

chapter 11

Applications of the Cognitive Academic Language Learning Approach (CALLA) to Special Education

Anna Uhl Chamot
J. Michael O'Malley

The Cognitive Academic Language Learning Approach (CALLA) is designed for limited-English-proficient (LEP) students who are being prepared for participation in mainstream content-area instruction. The approach is designed to further academic development in English through special content area instruction in science, mathematics, social studies, and language arts. Some of the important features of CALLA are its grounding in cognitive theory, the focus on academic language development, the integration of language and content area instruction, and the use of learning strategies to support the acquisition of both language and content area knowledge (Chamot & O'Malley, 1987). For each of these key features, parallels with special education can be found which suggest that CALLA will be a useful approach for limited-English-proficient students with learning disabilities.

This chapter provides some brief background information on the important features of CALLA while indicating specific applications of CALLA in the instruction of LEP students with learning disabilities. CALLA is appropriate for the instruction of learning disabled LEP in four major ways: content selection and presentation, language development, learning strategy instruction, and lesson plan design.

CONTENT SELECTION AND PRESENTATION

The purpose of integrating language with content in CALLA is to provide students with opportunities for learning academic language in a manner that is intrinsically interesting and motivating. The intent is to go beyond the less rewarding form of instruction in which language is learned as an end in itself by enabling students to use the language as a vehicle for learning ideas that are new and important in an academic context. What this requires is for ESL teachers to draw upon mainstream teachers as a resource to identify key concepts and activities in each content area that are essential for the student to progress effectively in mainstream classrooms. CALLA does not replace or substitute for mainstream classrooms but provides instruction in key areas that will build the information, schemata, and procedural knowledge required for mainstream success.

Academic content is made accessible to special education LEP students through:

- Selection of high-priority, central content topics which are carefully aligned with the school district's mainstream curriculum.
- Content presentations that are contextualized through graphic representations, active demonstrations, and audio, visual, and kinesthetic experiences.
- Content that is integrated into students' existing knowledge frameworks through concrete, hands-on experiences.
- Content that is absorbed through extensive discussion before, during, and after content presentation and practice.
- Content that is internalized through application to cooperative learning activities.
- Different learning styles that are addressed by using different modes to present and practice content.
- Thinking skills that are developed as teacher leads students to discover how new content can be related and applied to the everyday world.

ACADEMIC LANGUAGE DEVELOPMENT

Academic language is that special form of language used in content area classrooms that is cognitively demanding and is provided with limited contextual clues to support meaning (Cummins, 1982, 1983). Such clues might include concrete objects or diagrams, and elaborated language which restates the meaning using simplified grammatical structures. The language is cognitively demanding because students need to do more than simply comprehend the message, but are required to manipulate ideas, relate one idea to another, critically analyze arguments, infer missing information, predict consequences, and structure complex discourse in writing and in speaking.

The language skills that will be essential for students' further progress in the mainstream curriculum can be supported through activities which provide for: (a) contextualized development of academic vocabulary, (b) development of reading comprehension of expository prose so that students learn to gain information from textbooks, (c) practice in listening to and comprehending information presented orally, (d) practice in using speaking skills to discuss, explain, and elaborate information presented by the teacher and through reading, and (e) development of expository writing skills through a process approach.

LEARNING STRATEGY INSTRUCTION

Learning strategy instruction is an integral component of CALLA for at least three reasons: (a) strategic modes of processing information are characteristic of more successful students; (b) strategies can be taught to students who use them infrequently or inefficiently; and (c) given the right circumstances, strategies will transfer to new learning activities (O'Malley, Chamot, Stewner-Manzanares, Russo, & Kupper, 1985; Weinstein, Goetz, & Alexander, 1988). Students may nevertheless need special assistance to ensure that strategies transfer to new tasks. Three types of strategies are described in CALLA:

1. Metacognitive strategies, which involve executive processes in planning for learning, monitoring one's own comprehension or production, and evaluating how well one has achieved a learning objective.
2. Cognitive strategies, or strategically rehearsing the material to be learned, grouping or classifying concepts, elaborating on the material through one's own knowledge, or developing images related to the material.
3. Social/affective strategies, which entail interacting with another person as in asking questions or cooperating, or using affective control to influence learning.

The use of learning strategies in CALLA parallels the use of learning strategies for students in special education where limitations in strategic processing skills have been one of the defining characteristics of students with learning disabilities (e.g., Deshler & Schumaker, 1986; Deshler, Schumaker, & Lenz, 1984; Finch & Spirito, 1980; Loper, 1980; Rabinowitz & Chi, 1987). Learning-disabled students have been said to have limitations in metacognitive awareness of the variables which influence learning, in the ability to manipulate conceptually the information required to learn, and in the awareness of relevant and irrelevant characteristics of the task (Loper, 1980). Because academic language and academic content are cognitively demanding, learning in these areas will be particularly sensitive to limitations in the ability to use strategic modes of thought.

Direct instruction in learning strategies is central to CALLA. By modeling, explaining, and providing practice in the strategies that characterize effective learners, teachers provide students with techniques that help them understand and remember information, solve problems, and organize learning tasks. Teachers also encourage students to share information with other students about the strategies they use while learning and, whenever possible, embed strategies in curriculum materials that students work on to guarantee that strategy use is perceived as an intrinsic aspect of learning.

The following major strategies would be particularly beneficial for limited-English-proficient students with learning disabilities:

1. Selective attention, or attending selectively to key words, phrases, or details that signal important aspects of the learning task (metacognitive).
2. Self-monitoring, checking, verifying, or correcting one's comprehension or performance in the course of a language task (metacognitive).
3. Self-evaluation, checking the outcomes of one's own language performance against an internal measure of completeness and accuracy, or checking on one's resources to perform the task at hand (metacognitive).
4. Elaboration, relating new information to prior knowledge, or relating different parts of the information to each other (cognitive).
5. Inferencing, using available information to make an informed guess at the meaning of unfamiliar language items, to predict outcomes, or to fill in missing information (cognitive).
6. Grouping, looking for similarities in new information that can be used to group or classify common items which need to be learned (cognitive).
7. Summarizing, looking for the main ideas and associated details that can be used to get the gist of what was learned (cognitive).
8. Cooperation, working together with peers to solve a problem, pool information, check a learning task, model a language activity, or obtain feedback on an oral or written activity (social/affective).
9. Self-talk, reducing anxiety by using mental techniques that make one feel competent to the learning task (social/affective).

CALLA LESSON PLAN MODEL

One of the key aspects of CALLA is the five-phase lesson plan. The five phases of the CALLA lesson plan are designed to be particularly helpful for students experiencing difficulty in learning academic content. In CALLA lessons, students are exposed to new information in various modes; they are shown how to activate prior knowledge and link it to new information; they use all four language skills to mediate learning; and they learn how to use strategies that make learning more efficient and effective. At the beginning of each lesson, teachers indicate the content area objectives for learning, the language objectives, and the learning strategies that will be used in the lesson. By specifying the objectives of the lesson, the teacher generates information that can be used in the Individual Educational Plan (IEP) required in special education. A description of each of the five phases of the CALLA lesson plan model is as follows (typical learning strategies that might occur in each phase are identified in parentheses):

1. *Preparation:* The teacher provides a schematic framework for the lesson (advance organizers), asks students to identify what they already know about the topic (elaboration), and identifies key terms or concepts that will be introduced (selective attention).
2. *Presentation:* The teacher presents new information and suggests ways in which the new ideas can be effectively remembered (rehearsal, grouping, imagery, inferencing, elaboration).
3. *Practice:* Students are given small group assignments to apply in class what they heard or read during the Presentation Phase or to write syntheses or practical applications of the new information (summarization, cooperative learning).
4. *Evaluation:* The students evaluate the success of their learning activities by checking their answers with other students or by comparing their responses against a standard (self-evaluation).
5. *Expansion Activities:* Students collect further information about the assignment and apply what they learned to other classroom assignments or to activities assigned outside of class (elaboration, inferencing).

In each phase of the lesson plan above, students have ample opportunities to use all four language skills while accomplishing the objectives of the lesson. Furthermore, they experience the material to be learned through a variety of language and cognitive modes and interact with the information in a strategic manner rather than being a passive recipient of information.

SUMMARY

CALLA was designed for LEP students who are preparing for instruction in mainstream classrooms. The approach integrates academic language development with content area instruction and provides students with learning strategies to increase their command over the new information. Learning strategies are important to facilitate the acquisition of new and difficult information and to enable the teacher to introduce grade-appropriate academic content successfully. The approach was shown to be compatible with current views in special education and to have potential for extension to limited-English-students with learning disabilities.

REFERENCES

Chamot, A.U., & O'Malley, J.M. (1987). The Cognitive Academic Language Learning Approach: A bridge to the mainstream. *TESOL Quarterly, 21,* 227-249.

Cummins, J. (1982). Tests, achievement, and bilingual students. In *Focus* (No. 9). Washington, DC: National Clearinghouse for Bilingual Education.

Cummins, J. (1983). Conceptual and linguistic foundations of language assessment. In S.S. Seidner (Ed.), *Issues of language assessment: Vol. 2. Language assessment and curriculum planning* (pp. 7-16). Washington, DC: National Clearinghouse for Bilingual Education.

Deshler, D.D., & Schumaker, J.B. (1986). Learning strategies: An instructional alternative for low-achieving adolescents. *Exceptional Children, 52,* 583-590.

Deshler, D.D., Schumaker, J.B., & Lenz, B.K. (1984). Academic and cognitive interventions for LD adolescents: Part I. *Journal of Learning Disabilities, 17,* 108-117.

Finch, A.J., Jr., & Spirito, A. (1980). Use of cognitive training to change cognitive processes. *Exceptional Education Quarterly, 1,* 31-40.

Loper, A.B. (1980). Metacognitive development: Implications for cognitive training. *Exceptional Education Quarterly, 1,* 1-8.

O'Malley, J.M., Chamot, A.U., Stewner-Manzanares, G., Russo, R.P., & Kupper, L. (1985). Learning strategy applications with students of English as a second language. *TESOL Quarterly, 19,* 557-584.

Rabinowitz, M., & Chi, M.T. (1987). An interactive model of strategic processing. In S.J. Ceci (Ed.), *Handbook of cognitive, social, and neuropsychological aspects of learning disabilities* (pp. 83-102). Hillsdale, NJ: Erlbaum.

Weinstein, C.E., Goetz, E.T., & Alexander, P.A. (Eds.). (1988). *Learning and study strategies.* San Diego, CA: Academic Press.

Author Index

A

Abbott, M.M., 49, *61*
Abramson, M., 54, *63*
Agard, R., 93, *104*
Alexander, P.A., 220, *223*
Algozzine, B., 50, 52, *66*
Allen, V., 205, *213*
Ambert, A., 132, 133, *145*
Anderson, J.R., 200, *214*
Anderson, R., 154, *166*
Aphek, E., 201, *214*
Applebee, A.N., 40, *45*
Arkell, C., 116, *131*
Asher, J.J., 43, *45*, 78, *87*, 116, *129*
Audette, R., 55, *62*

B

Baca, L.M., 7, *23*, 49, 50, 53, *62*, 106, *129*, 135, *145*, 156, 163, *166*
Backman, L.F., 181, *193*
Bailey, D.B., Jr., 49, *62*
Behrmann, M., *129*
Benavidez, A., 56, 57, *62*, 126, *129*
Ben-Zeev, S., 6, *23*
Bernstein, D.K., 171, *193*
Bialystok, E., 25, *45*
Bilsky, L.H., 117, 118, 119, 120, *129*
Blackman, L.S., 117, 118, 119, 120, *129*
Borkowski, J.G., 43, *45*
Bozinou-Doukas, E., 170, *194*
Braden, J.P., 56, *62*
Bradley, C.H., 120, *130, 194*
Bransford, J., 7, *23*, 154, *166*
Brophy, J.E., 42, *45, 194*
Brown, D., 75, *87*
Brown, G., 55, *62*
Bruck, M., 80, *87*
Bryan, J.H., 68, 71, 72, *87, 89*
Bryan, T.H., 68, 71, 72, *87, 89*
Burke-Guild, P., 123, *129*

Burt, M., 31, 32, *45*, 53, *63*, 74, 75, 76, *87*, 132, *145*
Byrne, M.C., 72, *89*

C

Carbo, M., 123, *129*
Carpenter, L., 91, *104*
Carrasquillo, A.L., 182, *194*
Carrell, P.L., 170, *194*
Carrow-Woolfolk, E., 158, 160, *166*
Castaneda, A., 39, 41, *47*, 162, *166, 168*
Cazden, C.B., 75, *87*
Ceci, D.J., 72, *87*
Cervantes, H.M., 49, 50, 53, *62*, 106, *129*, 156, 163, *166*
Chalfant, J.C., 68, 69, *88*
Chamot, A.U., 118, *129*, 132, 135, *145*, 181, *194*, 196, 200, 201, 202, 206, 208, 209, 210, 211, 212, *214*, 218, 220, *223*
Chapman, G., 1, *3*
Cheng, L., 138, *145*
Chi, M.T., 201, *215*, 220, *223*
Chinn, P.C., 38, *45*
Chipman, S., 208, *214*
Chomsky, N., 70, *87*
Christiansen, J., 108, *130*
Christiansen, J.L., 108, *130*
Christison, M.A., 92, *104*
Cochran-Smith, M., 183, *194*
Cohen, A.D., 201, *214*
Colley, D.A., 157, *166*
Collier, C., 133, 143, *145*
Collier, V., 132, 135, *145*, 175, 188, *195*
Craig, H., 151, *166*
Cumbo, R.F., 49, *65*
Cummins, J., 7, 8, 9, 12, 19, 20, 22, *23*, 25, 26, 27, 31, 36, 42, 43, *45*, 49, 50, 51, 52, 56, 57, 59, 60, *62*, 74, 76, 77, 78, 79, 81, 82, 84, *87*, 91, 103, *104*, 123, *129*, 134, 135, 137, 139, 140, *145*, 156,

157, 158, 161, *166, 167,* 171, 176, 181,
194, 197, 205, 207, *214,* 219, *223*
Curran, C., 119, 122, *129*
Cziko, G.A., 53, *63*

D
Dalton, E., *45*
Damico, J.S., 32, *45*
Daniels, H., 139, *145*
Davidson, R.G., 205, *214*
De Avila, 7, *23,* 32, *45, 145,* 157, *167*
De Blassie, R., 13, *23*
Derry, S.J., 208, *214*
Deshler, D.D., 118, *129,* 220, *223*
Dever, R., 119, *129*
de Villiers, J.G., 132, *145*
de Villiers, P.A., 132, *145*
Dew, N., 106, 107, *129*
Donahue, M., 72, *87, 89*
Doris, J., 49, *65*
Duchen, J.F., 154, 158, *167*
Dudley-Marling, C., 150, 151, *168*
Dulay, H., 31, 32, *45,* 53, *63,* 74, 75, 76,
87, 132, *145*
Duncan, S.E., 7, *23,* 32, *45, 145,* 157, *167*
Dunn, K., 123, *129*
Dunn, L.M., 32, *45*
Dunn, R., 123, *129*
Duran, E., 128, *129*

E
Eisterhold, J.C., 170, *194*
Ekwall, E.C., 184, *194*

F
Farr, M., 139, *145*
Feagans, L, 69, 72, *87*
Fenton, K.S., 50, *63*
Feuerstein, R., 115, *130,* 161, *167*
Finch, A.J., Jr., 220, *223*
Finn, J.D., 54, *63*
Finocchiaro, M., 170, *194*
Fishground, J.E., 60, *63*
Flavell, J., 153, *167*
Flores, B., 139, 141, *145*
Fradd, S.H., 56, 62, *63*
Franse, S.R., 56, *65*
Friedenberg, J.E., 120, *130, 194*
Frohlich, M., 201, *214*

G
Gaardner, A.B., 175, *194*

Garcia, E., 77, *87*
Garcia, S.B., 9, *23,* 34, 35, 39, *45, 46,* 54,
57, *63,* 67, 74, 80, *88, 89,* 91, *104,*
114, *130,* 179, *195*
Gardner, R.C., 11, *23,* 78, *88,* 92, *104*
Garger, S., 123, *129*
Gearhart, B.R., 69, *88*
Genesee, F., 92, *104*
Glaser, R., 50, *63,* 208, *214*
Glass, R.M., 108, *130*
Glyn Carr, E., 180, *194*
Goetz, E.T., 220, *223*
Goldman, P., 106, *130*
Goldman, S.R., 142, *145*
Gollnick, D.M., 38, *45*
Good, T.L., 42, *45*
Gould, L.J., 49, 54, *63*
Gould, P., 1, *3*
Gould, S.J., 50, *63*
Greenlee, M., 26, *45*
Grosjean, F., 6, 7, *23*

H
Hagerty, G.J., 54, *63*
Hakuta, K., 49, 54, *63,* 132, *145*
Halliday, M., 151, *167*
Hammill, D., 32, *46,* 69, *88*
Harbin, G., 49, *62*
Harris, A.J., 182, *194*
Harris, K.C., 135, *145*
Hayes-Roth, B., 154, *168*
Heath, S.B., 40, *46*
Heather, N., 54, *63*
Henderson, R., 43, *46,* 161, *167*
Herbert, C.H., 32, *46*
Hernandez-Chavez, E., 32, *45*
Higgins, J., 121, *130*
Hoefnagel-Hohle, M., 132, *146*
Holdaway, D., 90, *104*
Holobrow, N., 92, *104*
Holtzman, W.H., Jr., 27, 31, 33, *46*
Holubec, E.J., 122, *130*
Honeyfield, J., 209, *214*
Hoover, W.A., 132, 137, 138, *146*
Howell, K., 165, *167*
Hudelson, S., *145*
Huebner, S.E., 51, *62*
Hutchens, P.W., *195*

I
Idol-Maestes, L., 72, *88*
Ingram, D.E., 53, *63*

J

Jacobson, R., 175, *194*
Jeffree, D., 183, *194*
Johns, T., 121, *130*
Johnson, D.W., 122, *130*, 158, *167*
Johnson, J., 1, *3*
Johnson, M.A., 121, 122, *130*, 154, *166*
Johnson, R.T., 122, *130*
Jones, B.F., 180, *194*
Juarez, M., 159, *167*

K

Kalk, M., 143, *145*
Kaminsky, S., *65*
Kaufman, M.J., 50, *63*
Keeton, A., 93, *104*
Keller-Cohen, D., 75, *88*
Kirk, S.A., 68, 69, *88*
Kirk, W.P., 68, 69, *88*
Kline, S.B., 205, *214*
Krahonke, K., 92, *104*
Krashen, S.D., 26, 43, *46*, 59, 60, *63, 64*,
    78, 79, *88*, 103, *104*, 116, 125, *130*,
    132, *145*, 171, 174, 181, *194*, 195
Kupper, L., 201, 202, 208, 209, 210, *214*,
    215, 220, 223

L

Lambert, W.E., 6, 11, *23, 24*, 92, *104*
Lambie, R.A., *195*
Landurand, P.M., 106, *130*
Langdon, H.W., 8, *23*, 69, 77, *88*
Langer, J., 40, *46*
Larsen, S., 69, *88*
Lee, L.L., 71, *88*
Legarreta-Marcaida, D., 59, *64*
Leigh, J., 69, *88*
Lennenberg, E., 71, *88*
Lenz, B.K., 220, *223*
Leopold, W.F., 136, *146*
Lerner, J., 149, 151, 155, 158, 163, *167*
Lin, N.H.J., 53, *63*
Linares, N., 69, *88*
Long, M.H., 78, *88*
Longstreet, W., 161, 162, *167*
Loper, A.B., 220, 221, *223*
Lund, N.J., 154, 158, *167*
Lynch, J., 158, 160, *166*

M

Mace-Matluck, B.J., 132, 137, 138, *146*
Macmillan, D.L., 50, *64*

Maldonado-Colon, E., 38, *47*, 91, *104*, 106,
    126, *131*, 135, *146*
Maltitz, F.W., 10, *24*
Mann, L., 153, *167*
Markman, E., 154, 155, *167*
Mattes, L., 27, *46*, 159, *167*
Maxwell, J.P., 50, *63*
Mayer, R.E., 208, *215*
McCahill, P., *130*
McCollum, P.A., 35, *46*, 51, *64*
McIntyre, R.B., 93, *104*,
McKeon, D., 107, *130*
McLaughlin, B., 132, 133, *146*
McLesky, J., 51, *62*
McNeely, S.N., 56, *62*
McNeil, D., 70, *88*
McNett, I., 67, *88*
McNutt, J.G., 69, *88*
Mendoza, P., 49, *64*
Menyuck, P., 71, *88*
Mercer, C., 163, *167*
Mercer, J.R., 49, *64*
Merino, B.J., 52, *64*
Messick, S., 54, 55, *64*
Meyen, E., 158, *167*
Meyers, C.E., 50, *64*
Miller, S.E., 55, *66*
Milson, J.L., 184, *194*
Mitchell, J., 50, *52, 66*
Mohan, B.A., 202, *214*
Moran, M.R., 72, *89*
Morehead, M., 165, *167*
Murphy, D.A., 208, *214*
Myklebust, H., 158, *167*

N

Naiman, N., 201, *214*
Newcomer, P.L., 32, *46*
New Levine, L., 170, *195*
Nine-Curt, C.J., 162, *167*
Nodine, B., 148, *168*
Nuttal, E.V., 106, *130*

O

Oakland, T.M., 49, *64*
Ochoa, A.M., 56, *64*
Oka, E.R., 44, *47*
Oller, J.W., Jr., 27, 32, *45, 46,* 91, 100, *105*
Olson, D., 55, *62*
O'Malley, J.M., 106, 108, *131*, 132, 135, *145*,
    181, *194*, 196, 200, 201, 202, 208, 209,
    210, 211, 212, *214*, 218, 220, *223*

O'Malley, M.O., 118, *129*
Omark, D.R., 27, *46,* 56, *64,* 159, *167*
Ortiz, A.A., 7, 8, 13, 22, *24,* 26, 27, 31, 33,
　　34, 35, 36, 37, 39, 42, *45, 46, 47,* 53,
　　54, 61, *65, 66,* 72, 80, *89,* 91, 100,
　　102, 103, *105,* 114, 126, *130, 131,* 135,
　　146, 168, 175, 179, 181, *195*
Ovando, C.M., 175, 188, *195*
Oxford-Carpenter, R., 110, 118, *131*

P

Pacheco, R., 56, *64*
Padilla, A., 56, *65*
Paris, S.G., 44, *47*
Patton, J.R., 155, 162, 163, *168*
Payan, R., 27, *47*
Payne, J.S., 155, 162, 163, *168*
Peal, E., 6, *24*
Pearl, R., 72, *87, 89*
Pennington, B.F., 71, *89*
Perlmutter, B., 72, *89*
Perozzi, J.A., 76, *89*
Piaget, J., 172, *195*
Plata, M., 107, *131*
Podell, D.M., *65*
Polloway, E., 158, *168*
Polyzoi, E., 27, 31, 33, *46*
Porter, B., 139, 141, *145*
Prieto, A.G., 54, 55, *65*

R

Rabinowitz, M., 201, *215,* 220, *223*
Raimes, A., 141, *146*
Raimondi, S.L., *129*
Ramirez, A., 5, *24,* 79, *89*
Ramirez, M., 39, 41, *47,* 162, *168*
Reid, J.M., 122, *131*
Reschly, D.J., 54, 55, *65*
Resnick, L.B., 54, *63*
Rhodes, L.K., 150, 151, *168*
Richards, J.C., *215*
Rodriguez, A., 140, *146*
Rodriguez, R.F., 54, 55, *65,* 162, *168*
Rogers, P., 92, *104*
Rosenshine, B.V., 34, *47*
Ross, A.O., 162, 163, *168*
Rossell, A., 184, *195*
Roy, P., 122, *130*
Rubin, J., 202, *215*
Rueda, R.S., 54, 55, *65,* 135, 136, 139, 141,
　　143, *145, 146*
Russo, G.M., 141, *146*

Russo, R.P., 201, 202, 208, 209, 210, *215,*
　　220, *223*

S

Sabatino, D., 153, *167*
Salend, S.J., 121, *131*
Sarason, S.B., 49, *65*
Savignon, S.J., 122, *131,* 181, *193*
Saville-Troike, M., 161, 162, *168,* 197, *215*
Schniedewind, N., 121, *131*
Scholl, H., 151, 158, *168*
Schumaker, J.B., 118, *129,* 220, *223*
Sederburg Ogle, D., 180, *194*
Segan, F., 143, *146,* 184, *195*
Semel, E., 158, *168*
Short, E.S., 72, *87*
Shuy, R.W., 48, 51, 52, *65*
Sigel, J., 208, *214*
Simich-Dudgeon, C., 138, *146*
Sipay, E.R., 182, *194*
Skeffington, M., 183, *194*
Skinner, B.F., 70, *89*
Slater, G.M., 56, *65*
Smith, F., 90, *105,* 148, *168*
Smith, J., 158, *168*
Smith, S.D., 71, *89*
Snell, M., 163, *167*
Snell, W.E., Jr., 27, 31, 33, *46*
Snow, C.E., 132, *146,* 205, *214*
Spencer, M., 52, *64*
Spirito, A., 220, *223*
Spolsky, B., 48, *65,* 110, *131,* 133, 134, *146,*
　　147
Sridhar, K., 151, *168*
Stark, I., 69, *89*
Steffensen, M., 138, *147*
Stern, H.H., 201, *214*
Stevick, E., 90, 100, *105*
Stewner-Manzanares, G., 201, 202, 208, 209,
　　210, *214,* 220, *223*
Storey, M.E., 32, *45*
Sue, S., 56, *65*
Sullivan Palinscar, P.A., 180, *194*
Swain, M., 7, *24*
Swedo, J., 22, *24*

T

Taylor, O, 159, *168*
Terrell, T.D., 43, *46,* 60, *64,* 79, *88, 89,* 116,
　　130, 171, *195*
Thonis, E.W., 54, *65,* 157, *168,* 171, 182,
　　195

Thorndyke, P., 154, *168*
Tiegerman, E., 171, *193*
Tikunoff, W.J., 17, *24*, 55, 56, *65*, 174, *195*
Tilis, H.S., 49, *65*
Toch, T., 54, *66*
Todesco, A., 201, *214*
Torgesen, J., 163, *168*
Trachtman, G.M., 51, *66*
Trueba, H.T., 161, *168*
Tucker, J., 34, *47*
Turner, L.A., 43, *45*

V

Valadez, C., 132, *147*
Valdez, G., 181, *195*
Van Ek, J.A., 119, *131*
Van Etten, C., 116, *131*
Van Etten, G., 116, *131*
Vega, J.E., 56, *63*
Vellutino, F.R., 69, *89*
Ventriglia, L., 122, *131*
Vogel, S.A., 72, *89*
Vygotsky, L.S., 90, *105*, 142, *147*

W

Walker, C., 200, 201, 202, *215*
Walker, L., 14, *24*

Wallace, C., 138, *147*
Wallach, G.P., 69, *89*
Weichum, W., 49, *65*
Weinstein, C.E., 208, *215*, 220, *223*
Weiss, R., 26, *47*
Wenden, A., 202, *215*
Westby, C.E., 40, *47*
Weyhing, R.S., 43, *45*
Wiig, E.H., 158, *168*
Wilkins, D.A., 119, *131*
Wilkinson, C.Y., 27, 31, 33, *46*, 54, *66*
Willig, A.C., 7, *24*, 27, 31, 33, 36, 42, *46*, *47*, 49, 57, *66*, 72, *89*, 106, *131*, 139, *147*
Wilner, R., *105*
Wode, H., 76, *89*
Wong-Fillmore, L., 78, *89*, 92, *105*, 132, 133, *147*, 175, *195*

Y

Yates, J.R., 9, *23*, 36, 37, 39, 42, *46*, 54, 57, 61, *63*, *65*, 67, 88, 91, *105*
Yoshida, R.K., 50, *63*
Ysseldyke, J.E., 50, 52, *66*

Z

Zigmond, N., 55, *66*

Subject Index

A

Academic language development, 219-220
Art, 188, 188-189
Assessment, 25-44, 49-51, 111-112
  assessing language skills, 27-32
  tests, 32-33
  achievement, 33-35

B

Bilingual education, 4-6, 10-11
  cognitive benefits, 6
  linguistic benefits, 8
  sociocultural benefits, 9-10
Bilingual handicapped students, 134-136
Bilingual special education, 14-18

C

Cognitive, academic, language learning approach, 196-213, 218-223
Court cases, 6
Cooperative learning, 121-122

D

Decision making, 51-52

E

Education For All Handicapped Children Act, 4
English as a second language, 107-110
  program, 110-111, 124-126, 181-182
  developmental, 116-117, 204-206
  content based, 117, 202-204
  strategies, 117-121
  vocational, 119-120
Evaluation, 20-21

I

Instruction, 25-27, 35-44
  instructional environment, 21
  instructional planning, 37-42
  instructional strategies, 42-44, 206-212, 220-223
  students' preferences, 90-105
  computer-based, 121
  content area, 169-172

L

Language arts, 180-181
Language differences, 100-102
Language proficiency, 156-158
Learning disabilities, 68-73
  students' characteristics, 73-74, 162-164
  learning disorders, 100-102
  language disabilities, 158-160
Literacy skills, 132-144
  reading skills, 136-138, 182-183
  content areas, 143-144

M

Mathematics, 183-186
Multicultural education, 172-173
  cultural experiences, 161-162
Music, 188-189

N

Native language, 58-59, 133
  primary language skills, 17-18

O

Occupational education, 187-188

P

Parental involvement, 22
  home support, 115-116

R

Reading, *see* Literacy skills

S

Science, 186-187

Second language, 18, 106–128
  acquisition, 59–61
  English development, 18, 95–100
  program, 74–81
  strategies, 81–86

Social studies, 186–187

W

Whole language, 123–124
Writing, 139–143, 148–166